Advertising Media Planning

Advertising
Media Planning
A Brand Management Approach
THIRD EDITION

Larry D. Kelley
Donald W. Jugenheimer
and Kim Bartel Sheehan

M.E.Sharpe
Armonk, New York
London, England

Library of Congress Cataloging-in-Publication Data

Kelley, Larry D., 1955–
  Advertising media planning : a brand management approach / by Larry D. Kelley, Donald
W. Jugenheimer, and Kim Bartel Sheehan.—3rd ed.
    p. cm.
  Includes bibliographical references and index.
  ISBN 978-0-7656-2635-6 (hardcover : alk. paper)
    1. Advertising media planning. 2. Brand name products. 3. Marketing. I. Jugenheimer,
Donald W. II. Sheehan, Kim. III. Title.

  HF5826.5.K45 2012
  659.1'11—dc22   2011012296

Printed in the United States of America

The paper used in this publication meets the minimum requirements of
American National Standard for Information Sciences
Permanence of Paper for Printed Library Materials,
ANSI Z 39.48-1984.

IBT (c)   10   9   8   7   6   5   4   3   2   1

Contents

Preface

This is the third edition of *Advertising Media Planning: A Brand Management Approach,* a book that can be used by anyone making advertising and promotional media decisions. Media planning is a crucial part of the advertising process—and ultimately of the brand management process—yet little has been written on how brand management can impact the media process. Our goal with the first two editions was to fill the void in the market and, additionally, with the second edition, to show the media planning process from the viewpoints of both the media planner and the brand manager. All of the stakeholders of a media plan have input and control over various aspects of its outcome.

This, the third edition, expands on these important concepts while continuing to focus on media planning as a consumer engagement process. We have provided new, detailed chapters on media planning for traditional broadcast, print, and outdoor advertising. Today's media planners and brand managers are involved in decision making beyond the traditional media realm, and so we have included information on digital and social media, in-store media, and direct response. You will also find chapters on ethnic media and alternative media (coffee sleeve advertising, anyone?). We believe that media planners and brand managers must think of media's place in the advertising process more holistically, and so we have included chapters on sponsorships, promotions, and publicity.

Because many who read this book might never work in a media department but still want to understand how the agency and media businesses work, we have included new information on the advertising agency business, including chapters on effects of media ownership, agency organization, and agency compensation.

Like our previous books, this edition of *Advertising Media Planning* ties into the new, third edition of *Advertising Media Workbook and Sourcebook,* also published by M.E. Sharpe. For students and instructors of media planning courses, the workbook offers a detailed perspective of each facet of media, along with practical exercises offering students the opportunity to put sometimes-abstract concepts into real-world situations.

Within this ever-changing field of media, there are more reasons than ever to have a "go-to" source that any level of media decision maker can use to help make crucial decisions that affect a brand's value. Brand managers who have little formal training in advertising, students of advertising and integrated marketing communications programs, and other practitioners such as account supervisors and media salespeople can benefit from this book's straightforward, hands-on approach to the business of advertising media.

Acknowledgments

The authors wish to thank Harry Briggs, our editor, Elizabeth Granda Parker, our responsive and creative associate editor, and Stacey Victor, our production editor. We also thank our spouses and families for all their support, without which this project would not have been possible.

Advertising
Media Planning

Chapter 1

The Role of Communication in Advertising and Marketing: Why Media Are Important

Advertising involves communicating information. The communication is often persuasive. The media are the conduits through which the advertising is communicated to the members of the audience.

Communication is critical to advertising success. You may recall the four Ps, the four components of the marketing mix: product, price, place, and promotion. Advertising is communicated promotion.

Advertising is also part of marketing communications. Some marketers break up the marketing mix into the four Cs: commodity, cost, channel, and communication. These four elements are analogous to the four Ps, but this view makes it even more obvious that communication is a critical process in the success of advertising, which in turn is critical to marketing success.

Now let's say that you are a brand manager. You are responsible for the marketing success of a product or service, or a brand, or maybe an entire line of goods. Your personal and professional success depends on your brand's success. Perhaps you are an advertising account executive or account supervisor, or even a top-level executive who wants the entire company or corporation to do well. The success of your advertising is crucial to your product's welfare and success.

Whatever your job title, you are concerned with the sale of the product or service that you are marketing. Sure, you are interested in the advertising campaign strategy, and you review and approve all the advertising copy and themes before they go to production. Nevertheless, the media portion of the campaign may not really interest you. After all, it is detailed, it is somewhat abstract, and it is invariably complicated. You may believe that the heart of advertising is the message, so you probably concentrate on the theme, headlines, visuals, and copy. You may give cursory review to the research and to the media plan, but they are not your primary focus. Or maybe you

3

do not delve deeply into the media plan because you do not fully understand the concepts and workings of advertising media.

So why should you be so interested in advertising media and the media plans that underscore your campaign? There are several reasons why advertising media, the conduits that carry advertising communication, are important to you and critical to the success of your advertising.

Media: Most of the Budget

First, advertising media take up most of the advertising budget. Media time and space are expensive: in a typical advertising campaign, the media costs account for 80 to 85 percent of the advertising budget; the remaining 15 or 20 percent covers research, message, production, evaluation, and profits for the advertising agency (see Exhibit 1.1).

If advertising media control the bulk of your advertising budget, you should spend sufficient time and effort making sure that the media plans are sensible and that the media selection and purchases are relevant and efficient. In most situations, 20 percent of the effort produces 80 percent of the revenue. You may be spending only 20 percent of your effort on the 80 percent of the advertising campaign that will make or break your campaign success. Anything that accounts for 80 percent of the monies and a large share of the campaign success deserves a large share of your attention and effort.

Advertising media may seem complicated and somewhat arcane to you. The purpose of this book is to give you the background and information you need to be an informed and capable manager, one who understands and administers the entire advertising effort, including the media planning, selection, and buying.

So advertising media account for most of your advertising budget and are therefore worthy of your attention and interest. But there are more reasons why advertising media are important to you.

A Poor Media Plan Sabotages an Entire Campaign

Let's say you have a great advertising campaign plan. The theme is memorable, the visuals are impressive, and the words are emphatic. What good is it if those message elements do not reach the intended audience?

Suppose you're selling canned soup. The media team targets traditional users of canned soup—mothers of young children—but the copy team prepares advertisements intended to encourage single people to use the soup for a quick, wholesome meal. The message will not make much sense to the media audience because the media and copy strategies do not match.

Exhibit 1.1

Typical Allocations for a Consumer Advertising Campaign

A typical advertising campaign budget is divided up for a variety of needs and purposes. Here is a sample advertising budget from a campaign to promote a consumer packaged good.

Budget item	Budget allocation (%)
Research, precampaign, and postcampaign evaluation	3–6
Message development	5–8
Advertising media	80–85
Production	4–7
Overhead, administration, agency profits	1–3

Source: Advertising Research Foundation.

A great advertising message in front of the wrong audience is a total waste of time and effort. If you focus on the message strategies and ignore the media strategies, you risk sabotaging the entire package: the campaign, the budget, and everyone's hard work.

That, of course, is where the advertising media plan plays its role. A solid media plan with good media selection and media buying can ensure that the message reaches the right people at the right time and in the right mood. Based on solid research, a good media effort is what makes the rest of the advertising campaign work—or not work.

Media Are Least Understood

Most advertising campaigns are sold to the client advertiser based on the message. If the message is good, the campaign is more likely to be adopted. That's because the message is inherently the most interesting part of the advertising campaign. And it should be. The message is what is going to attract, inform, entertain, promote, convince, and sell your service or product. It is supposed to be attractive and interesting.

The advertising agency stresses the message, the advertiser client sees and hears the message, and the prospective campaign is adopted based largely on the message. Typically, the advertiser (the client) pays attention to messages and promotions, and maybe even to research, but not to the media plan. To match the client's interests in a proposed advertising campaign, the advertising agency presents more material dealing with the message and not as much dealing with research, production, evaluation, or media.

So most proposed campaign presentations spend the most time on the message strategies and relatively little on the media portion of the campaign. The top executives may assume that the media plan is complete and logical, but that is not always the case.

This is precisely why you need to pay attention to the media plan. Whereas others might be apt to downplay or overlook it, you are the one responsible for making sure that the media plan makes sense and can be accomplished efficiently and accurately for the complete success of the advertising campaign.

Media Are Critical to Success of the Brand

Obviously, then, advertising media are critical to advertising success. Advertising success brings with it the achievement of the marketing goals: more sales, positive opinions, increased awareness, word-of-mouth recommendations, competitive advantages, or whatever your goals may happen to be. Accomplishing those goals makes your brand successful, and hanging on that brand success is your success as a brand manager, or as an account executive or supervisor or administrator.

Advertising media are critical to the success of the brand and thus critical to your success as a manager. As we have already seen, poor media choices can waste an entire advertising campaign. On the other hand, proper and efficient use of advertising media can ensure its success, and it is up to you to be certain that the media contribute all they potentially can to that end.

Client Exposure to the Advertising

Advertisers like to see their own advertising. Top executives know how much is being spent on advertising, and they want to see and hear that advertising in the media. Top executives who know and approve total advertising budgets are not likely to understand the nuances of advertising, including media. They simply know they are spending large sums of money to promote their products and services, and they want to see effective outcomes. These outcomes will eventually be product sales and brand preference, but in the meantime executives want to see their advertising running in the media.

You may not target media specifically to reach those executives. You may not even know which media the executives read, listen to, or watch. But if your media plan reaches your industry and your prospects, you will be reaching your own executives and supervisors as well.

Good media plans make sure that the advertisements appear in places where they will be exposed to your firm's executives. The only way to be certain that will happen is if you are on top of advertising media in general, and your specific advertising media plan in particular.

Media Support Product Positioning

Perhaps the most crucial decisions you make involve positioning for the product or service that you are marketing. Brand positioning plays a critical role in the success or failure of your marketing program. Once the position has been determined, it must be translated into advertising; the positioning is meaningless if it is not supported in the advertising.

One of the most sensible and direct ways of translating positioning into advertising is through advertising media. The media reach those same customers whom you have selected as the target audience for the brand and its position. There is no way that positioning will be successful if it is not supported adequately and accurately through the media selections and placements.

So successful marketing depends on successful positioning. If you want your positioning to be successful, you must select and utilize advertising media effectively, efficiently, and, above all, accurately. Advertising media play an essential role in your brand's success and, ultimately, in your own success and progress.

The Ever-Changing World of Media

The basics of good marketing communications have remained constant over the years, and positioning strategy has changed only slightly since the late 1980s. Still, advertising media have evolved rapidly over the past 10 years, led principally by the digital media revolution.

We have certainly seen the rise of new kinds of advertising media over the past decade. The Internet has led the way with a wide variety of media such as search-engine marketing, rich media, and streaming audio and video. Other media channels have come into play, including the iPod, cellular phones, video games, and satellite radio. Existing media have evolved as well. The area of point-of-sale advertising has been transformed in the 21st century, with opportunities appearing in seemingly every venue. Malls now have digital signs that show television commercials. In some major markets, buses contain television sets that are programmed to show a retail ad within a block or two of the advertising establishment. Ads are popping up in elevators, inside fortune cookies, and even on celebrity and wannabe-celebrity body parts.

The rise of consumer-generated media is redefining the media landscape as well. Now, anyone with a video camera can shoot a commercial and post it on the Internet. Blogs, which are personal journals posted on the Net, allow everyone the freedom to comment on whatever they want. Fundamentally, anything can become a medium these days for good or bad.

This digital revolution has changed the way that advertisers and marketers approach media. Before the digital revolution, advertising pushed a message out to consumers with little direct feedback. Today, consumers are providing feedback to marketers through their own media and by asking for deals from select advertisers. This type of marketing is dialogue-based rather than push-based messaging.

The advertising industry has also undergone major structural changes. At one time, media ownership was largely a mom-and-pop business. An individual family owned a local newspaper, radio station, or television station. Today, there has been massive consolidation of media outlets. There were once hundreds of radio station owners; at one time Clear Channel owned more than half of all radio stations in the United States. Time Warner controls a host of mass and interpersonal media, from magazines to television to Internet to motion pictures. Within the past 10 years, the power of search-engine marketing companies such as Google has brought a new wave of corporations to what used to be a very clubby business.

The jury is still out on the social and marketing impacts of this media ownership consolidation. Many believe that news and information, because it is controlled by just a few companies, has become stilted, or fixed. Counter to that argument, we have seen the rise of consumer-generated media as a collective voice in many social circumstances. From a marketing viewpoint, advertisers fear that media mergers will bring about higher advertising rates. But with so many new media on the horizon this has also become moot. What we are seeing is the rise of multimedia companies providing advertisers with content that crosses a variety of platforms.

The Changing Nature of Media Effectiveness

Media plans and media buys have long been judged on their efficiency. Today, new emphasis is on how consumers use media, how media impact the creative content, and when consumers are most susceptible to the message.

Let's tackle the area of susceptibility first. Psychologists have long debated whether primacy or recency is more important in advertising. Does it help more to be the first advertisement seen or heard in your product category, or is it better to be the last advertisement seen or heard before the consumer makes a purchase decision? The current trend is for recency, which affects both the frequency and placement of advertising. For example, if you know that most consumers make a meal decision an hour or two before they eat, then you may want to load up your advertising to intercept them at that moment. Looking at the media world through the consumers' eyes is an evolving area in media studies. In the past, media planners traditionally used syndicated research to determine what consumers watch, read, or listen to. They then constructed media plans that were the most efficient combination of those elements. Today, media planners continue to look at syndicated data, but they are more likely to conduct their own consumer research. They may observe how consumers use media, or how various media influence consumers' decisions about a brand. For example, a recent study showed marked differences in consumers' views of media for impulse items versus planned purchases. So effectiveness in a particular case might mean finding the medium that fits best with, say, an impulse-purchase decision. This type of thinking is much more in line with consumer behavior theory than media theory and has led to a number of studies regarding the role of media in the creative message. For example, if a brand's success is based on a high degree of trust, would you be better off placing it on the nightly news or during a soap opera? This study found that there is a significant copy-recall benefit for such a brand if it is on the nightly news rather than during a soap opera. Media effectiveness is certainly an evolving aspect of the media landscape.

Media are also looked at from a return-on-investment perspective. In fact, media are sales channels for many brands. Retailers may have stores, website sales, catalogs, and kiosks. They may know exactly what a particular Sunday insert does for their business. Most service brands track the source of their leads, whether through the Yellow Pages, local search-engine marketing, or word-of-mouth. Brand marketers conduct rigorous analyses to determine the lift that each medium and vehicle gives to incremental brand sales. And business-to-business brand managers are using media to sell merchandise directly. The PC company Dell is a primary example of this type of advertising, where each sale is coded to a particular media and message source.

All these recent changes and future developments make it mandatory that everyone who works with advertising—and especially brand managers—has a working knowledge of how advertising media operate and the role they play in the overall advertising and marketing efforts.

Good Media Planning Increases Efficiency

As we have said, media efficiency is a primary goal of advertising media planning and buying. Efficiency, though, does not always mean getting the lowest price. In this case, we look at efficiency in terms of having the optimum amount of advertising to do the job. No firm wants to waste money, and that includes not wasting the advertising budget.

Too much media overlap is inefficient. If the selected media and vehicles all reach the same audience, advertisers risk losing out on a broader audience that could help build market breadth.

Too much frequency is also inefficient. You want to advertise enough so that your customers do what you want them to do: switch brands, think favorably of your brand, know your product's attributes, or simply buy your product. You want your advertising to reach them enough times to accomplish those goals. More than that may be unnecessary.

To be efficient, your advertising should reach genuine prospects. Advertising that does not focus on those who are genuine prospects is wasteful.

A solid advertising media plan can avoid the inefficiencies of excessive overlap, frequency, and waste. Certainly, some media overlap is desirable to reinforce the message in a variety of ways and from a variety of sources. Frequency of exposure is also important: an advertising message that is seen or heard only once is unlikely to work. Similarly, it is impossible to reach all your prospects and only your prospects; some coverage will go to nonprospects. A golf equipment campaign that uses both *Golf Digest* and *Sports Illustrated* will find that some audience members read both publications; that is not necessarily bad, but make sure that you count the double exposure in your calculations of total audience impressions to minimize the possibility of wasteful overlap. For a bread account, an average exposure level of 20 times a week is probably excessive; frequency is important, but overdoing it wastes money. If you sell dog food, it may not be possible to reach dog owners and only dog owners; still, you do not want too much of your advertising to appear before those who do not have dogs and are not likely to buy your dog food. Knowledge of advertising media and media planning will help you avoid these excessive and wasteful practices, which will lead to yet another benefit.

Media Efficiency Provides Budget Flexibility

If you reduce waste, you save money. Saving money means that your budget will go further, you will have money left over for other uses, and you can afford to underwrite additional promotions.

Your knowledge and understanding of advertising media planning can help you avoid the excesses of overlap, frequency, and waste, achieving the correct levels of exposure without going beyond them. In turn, you will then have more money left in your budget. Leftover monies mean

Table 1.1

Media Expenditures in the United States (in %)

Television	45.4
Network TV	18.6
Cable TV	13.2
Spot TV	10.6
Syndicated TV	3.0
Magazines	20.0
Newspapers	17.6
Internet	6.8
Radio	6.6
Outdoor	2.7
Other media	0.9

Source: Figures compiled from industry sources by In-Telligence, Inc. Used by permission.

greater flexibility; more advertising and promotions; increased product awareness, knowledge, and sales; and quicker and greater brand success. And those are your goals. Efficiency in your use of advertising media helps you have more funds to achieve all your goals, making you and your brand successful.

If your automotive service campaign reduces excessive media overlap, cuts frequency of advertising closer to the minimal effective level, and avoids reaching audiences who do not own cars, you may be able to save enough money from your advertising budget to run additional promotions, to introduce a new add-on service, to promote dollars-off or coupon offers, or perhaps to start a special selling effort aimed at getting competitors' customers to switch to your service. These new additions are certain to increase your chances of higher sales and more revenue.

Gaining efficiency makes sense, whether to save money or to provide remainder funds for new efforts.

Here at the beginning of your study of advertising media, it may be useful to understand what the overall media business looks like in advertising. Look at Table 1.1, which shows the share of total advertising revenue that each of the major advertising media receives in the United States. You will see that although television captures the bulk of advertising investments by far, its share is somewhat static. It is even in a bit of a decline. This is partly because of the economy, partly because of the huge expense of advertising in television, and partly because other media, such as the Internet and social media, are growing rapidly, taking away from some of the more established media—what we call the traditional media.

The shares held by print media, newspapers, and magazines have been shrinking in recent years. Some individual publications have been doing quite well, but the numbers of magazines and newspapers have been falling, and many of the remaining publications are attracting fewer advertising dollars and certainly a smaller share of the advertising investment total.

To use advertising media effectively, it is useful to have an overall perspective of the size of the advertising marketplace.

Chapter 2

Outlining the Components of a Communication Plan

Every communication plan should begin with an outline. Outlining what is contained in the plan is an efficient way to begin the communication planning project. Of course all plans are unique depending upon the advertiser, but there are some fundamentals that should be part of any communication plan.

Exhibit 2.1 contains an outline for a communication plan. There are ten broad areas that are covered. They begin from an executive summary to how you would measure the results of your plan. Other than the executive summary, each component of the plan builds on the prior component. For example, marketing objectives/strategies lead into the role that communication plays in solving the marketing challenge. This leads to communication objectives which then lead to communication strategies and tactics. Each communication plan is not unlike a book. It tells a story. In this case, the story is how you plan to solve the brand's marketing challenge.

Communication Plan versus Media Plan

A communication plan and a media plan have very similar components. The difference between a communication plan and a media plan is the approach to solving the marketing problem. In an advertising media plan, it is assumed that advertising is the solution to the marketing problem. Therefore, a paid media plan is necessary to convey the advertising message to the appropriate target market.

In a communication plan, advertising is one of a myriad of alternatives to solve the marketing challenge. It may be the solution or not. Or advertising may be a part of the solution in combination with other communication alternatives. A communication plan then assesses advertising, promotions, publicity, direct response, and any other form of communication. The com-

Exhibit 2.1

Components of a Communication Plan

1. Executive Summary
   a. Summary of marketing objectives/strategies
   b. Summary of communication objectives/strategies
   c. Budget summary
2. Situation Analysis
   a. Marketing
   b. Communication
   c. SWOT
3. Marketing Objectives/Strategies
   a. Business
   b. Brand
4. Role of Communication
   a. Message
5. Communication Objectives
   a. Target segment
   b. Geography
   c. Seasonal/Timing
   d. Reach/Frequency/Continuity
6. Communication Strategies
   a. Mix
   b. Scheduling
7. Communication Tactics
   a. Vehicle
   b. Rationale
   c. Costs
   d. Impressions
8. Communication Budget
   a. Dollars by communication channel
   b. Dollars by month
9. Communication Flowchart
   a. Weekly schedule
   b. Recap of dollars
   c. Recap of impressions
   d. Reach/Frequency
10. Testing and Evaluation
    a. Test programs
    b. Evaluation methods

munication plan should be strategy neutral. It doesn't assume that one method of communication is better than another going into the planning process.

Components of a Communication Plan

There are ten components to the communication plan, as highlighted in Exhibit 2.1. The following are brief descriptions of what is contained in each of these elements.

1. Executive Summary

An executive summary focuses management on the link between the marketing objectives and strategies and the communication objectives and strategies. From a management viewpoint, it is crucial to understand how communication is tied to the business goals of the brand. Management will also want to understand the strategic nature of the plan and the budget necessary to implement it. All of that is contained in the executive summary.

2. Situation Analysis

The situation analysis forms the context for the plan. It should contain a marketing analysis as well as a communication analysis. A marketing analysis contains a review of pricing, distribution, resources, and product differentiation compared with competing brands in the category. Communication analysis contains message, copy, and communication channel comparisons to competing brands in the category. Both should roll up into a strengths, weaknesses, opportunities, and threats summary. This is called a SWOT analysis.

3. Marketing Objectives/Strategies

All communication plans derive from a marketing strategy. It is paramount to recap the marketing objectives and strategies. These objectives and strategies should have two aspects. One is business objectives, typically defined by number of customers and sales. The second is brand aspects, which may be defined by specific brand attributes such as quality or value.

4. Role of Communication

The role of communication defines how communication is going to solve the marketing challenge or meet the objectives. The role of communication is how the brand is going to communicate with its consumers. Some typical roles of communication are to increase awareness, change perceptions, announce new "news," and associate the brand with quality perception. Within this section should be the role that communication plays as well as the creative message strategy. This is the foundation for the communication plan.

5. Communication Objectives

Communication objectives include whom you are going to target with the message, where you are targeting, when you are targeting, and how much pressure you plan to provide the message. The Big Four communication objectives are target market, geography, seasonal/timing, and reach/frequency/continuity.

6. Communication Strategies

Communication strategies are the ways you plan to achieve the objectives. Each objective should have a corresponding strategy. There are two major strategies for a communication plan. The first is the communication mix. This is the mix of communication channels you plan to use to achieve the objectives. The second is scheduling, that is, when you plan on deploying each channel.

7. Communication Tactics

Communication tactics reflect the details of the strategies. For example, if a strategy to support a specific local market contains print and radio, then the tactics would be what print vehicles and radio formats or stations to recommend. Tactics are the specifics of the plan. They should address each vehicle recommended, the creative unit, costs, and the impressions that the vehicle will deliver.

8. Communication Budget

Communication budget is a recap of the dollars allocated to each communication channel and not to the specific vehicle. For example, funds would be allocated to magazines as a category, that is, the communication channel, not *Vanity Fair, Wired,* and *GQ* individually. Communication budgets include dollars by channel and also a recap of dollars by month.

9. Communication Flowchart

A communication flowchart is a schematic of the plan on a single page. It contains a weekly schedule of activity, a recap of dollars by vehicle and category, a recap of impressions by vehicle and category, and a reach/frequency analysis. The communication flowchart is a summary of all activity, scheduling, and costs.

10. Testing and Evaluation

Testing and evaluation are optional aspects of a communication plan. Many communication plans have test programs. A test program may be to test how an increase in media pressure might impact a specific market, or it may be to test an emerging medium. Any test would be covered in this section. The other aspect of this section is how to evaluate the success of the plan. This may be a recap of a research method or a recap of the measure and methods to ensure that the communication plan reaches its impression objectives.

Summary

Before exploring a particular communication plan, it is important to outline its components. Doing so will provide the best and most efficient method for developing the plan. It is vital that each section of the plan build on the prior section. A communication plan is a strategic road map on how you plan to solve marketing challenges.

Chapter 3

How Marketing Objectives Impact Communication Planning

Never, under any condition, should you begin an advertising media plan without first establishing your objectives. But establishing objectives for your media effort is not the first thing you should do.

This seemingly contradictory advice is not really so puzzling. Establish your objectives before you begin your planning effort, whether in media or any other aspect of your marketing program. Media objectives rely on other objectives, and those other objectives must be established prior to laying out your media objectives.

Objectives: Marketing, Communication, Advertising, Then Media

Always begin by establishing the overall marketing objectives. Then set separate advertising objectives, which must be in concert with and derived from the overall marketing objectives. Finally, set the communication and media objectives, which are based on the advertising objectives, which, as we just saw, are based on the marketing objectives. Again, the communication and advertising media objectives will be stated separately from the other objectives, but they will derive from and support both the advertising objectives and the marketing objectives. Advertising media do not operate in a vacuum; they must be part of the overall marketing, communication, and advertising plans. Of course, not everything goes as planned, which is why contingency plans are also necessary (see Exhibit 3.1).

Along with media objectives, you are likely to include specific advertising message objectives and perhaps research, production, or other types of objectives for your advertising campaign.

Exhibit 3.1

Contingency Plans

Perhaps the best time to prepare for next year's taxes is right after you finish this year's taxes. That way, you'll have all your documents and figures, and you will know what you wish you had done better for the current year.

Similarly, the best time to do a contingency media plan is right after the proposed media plan has been completed. That way, you have all your documents and figures, and you are well aware of the other options that came to mind.

A contingency plan is not the same as a reserve fund. A reserve takes part of the advertising media budget and sets it aside for unanticipated emergencies. Doing that indicates two negative ideas: you are not confident about your proposed plan, and you don't need your entire budget.

A better strategy is a contingency plan, which is an alternative to the plan that has been proposed. Rather than setting aside budgeted monies, it allows for transfers among media choices.

Contingency plans usually answer three questions, all of which start with the same phrase: What will you do during the year if . . . ? The questions are these:

1. What will you do during the year if sales expectations are not being met?
2. What will you do during the year if sales expectations are being exceeded?
3. What will you do during the year if a competitor takes some unexpected action?

If the campaign proposal is for some period other than a year, substitute "during the campaign period" for "during the year."

The more complete and accurate you can make your contingency plans, the better. If they are actually needed, it will likely be an emergency situation, so you will not have time to re-do media plans or to finalize details. You need contingency plans that you can put into action on short notice.

Based on Research

Ideally, all objectives will be based on research. Be wary if someone proposes to use advertising media, or to use advertising at all, without first doing research. Some people seem to have an innate feeling or sixth sense about advertising and media, but they are not really operating without research foundations; instead, they are using their own experience and expertise, which are a type of research, based on the results of past efforts.

Most people, though, must make manifest their research efforts. You draw up a list of questions to which you need the answers, and then you design or contract for research that will provide insights into those answers.

Perhaps surprisingly, the research may not include such questions as, what advertising media should we use in the upcoming campaign? Instead, questions may focus on the best kinds of people to target or the best kinds of locations in which to market. The answers to these questions will help you derive your target markets and target groups and, then, your media selections.

Utilizing research makes the task much easier when it is time to establish the marketing, advertising, communication, and media objectives.

Objectives as a Road Map

Imagine that you are in Kansas City and you want to drive to Tulsa. Unless you are familiar with the route, you would likely consult a road map.

When you look at the map, you first find Kansas City, then you find Tulsa, and on the map you might work your way back from Tulsa to Kansas City. If you just start out driving from Kansas City, you have no idea which way to go: north, south, east, west, or, in this case, southwest. So knowing where you already are is important, but knowing that alone is not enough. You need to know your destination, too.

If you track back from Tulsa to Kansas City, you are working from your objective back to your starting point. That is not the way you will drive it; you will drive just the reverse, from Kansas City to Tulsa. But you will plot your course from the destination back to the point of origin.

That's the way you make a plan work, too, whether it is a marketing plan, an advertising plan, a communication plan, or a media plan. You know your point of origin, and then you set up your objectives. Finally, you plan how to make your way from the origination point to the objective, and you often do it by first working backward to find out what is needed to meet your goals.

Objectives, Strategies, and Tactics

So far, we have used the term *objectives* for the place you wish to go. Sometimes the term *goals* will be used. In advertising, objectives are what you want to accomplish in the long term and goals are what you want to accomplish in the short term. In business, the short term is usually within the coming year, and the long term applies to things beyond the coming year. Use this vocabulary consistently with your co-workers.

Most of the time, you will have a five-year plan, which is the long term, with details for the coming year, which is the short term. Each year, you will update the short-term goals and plans, and then extend the long-term plans and objectives for another year, always working about five years ahead. Whether it is three years or five years or ten years does not matter so much as the fact that you always have short-term and long-term achievements and plans, and that they are updated regularly—because things often change rapidly in advertising. The long-range plans may be for a shorter period and the updating may occur more often.

So objectives and goals are what you want to achieve. The plans you establish to meet these objectives and goals are called strategies. Then, the implementation or execution of those plans is called the tactics. Remember that distinction. Tactics are putting the plans into action.

You always have these three stages: first, objectives and goals, what you want to achieve; second, your strategies, the plans to achieve those goals and objectives; and third, the tactics, by which you implement your plans.

Advertising Media Are Strategies, Not Objectives

Even though you will eventually establish media objectives and goals, the advertising media themselves are not objectives or goals. Media are strategies.

Your advertising media goals may be to reach a certain number of persons, with a certain frequency, with some impact. The media goal is not to use newspapers or television or outdoor billboards. The media themselves are strategies; they are ways that you plan to achieve those goals of reach, frequency, and impact, and maybe continuity, cost efficiency, and creative considerations.

Keep this distinction in mind. Media are strategies, not goals or objectives. Do not establish goals to use certain media. Instead, establish goals of things that you hope to accomplish with your advertising media, and leave the actual media selection to the strategy stage.

Why make this differentiation? Because if you establish the use of certain types of media as part of your goals, you are setting out on your trip without knowing where you want to go. It would be like driving in any direction from Kansas City, on any highway, without knowing in which direction is Tulsa. If you spell out the media as goals, you are likely to overlook some good alternatives, because your mind is already made up.

Make this a three-stage process. First, set your media goals and objectives, without detailing which actual media might be used. Then plan how to achieve the goals and objectives, using the best types of media. Finally, implement the plan and execute the actual advertising campaign.

Setting Good Objectives

Good goals and objectives, then, help you determine where you want to go with your marketing, advertising, communication, and media efforts. So setting good objectives and goals is crucial to success.

Good objectives usually use the infinitive form of a verb, as in "to do" something. Your objectives might be to accomplish, to sell, to convince, to change, to increase, to communicate, to eliminate, to compete, to modify, to promote, to reach, or to do any of a host of other things, or some combination of these things.

Note that the advertising media themselves could not possibly be objectives and goals because they are not verbs. You could not have "to newspaper" or "to outdoor" as a media goal.

Good objectives will also be quantifiable. It is easy to say that you wish to increase sales. Then, if this year you sell 3,000,000 items, you will have met your goal if next year you sell 3,000,001. But is that a real increase? It is more helpful to state quantifiable terms. Say "next year, we will increase our sales by 2.2 percent" or "next year, we will increase sales by 60,000 units." Then you will know for sure whether you have increased your sales, and you will know for sure whether you have met your goal.

Consistency with Message Strategies

It is also important for your media goals and objectives to be consistent with other goals and objectives, as well as with other strategies. We have already seen that advertising media goals must be consistent with marketing and advertising goals.

Your advertising media goals must also be consistent with strategies from other aspects of the campaign, especially with message strategies. If, for example, the copy and art teams have already decided that they must use

Exhibit 3.2

Examples of Marketing, Advertising, Communication, and Media Objectives

Here are examples of categories that might be used for objectives in marketing, advertising, communication, and media.

Marketing objectives	Advertising objectives	Communication objectives	Media objectives
Sales levels (in dollars and in units)	Merchandising support Creative considerations	Message Points of recall	Efficiency CPP and CPM—
Sales shares (in percentages and in competitive indices)	Media considerations: Flexibility Contingency	Major stressed items Order of items	Then, TAI and GRP targets can be derived
Product position	Timing:	Target audiences	Reach
Geographic distribution	Flights Hiatus periods	Need for awareness,	Frequency Impact
General consumer profile	Sustaining periods Budget considerations:	knowledge Product or service	Continuity Targets:
Competitive goal	Allocations to:	strengths	Groups
Timing during year	Regions	Geographic	Regions
Timing by seasons	Markets	distribution of	Markets
Packaging	Media functions	messages	Audiences
Pricing	Targets	Formats	Creative
Types of store or other outlets	Target markets:[a] Areas or regions	Audience calculations	considerations and support
Relative needs for awareness, knowledge, interest, desire, and sales	Target groups[a] Target audiences[a] Levels of awareness, Circulation numbers desire, and purchase Competitive	Size Composition	Media capabilities Flexibility Merchandising support Competitive
Distribution knowledge, preference, considerations	prospects numbers Show package? concentration[c]		strategies Audience sizes[b] Matched with Media mix vs.
Tell price? Coupons	Advertising units		media

[a]Target markets, target groups, and target audiences are often left to the strategy stage, rather than included as objectives.

[b]All given in audience terms, not simply in demographics.

[c]Note that media types to be used are usually considered strategies rather than objectives.

demonstration to make the advertising campaign effective, then the media goals must reflect the need for media that allow for demonstration. Such media include television and cinema, but it is too early to state what media type will be used; in the goal-setting stage, it is enough to state that the eventual media selection must include media that permit ease of demonstration.

There has long been a controversy over which should be decided first, the advertising message or the advertising media. It makes sense for media to come first, because it would be silly and wasteful for the message and creative strategies to develop messages for, say, billboards if outdoor advertising is not included in the schedule. In fact, however, most often message dictates media. If the creative, message, or copy staff needs certain capabilities, it is usually up to the media goals and plans to accommodate them. In the best case, both media and message will be developed alongside each other, simultaneously, so that each can draw upon the expertise and capabilities of the other. Because of the time constraints involved in advertising, this ideal situation too often does not occur (see Exhibit 3.2).

Marketing Goals Bring Media Plans

So there you have the outline of how to establish goals and objectives, whether for marketing, communication, advertising, media, or any other phase of the marketing effort. You also have an understanding of the process: first, goals and objectives, then strategies, and finally tactics. And you can see how the various phases must work together and support each other.

Good objectives and goals are essential in every phase of your work, and advertising media work is no exception.

In some cases, the campaign targets are established as part of the goals and objectives, but more often, targets are part of the strategies. In the next chapter, you will learn more about setting up and reaching your advertising media targets.

Chapter 4

Working with a Situation Analysis

Before providing a strategic recommendation, assess the situation. That is the first step in the planning process. A properly constructed situation analysis should provide you with the necessary information and insights to construct a communication plan that will meet the brand and marketing objectives.

SWOT Analysis

The situation analysis is typically called a SWOT analysis. SWOT stands for strengths, weaknesses, opportunities, and threats. Exhibit 4.1 diagrams the SWOT analysis and the components of it. Here is an overview of what each of the four areas contains.

1. Strengths

Strengths are something that the brand has that will be helpful in achieving the marketing objectives. For example, Frito-Lay has a sophisticated and highly developed distribution network for providing its products to all types of retail outlets including grocery stores, convenience stores, and institutions. If Frito-Lay is introducing a new product, this would be a great asset.

2. Weaknesses

Weaknesses are items the brand has that are harmful in achieving the marketing objectives. For example, Cadillac has an old and stodgy reputation that would impact the ability to attract a younger buyer to the company's automotive products.

Exhibit 4.1

SWOT Analysis

Helpful	Harmful
Strength	Weakness
Opportunity	Threat

3. Opportunities

Opportunities are external forces that will be helpful or will aid the brand in reaching its objectives. For example, if birthrates for young women are rising by 5 percent, that is a good trend for Pampers. Or if the U.S. government taxes soft drinks, that could be an opportunity for bottled water brands.

4. Threats

Threats are external forces that will be harmful or will get in the way of the brand achieving its objectives. For example, if Pepsi increases its marketing budget by 50 percent, that could negatively impact Coke and other brands in the soft drink category. Another example is the government banning soda machines from all public schools.

Putting SWOT in Context

It is important to construct a SWOT analysis with a goal in mind. Otherwise, the SWOT analysis becomes a listing of unrelated items that do not impact the future strategy of the brand. So, if the brand's objective is to grow by 5 percent and the strategy for doing this is by expanding the user base of the brand, then the SWOT analysis should be done within that context.

In this case, it means looking at consumers who do not use the brand. A brand strength may be that the brand is accessible to new users. But a weakness may be that it is perceived as being too expensive. An opportunity could be that there is a movement toward quality within the category. A threat could be that another brand completely dominates this sector of the market.

Instead of just listing items to fill in each box in the SWOT analysis, always think about how each item will either help or hurt the brand's cause. That will make your SWOT analysis more powerful and actionable.

Integrated Marketing Communication SWOT

As you develop a SWOT analysis for an integrated marketing communication plan, you should identify both marketing and communication elements that can impact the brand. The third category is consumer trends that impact both areas. Here are examples of marketing and communication items that should be considered for the SWOT analysis.

1. Marketing

Marketing elements include distribution, pricing, and product comparisons between the brand and its competitors. Marketing can also include items such as how financially strong the company is, how experienced the management is, and any patents or other proprietary items that the company has of value. It can also include brand perceptions by the consumer and other perceptual items related to the brand.

2. Communication

Communication elements include message, copy platforms, and communication outlet comparisons between the brand and its competitors. Communication can also include perceptual elements such as how strong the creative message is and if there are any media or sponsorships that are associated with the brand. It can also be cost or consumer trends in media consumption.

This is not an exhaustive list of items for either marketing or communication. The key is to identify all the elements that are relevant to the brand and its competitive set. It is also important to view the brand from the consumer's viewpoint. How the consumer sees the brand is crucial in determining how to tackle the marketing challenge. This should be captured in the SWOT analysis.

Summary

The SWOT analysis is a tremendous tool for determining future communication strategy. Remember that the best SWOT analysis starts with an objective in mind. This puts the SWOT analysis in proper context. Ensure that the SWOT analysis contains both marketing and communication elements. These suggestions and a thorough review of consumer trends will aid in developing a meaningful analysis.

Chapter 5
Defining the Target Audience

Nothing is more important in building an effective media plan than properly defining the target market and audience. An efficient execution of an improperly targeted media plan is not going to matter. As brand manager, you need to ensure that the media plan and the creative execution are working together. If the agency's creative group is crafting commercials for an upscale, suburban soccer mom while the media group is working on an efficient media plan aimed at a downscale, rural, single mom, then your advertising program is likely to be ineffective and maybe even offensive.

The term *target* can have a wide variety of uses and meanings. A *target market* typically refers to the geographic market you are considering for your advertising. Some advertisers use the term *target group* to define a demographic target, whereas others use *target audience* to mean just the media target. In this chapter, we use the term *target audience* to mean the media audience.

Arriving at the right target audience appears on the surface to be a simple exercise, but it takes careful crafting and tremendous coordination to get the most out of your marketing budget. The target you choose must make sense from a business perspective, a marketing perspective, a media perspective, and a creative perspective. Unless all your stars are aligned, your spaceship will likely hit an asteroid.

For example, in the late 1990s, Chef Boyardee changed its target emphasis to teen-aged boys, who made up the largest consumer category of the brand. Message strategy was crafted and tested, and a media plan was fully developed. The program resulted in a double-digit decline in brand sales for Chef Boyardee. But doesn't targeting your best consumers make sense? The answer is, only if they are buying the product. In this case, mom still bought the brand and, although kids were the ultimate consumers, mom was still making the purchase decision. When the target was subsequently changed to favor mothers, brand sales began to rise. The moral is that you must start with the right objectives before moving toward a proper target.

Start with the Right Objectives

Isn't getting the proper target as simple as finding out who is using the brand and getting your message to them? As we saw in the Chef Boyardee situation, teen boys may be the consumption target, but they are rarely near a grocery store to buy the product. Obviously, understanding who uses your brand is paramount to the targeting process, but it is not the best place to begin.

The place to begin to define the target is with the behavior you want to change. This behavior may be included in the creative brief but is many times left out of the media discussion. For example, you may have a marketing objective of increasing the user base of your brand. You need to attract new users. If your media plan targets heavy users of the brand, are you going to meet that goal? Of course not.

It is important to outline the specific objective that your marketing plan seeks to accomplish before evaluating the appropriate media target. As we will see, the media planning group should be right in the midst of defining the target, but it is more than strictly a media exercise.

Let's take a look at the soup category. Campbell's soup dominates the U.S. market, so the company must try to expand the category in order to attain growth. Campbell's can do this either by getting more people to eat soup or by getting current users to use it more frequently in recipes. Brands such as Progresso and Healthy Choice need current soup users to switch to their brands. Other brands, such as Lipton and Knorr, look for niche markets: Lipton wants people who will cook with dry soup, and Knorr wants people who rarely if ever use prepared soups.

As brand manager, you need to assess the strengths and weaknesses of the brand in question. If your charge is to grow the brand by 5 percent, then you have a number of ways to get there.

One of the most likely ways to accomplish this goal is to get your current users to use your brand more often. In this case, you would target your current user base. You may also have to attract new users away from other brands (stealing share) or grow the category. This would lead to a target that might not necessarily be your brand's existing audience. Perhaps there is an ethnic niche that hasn't been mined. Or there may be a purchase influence dynamic at play, where the influencer, rather than the actual purchaser, drives the business.

Again, all your goals must align. Start with the business goal, which is typically growing the business at X percent. Then ask yourself how you are going to get there. From this point, you should assess your brand versus the category and the competition. Is the product category growing at the same rate as the brand? Is there a gap between your brand and the category that could lead to a potential source of business? Or is there some sort of competitive threat or opportunity that would lead to a growth opportunity for the brand? Once these issues are raised with both the agency and the brand group, you can begin to define the proper target audience.

Tools for Defining the Target Audience

A number of secondary research tools can aid in defining the media target. Over the years, there have been several improvements in linking actual brand purchase data to media behavior. These have led to a recent rise in the ability to model schedules and to determine the sales impact potential of various media alternatives.

Historically, the two nationally syndicated research studies used by media planners have been those of Mediamark Research Inc. (MRI) and Simmons Market Research Bureau. Both annual studies were initially designed to support the magazine industry with sales and audience data. MRI has now become the standard for most brand media planning, and Simmons has moved into the custom research arena. Simmons recently teamed up with MasterCard to offer brand purchase data on an aggregate basis—a very powerful tool for goods that are not tracked by panel data from the Nielsen Company or Information Resources, Inc.'s (IRI) InfoScan. Nielsen and IRI are the two services that track manufacturers' brand movements through grocery store chains. Both have powerful databases of purchase behavior, which are used in helping media planners to understanding the purchase dynamics of a multitude of brands and categories.

MRI is currently the preferred national media planning tool. It provides information on more than 500 categories and 6,000 brands. MRI is the most widely used syndicated research service for determining magazine readership. Measuring 235 magazine titles for readership, MRI uses a "recent reading" technique with logo cards and a "sort board" with which respondents sort logos based on their reading habits of the past month. MRI also collects information on television, cable, radio networks and formats, newspaper readership, and Internet usage.

MRI's sample is 26,000 adults aged 18 and older (18+), so it is highly reliable. MRI surveys twice a year, so most media planners use the MRI Doublebase, which has 50,000 respondents as the key media targeting tool. The Doublebase is linked to other segmentation schemes such as PRIZM (Claritas's market segmentation system), Spectra, and NPD, which have developed consumer segmentation analyses that divide the population into common groups based on geography, demographics, and purchase behaviors. A typical segmentation study may have as many as 60 discrete groups. This brings us to the second major media planning tool—one used in the packaged-goods industry.

Nielsen and Spectra have developed a tool that bridges the gap between retail tracking and consumer targeting. This tool connects actual product purchase behavior with Spectra's lifestyle segmentation. Spectra's lifestyle segmentation grid allows the brand manager to analyze consumer behavior not only for media but for consumer promotion as well. With this segmentation scheme becoming very popular for brands, Spectra has become much more important in the media planning process with its link to MRI data.

Using this system, the media planner can get actual brand purchase data that can be linked to media behavior. Until this time, media planners used MRI for both media and marketing data. Now media planners can confirm MRI marketing data and use the same MRI data for media planning.

The Simmons National Consumer Survey (NCS) is another brand planning tool that is particularly powerful in the retail sector. It offers much the same data as MRI but is more extensive in terms of its own segmentation schemes. It is also a nice double-check for media planners to use in conjunction with MRI.

There are two local market tools available primarily for local retail planning. Scarborough Research, a service in joint partnership with the Nielsen Company and Arbitron, Inc., measures local media markets for the leading 75 U.S. markets. The Media Audit is a competitive product that offers a much deeper market list at 86 markets, but not quite the level of detail in terms of advertisers measured. Both are excellent sources for analyzing local market activity and can be manipulated to include custom regions.

Those are the key secondary resources used in broad-based media planning. Once a plan is developed, media buyers use specific audience measurement tools for negotiation purposes. The key broadcast sources are Nielsen for television and cable and Arbitron for radio. Recently, there has been a move toward primary research studies for the brand that can be geo-coded by either a PRIZM or Spectra database and linked back to other studies such as MRI.

Target Groups and Target Audiences

Keep in mind that not every target group can be reached by media. For example, if you are selling dog food, you might wish to target dog owners: all dog owners and only dog owners. But there is no advertising medium that reaches all of them and only them. Even media aimed at dog owners, such as *Dog Fancy,* reach some persons who do not have a dog. These people may still read the magazine even though they do not have a dog, perhaps because they do not have enough room for one or they travel too much, or they may have lost a dog. And, of course, even this publication cannot reach all owners of dogs. And there may be people who buy dog food who do not have a dog; perhaps they donate the food to a local humane shelter.

So you need to have a target group, but you also need to specify a target audience: a group that can be reached by media and that can be clearly defined.

At the same time, you also want a communication target. That may be the same as the target audience, but at times it might not be. Again, if you want to target dog owners, that is a target audience: households with dogs. But it's unlikely that the entire household is buying food for their dog. The principal purchasing agent is the communication target: the person who actually goes to the store to buy dog food.

The Heavy-User Definition

Now that you have the right tools, how do you go about defining an audience? There are a number of ways to look at an audience. We have identified some of these from the marketing objectives. An important way to look at your audience profile is in terms of consumption.

The Pareto principle states that 20 percent of the audience represents 80 percent of the consumption. There is a heavy-user segment for nearly every brand. The heavy user may not represent 80 percent of consumption, but there is usually a strong ratio that is typically in the 2-to-1 range for usage-to-users ratios. The procedure of looking at the heavy, medium, and light users of a brand is an excellent analysis tool and a viable way to target (see Tables 5.1 and 5.2).

Let's look at Hunt's tomato sauce. Here, the heavy user for tomato sauce represents 17 percent of the user base but accounts for 50 percent of the usage. This might suggest that Hunt's must not lose the heavy-user group because it is a small yet vital part of the category. The real opportunity may be in targeting those other 83 percent of the users to get them to use the brand more often.

You can extend the heavy-user analysis to look for gaps between how your brand attracts users and how the category attracts users. In this Hunt's example, suppose that the category of heavy users is concentrated in the age range of 25 to 34, but Hunt's heavy users are 35 to 49. This means that Hunt's has an opportunity to grow the brand by attacking this usage gap.

Table 5.1

Tomato Sauce Category Usage Analysis

Sauce category range	Users (000)	%	Volume (000)	%	Avg.
Heavy 6+	3,587	17	40,030	50	11.2
Medium 3–5	5,892	28	22,208	28	3.8
Light 1–2	11,395	55	17,359	22	1.5
	20,874	100	79,597	100	3.8

Source: MRI Doublebase.

Table 5.2

Diced Tomato Category Usage Analysis

Diced category range	Users (000)	%	Volume (000)	%	Avg.
Heavy 6+	1,867	14	15,406	41	80.0
Medium 3–5	2,481	18	8,487	22	3.4
Light 1–2	9,456	69	13,970	37	1.5
	13,804	100	37,863	100	2.7

Source: MRI Doublebase.

Another gap to analyze is the gap between competitive brands. For example, there is a definite difference in usage between Hunt's and its major competitor, Del Monte. After assessing the reason for this difference, the brand can determine if this gap is something that advertising can impact or if it is the result of a product trait.

The heavy-user concept is certainly one that packaged-goods brand managers use regularly. As well, retail and business-to-business brand managers can use this theory to segment their audiences.

For example, a grocery retailer knows that a mom with kids is likely to spend more on groceries than a single retired adult. The grocery retailer may use basket size (how many products and subsequently dollars a person is buying from the store) as a barometer of a heavy user. So, a shopper who spends $200 on an average visit is worth more than the one who spends $50 per visit. With sophisticated retail databases so prevalent in today's retail landscape, this type of analysis is relatively easy to conduct.

In the business-to-business world, transactions aren't usually as frequent as in retail or packaged goods. Nevertheless, there is still a size dimension that relates to heavy usage. One way that business-to-business marketers can evaluate their sales database is to see how large the sales are in rank order, or to have their financial department help them assess the profitability of each customer in terms of sales versus customer support required to service that customer. Each of these methods can be used to arrive at some form of ranking of heavy to light usage or of profitable to less profitable customer.

Lifestyle and Life Stage Segmentation

Beyond the usage method of targeting, there are a number of lifestyle and life stage assessment methods that affect media targeting. It is possible to gain insight into your target audience by looking at their lifestyles and life stages. We noted that the key tools for assessing lifestyles and life stages are PRIZM and Spectra. Both of these research tools define lifestyle largely by where you live and how affluent you are. For example, the lifestyle of a consumer who lives in an upscale suburb is very different from that of a consumer living in a downscale urban area. This type of analysis helps put a face on your target and may suggest that you need different media approaches to reach various lifestyle groups.

Another way to look at your target group is by their life stage. Consumer patterns of behavior are sometimes dictated by where you are in your life. There is a huge difference between a 25-year-old mother of two and a 25-year-old working woman with no kids. In many cases, life stages serve as marketing milestones that require different media approaches. For example, if you are a senior in college, it is likely that credit card companies have been soliciting you, because they know you will be getting a job soon and establishing credit. Similarly, new parents receive all sorts of coupons for various baby products as well as banking products to save for their children's education.

Let's look at an example of lifestyles and life stages of users of PAM Cooking Spray (Table 5.3). The PAM brand attracts an older and more affluent audience. The challenge for the PAM brand is to generate a new base of users with a younger audience.

Generations as a Target

We have discussed various demographic and brand usage approaches to targeting. One other method of targeting is to find common ground among various generations of consumers. Generations are brief periods of time that are connected with popular culture. Consumers of the same generation are connected not only by age but by the various milestones they have reached

Table 5.3

PAM Cooking Spray

	Life stage						
Spectra lifestyle	18–34 w/kids	18–34 w/o kids	35–54 w/kids	35–54 w/o kids	55–64	65	Total lifestyle
Upscale suburbs	105	53	112	104	136	154	116
Traditional families	73	55	93	107	130	178	111
Mid/upscale suburbs	62	60	108	82	122	142	108
Metro elite	78	34	88	71	121	130	83
Working-class towns	77	45	94	86	145	157	104
Rural towns and farms	48	44	86	103	127	145	99
Mid-urban melting pot	48	38	83	73	108	148	89
Downscale rural	49	35	90	86	119	162	103
Downscale urban	56	30	85	71	97	148	87
Total	65	42	94	87	124	151	100

Sources: AC Nielsen and Spectra/Media*PLAN.* Reprinted with permission.

together. Some unifying characteristics include music, fads, inventions, politics, and social movements. For example, the 1960s ushered in the British invasion of rock stars to the United States, led by the Beatles. World War II colored two generations: The first has been termed the G.I. Generation because its members fought in the war as adults; these Americans were later referred to as the "Greatest Generation" for defeating the Axis of Evil. The second generation impacted included those who were children during WWII; dubbed the Silent Generation, these Americans grew up in families that were preoccupied with the war. Table 5.4 offers a list of U.S. generations for the past 100 years.

Generations can be a very effective method of targeting. Members of these groups are connected not only demographically but also emotionally and historically. Many times an advertiser will choose music or images that stir emotions within a particular generation. From a media perspective, it is important to be sensitive to the demographic nuances of generations as well as to patterns of culture, either of which may be a good forum for delivering an advertising message.

Behavioral Targeting

Another way to target your market is by how its members behave. This type of targeting is very popular in the online world where it is possible to track the websites someone is visiting based on real-time. For example, if you have just visited a website on border collies, you are likely to be a pet

Table 5.4

List of U.S. Generations

Generation	Born	Notable Occurrences
Lost Generation	1883–1910	• Experienced WWI
G.I. Generation	1911–1924	• Fought WWII as adults • Called the "Greatest Generation"
Silent Generation	1925–1942	• Repressed childhoods due to WWII
Boomer Generation	1943–1965	• Civil Rights movement • Woodstock
Generation X	1965–1985	• Rise of mass media • End of Cold War • MTV
Generation Y	1986–2001	• Rise of Information Age • Internet
Generation Z	2002–	• Unknown

owner and receptive to a new dog food brand. That is how behavioral targeting works in the online world. But this type of targeting is not exclusive to cyberspace. Off-line, you can target people who drive Corvettes. Or you can target men who play golf. The idea of behavioral targeting is to have a relevant message for someone at the time it is most relevant to them—that is, when they are actually demonstrating or behaving in a way that indicates your brand is important to them.

This type of targeting can be stretched to more than just activities. You might consider targeting bargain hunters, those people who clip coupons or visit websites that sell discounted goods. In this way you are discovering some behavior outside of the brand's purchase dynamics that might be a good fit for the audience.

Purchaser versus Influencer

So far we have talked about the brand in terms of who is buying the product. For packaged goods, this is typically the mother in a household. But she is not always the one consuming the products. Whereas our secondary research tools do an excellent job of defining the purchaser, they do not necessarily define the actual consumer of the product.

To understand this dynamic, the brand needs to do primary research to understand whether or not there are influences that tip the scale beyond the actual purchaser of the product. For many items, the child in the household exerts the brand influence. Many households purchase private-label cereal and put that cereal in the branded box so children will think it is from their favorite branded source.

In James McNeal's book *The Kids Market: Myths and Realities,* the author offers estimates of children's influence on parents' spending for various items. These range from items such as toys, candy, and video games where you might guess the children's influence on purchasing is high, to items where children have smaller influences, such as sporting goods, sunglasses, and salad dressing (see Table 5.5).

The challenge for the brand manager and the media group is to determine how to balance these influences. In the case of cereal, do you target mothers or do you target only the children? Of course, you would like to do both, but if you do not have enough funds, which one do you pick? Or should you blend the funds in a ratio, say, 70 percent for mothers and 30 percent for children? These issues certainly need to be resolved before the media plan can be fully developed.

The issue of purchase influence is not confined to mothers and children. Many household purchases from the family car to the house to vacations are made with varying degrees of influence from both heads of the household. Recent trends in health care show that adult children assert influence over their now-senior parents. So the issue of purchase influence is very far reaching and can be the key decision in the media targeting process.

Other Brand Influencers

The issue of brand influence is not just the domain of brand purchaser versus brand user. In the retail and service area, the employee exerts a huge influence on the delivery of a service and is the key to customer satisfaction. As a result, a retailer or service brand manager often makes sure that the employees are a media target for the advertising.

Sometimes retail or service advertising is based around a promise made to consumers, which employees must fulfill. For example, a grocery chain ran this promotion: if you aren't checked out within five minutes, they will give you a discount off their groceries. To ensure that the employees were up for the challenge, the marketing manager ran an advertising campaign saluting the great employees of the store. This campaign led to a big increase in store pride on the part of the employees, so when the promotion hit, they were more than ready to execute it.

The world of business-to-business marketing has a very complicated set of influences. Because the purchase of a business item for your company doesn't involve your own money, it comes with an entirely different dynamic. For example, when a company buys a computer, the user of the computer wants something he or she can be comfortable with; the information technology (IT) group wants something that fits into their overall IT framework;

Table 5.5

**Estimates of Children's Influence on Selected Product
Purchases**

Selected products	Industry sales (billion $)	Influence (percent)	Influence (billion $)
Amusement parks	5.0	45	2.3
Athletic shoes	5.6	20	1.1
Autos	221.7	8	17.7
Bakery goods	26.1	10	2.6
Baking mixes/dough	2.8	15	0.4
Bar soaps	1.5	20	0.3
Batteries	3.5	25	0.9
Beauty aids (kids)	1.2	70	0.8
Bicycles	2.9	40	1.2
Blank audio cassettes	0.4	15	0.1
Bottled water	2.0	9	0.2
Bread	13.0	20	2.6
Cameras (still) and film	4.6	12	0.5
Candy and gum	19.0	35	6.7
Canned pasta	0.6	60	0.3
Casual dining	21.0	30	6.3
Cereal, cold	0.7	27	0.2
Cereal, hot	8.0	50	4.0
Clothing (kids)	18.4	70	12.9
Condiments	5.0	10	0.5
Consumer electronics	36.0	12	4.3
Cookies	5.4	40	2.2
Costume jewelry	4.0	12	0.5
Dairy goods	40.2	12	4.8
Deli goods	11.1	9	1.0
Eyewear	13.5	10	1.4
Fast foods	89.8	35	31.4
Fragrances (kids)	0.3	70	0.2
Frozen breakfasts	0.6	15	0.1
Frozen dinners	4.0	15	0.6
Frozen novelties	1.5	75	1.1
Frozen sandwiches	0.3	30	0.1
Fruit snacks	0.4	80	0.3
Fruits and vegetables, canned	3.0	20	0.6
Fruits and vegetables, fresh	52.1	8	4.2
Furniture, furnishings (kids)	5.0	35	1.8
Greeting cards	6.2	15	0.9
Hair care	3.8	10	0.4
Hobby items	1.0	40	0.4

(continued)

Table 5.5 *(continued)*

Selected products	Industry sales (billion $)	Influence (percent)	Influence (billion $)
Home computers	4.5	18	0.8
Hotels, mid-price	5.5	12	0.7
Ice cream	8.7	25	2.2
Isotonic drinks	1.0	15	0.2
Jellies and jams	2.6	23	0.6
Juices and juice drinks	11.8	33	3.9
Meats, fresh	43.1	12	5.2
Meats, packaged	17.1	18	3.1
Microwave foods	2.3	30	0.7
Movies	1.6	30	0.5
Over-the-counter drugs	11.0	12	1.3
Peanut butter	1.4	40	0.6
Pet foods	8.2	12	1.0
Pet supplies	3.7	12	0.4
Pizza, frozen	0.9	40	0.4
Pudding and gelatin	0.9	25	0.2
Recorded music	3.4	22	0.7
Refrigerated puddings	0.2	20	0.0
Salad dressing	3.0	10	0.3
Salty snacks	13.6	25	3.4
School supplies	2.3	35	0.8
Seafood	8.0	15	1.2
Shoes (kids)	2.0	50	1.0
Soda	58.0	30	17.4
Software, learning	1.3	50	0.7
Soup	3.0	20	0.6
Sporting goods	30.0	15	4.5
Spreadable cheese	0.3	20	0.1
Sunglasses	2.0	10	0.2
Toaster products	0.3	45	0.1
Toothpaste	1.5	20	0.3
Toys	14.0	70	9.8
Video games	6.0	60	3.6
Video rentals	11.0	25	2.8
Wristwatches	5.9	12	0.7
Yogurt	1.6	12	0.2
Total	$932.7		$187.7

Source: James McNeal, *The Kids Market: Myths and Realities* (Ithaca, NY: Paramount Market Publishing). Used by permission.

the finance group wants to minimize costs; and the CEO wants the greatest productivity. All of these customers have influence over the purchase. In many cases, the actual purchaser (the person who writes the check) has the least amount of influence over the purchase.

So, as a business-to-business brand manager, it is important to walk the advertising agency and the media group through the sales process so that they understand its various components.

Growing Ethnic Diversity

In the golden age of television, the media target was fairly easy to discern. Take a look at *Leave It to Beaver* and you have your audience. It consisted of a Caucasian family with a working husband, a stay-at-home mom, and two kids. Of course, that was 1960. The times have changed a lot since then.

Everyone knows that more women now work than stay at home, although that figure has topped out at about 60 percent, according to the latest U.S. Census Bureau data. The larger trend in the United States is the ethnic diversity of the population. There are many large markets, such as Los Angeles and Miami, where whites are not the majority. The most rapid growth in the population is coming from Hispanic and Asian populations, followed by African Americans.

Obviously, these growth patterns have a lot of bearing on media planning and targeting. Ethnic audiences do watch, listen to, and read media that would be considered general-market media; nevertheless, each ethnic group also uses specific media that are tailored to its specific culture. The media planning dilemma is to determine when additional resources should be funneled into ethnic media.

There are two schools of thought on this issue. The first is to determine what percentage of the ethnic population is underdelivered by the general-market media and then to make up that difference in ethnic media. For example, if you were targeting beer-drinking men, you might schedule a commercial on *Monday Night Football*. If MNF delivers a 12 rating for all men but only an 8 rating for Hispanic men, there is a 33 percent shortfall for Hispanic men. You can either accept this shortfall or look for programming that will balance the delivery for Hispanic men. Assessing underdelivery of various target groups is an excellent form of media analysis. This example suggests that the current buy of *Monday Night Football* might not be enough if Hispanic men are a key part of your target.

This brings us to the second school of thought, which is marketing versus media. If Hispanic men are a crucial target audience, then you should market to them. Scheduling support in ethnic media is as much a political statement as it is a method of reaching the right audience. It means that you recognize the importance of this group, and that that recognition has an impact that goes well beyond the impact of the standard media analysis.

It is important in ethnic markets to understand the media impact of the plan in terms of media delivery. If an ethnic segment is growing and is important, then develop a marketing program to cultivate that group. That is where the brand manager and the media team need to work together to ensure that all aspects of strategic thought are represented before proceeding.

Economic Impact of Targeting

We have looked at media targeting from the perspective of who is the best audience to reach in order to make your business grow. There are also economic implications of targeting. Each decision you make on defining your target audience has an effect on the cost of media. Thus, assessing the cost impact of your target decision is crucial to finalizing your target audience.

In your analysis of various target segments you will discover that each segment consumes media in a different way. This consumption leads to various cost trade-offs as you finalize your target audience. For example, research indicates that women watch more television than men. Therefore, the cost of reaching a certain number of men through television is more than the cost of reaching the same number of women. Suppose you decide that it is important to reach both men and women based on the purchase influence dynamics of the brand. If you change the target audience for the media plan from women to adults, you raise your costs by more than 10 percent. Why? You are paying a premium to reach men.

This same dynamic holds true for age. Older adults watch more television than do younger adults. It costs dramatically more, based on cost per rating point, to reach adults aged 18 to 34 than it does to reach adults aged 55 and over. If you change your target from the 18 to 49 group to the 18 to 34 group for a television plan, you will have to pay another 5 to 10 percent in costs.

The harder the group is to reach, the more it costs to reach them, which seems like a pretty basic maxim. The curve ball here is that some media are designed to reach a very narrow audience rather than a broad one. This holds true for the regular television networks, but it does not necessarily apply to cable, where programming is very specific (see Table 5.6).

Television and newspapers are very much alike: the broader the audience, the lower the cost to reach them. Radio is just the opposite. Radio formats are tailored for narrow age cells. Each station is trying to own a key demographic. On radio, the tighter the audience, the lower the cost. For example, if you are targeting all men with a radio buy, you would likely

Table 5.6

Media CPM Efficiencies Based on Target Size

Target	TV	Cable	Radio	Newspaper	Magazines	OOH	Online
Broad Target	*****	**	*	*****	*****	*****	*
	****	**	**	****	****	****	**
	***	***	***	***	***	***	***
	**	****	****	**	****	**	****
Niche Target	*	*****	*****	*	*****	*	*****
CPM Scale	*****		Highly Efficient				
	*		Not Efficient				

need to purchase a news station for the older men and a rock station for the younger men. If you are just targeting young men, you could cut the news and reduce your costs considerably.

Magazines have similar dynamics. There are broad-reach publications, such as *Time, Sports Illustrated,* and *Good Housekeeping.* If you are targeting just people who like spicy food, though, you might be better off with *Chili Pepper* magazine.

The Internet is cut from the same cloth as magazines, with large search engines as the broad-reach vehicles and individual sites as niche properties.

The other economic implications of targeting involve your media budget. If you are like most brand managers, you usually do not have enough resources to do what you want to do. Every brand is under pressure to deliver profits, and media support is one of the easiest budget cuts because it is one of the variable expenses.

If you are faced with marketing a national cereal brand with only $3 million for advertising, and the competition spends $15 million, you have some tough challenges. Your $3 million will not go far against a broad "mothers" target, but it is certainly enough to generate some noise in the children's market. Or you may want to tackle an ethnic market with your limited budget. Therefore, when working with the media-planning group, it is critical that you understand the cost impact dynamics of a target. The target audience is the cornerstone of the media plan. Defining the proper target is crucial for success. It begins with setting the right objectives and then using the tools at your disposal to better identify the audience. Once you have weighed your options from both the perspectives of opportunity and economics, you are ready to finalize this aspect of the media plan.

Chapter 6
Geography's Role in Planning

Where your product is marketed is just as important as to whom your product is marketed. Whether your brand is international or found only in the corner grocery store, when it comes to media planning geography is an essential strategic issue. How you define where you want to advertise and how much weight you give to one market versus another are key questions in deciding resource allocation.

Geography ties in to the target audience definition. As mentioned in Chapter 5, PRIZM or Spectra data can be mapped to provide a look at regional pockets of strength or weakness for a brand's target market. Then, as the brand manager, you can decide whether to support geography that has a high concentration of customers or to go fishing for new customers.

Before we get into geographic analysis and the impact of geography on media costs and media vehicle selection, we first need to define our geography.

How to Define Geography

You, the brand manager, tell the media planning group that you want to "heavy-up" (or apply more advertising weight to) Birmingham, Alabama. The media planning group walks away thinking that you simply want to advertise in the Birmingham designated marketing area (DMA). You, on the other hand, are thinking that the media planning group is looking at the Birmingham Information Resources, Inc. (IRI's) InfoScan market, which consists of seven different DMAs (see Table 6.1).

Obviously, you have a problem. One of the most common problems a brand manager faces is matching up marketing areas to media planning geography. This may sound fundamental, but it is a crucial area that is often overlooked until it is too late, or until a critical mistake is made.

The media planner will usually define geography with the television DMA from Nielsen. A DMA is a group of counties that get the majority of their

Table 6.1

IRI (InfoScan) Market to Nielsen Designated Market Area

INFOSCAN Market (ISM): Birmingham, AL

DMA	InfoScan market coverage	
	TVHH (000)	% of ISM
Birmingham	530.7	39.7
Huntsville–Decatur, Florence	317.8	23.7
Montgomery	211.2	15.8
Mobile/Pensacola	117.4	8.8
Tuscaloosa	59.4	4.4
Columbus, GA	50.7	3.8
Anniston	43.2	3.2
Other spill	7.8	0.6
Total	1,338.1	100.0

Source: IRI (InfoScan).

television viewing from the same home market. There are 210 DMAs in the Nielsen television system. DMAs are fairly static but changes can occur. For example, at different times Sarasota, Florida, was both its own DMA and a part of the Tampa/St. Petersburg DMA, depending upon how strongly its local station performed in its home market. Although counties may shift from one DMA to another, DMAs are fairly consistent from year to year.

A second geography, or geographic unit, used by media planners is the metropolitan statistical area (MSA). An MSA is a central metropolitan area as designated by the U.S. Census. Each MSA comprises a certain number of counties and is smaller than a DMA. Radio stations typically use the MSA as their geography for their signal strength. Some brands use the MSA as their trading area because the MSA contains a considerable amount of census data that can be used to analyze the area. There are approximately 280 MSAs in the United States.

Packaged-goods marketers use either Nielsen panel data or IRI data to analyze sales information. Each of these sources uses broader marketing areas than either a DMA or an MSA. To describe their geography, Nielsen and IRI use approximately 60 market areas, which incorporate the 210 DMAs.

Regardless of the source you are using, it is important to match up these market areas with DMAs before proceeding into media planning. Thus, when you say "Birmingham," you will get all the DMAs in the area and not just the 40 percent of the total marketing area that lies in the Birmingham DMA.

If you are a brand manager of a retail chain, then you define your market by the store's trading area. A trading area is a geographic area based on where your customers actually live or work. For example, most fast-food restaurants use a three-mile trading radius as their standard for defining their individual stores' trading areas. Other retail stores may draw from a wider area, but most retailers have a specific part of the market that makes up the majority of their customers. To market effectively to this group, a retail brand manager conducts a trade area analysis. This is usually done by evaluating the point-of-sale system used by retailers to capture customer names and addresses. Table 6.2 shows a zip code analysis for a fast-food chicken restaurant in Georgia.

As Table 6.2 shows, a concentration of sales comes from just a few zip codes. This provides the media planner with information to make an intelligent decision on a variety of media. Perhaps there is a billboard location that makes sense in this area. Or there may be a need to provide inserts or direct mail with coupon offers to area residents.

Geography can play a role in business-to-business marketing as well. The difference in business marketing compared with consumer marketing is that the decision process can involve more than one market. For example, a cellular phone company that markets to the offshore oil industry found that the users of their service lived in rural markets near the coasts of Louisiana and Texas; the decision makers, on the other hand, working on the oil rigs with the workers, lived in more-urban markets such as Houston, New Orleans, and Baton Rouge. In addition, the headquarters for most of the oil companies were in a western suburban area of Houston, more than 100 miles from the coast. In this case, the brand manager had to develop a different strategy for users of the service versus corporate headquarters.

So, any goods or services will have geographic influences, whether they are national, based on a local market, or even as micro as a city block. Regardless of your brand's situation, the same discipline and tools should be used to determine the appropriate geographic media approach.

How to Analyze Geography

Now that everyone is working with the same definitions, it is time to analyze your sales by geography to determine strengths and weaknesses. The classic method is to develop a BDI/CDI analysis.

BDI stands for *brand development index,* which tells how strong a market's sales are in relation to its population size. This index is the percentage of your brand's sales compared to the percentage of the population in a certain market. Suppose you have 3.4 percent of your sales in Dallas, a city that represents 1.7 percent of the population of the United States. The BDI would be 200 for your brand (3.4 ÷ 1.7 × 100).

Table 6.2

Georgia Trading Area Analysis: BoJangles Chicken

Zip Code	# Households	Sales	% Total	Sales per HH
30327	4,760	$150,000	10	$31.51
33110	5,110	$135,000	9	$26.42
32112	4,210	$120,000	8	$28.50
35333	4,510	$120,000	8	$26.60
30353	5,010	$105,000	7	$20.96
32121	4,420	$105,000	7	$23.76
31760	4,130	$90,000	6	$21.79
32211	4,610	$90,000	6	$19.52
30761	4,750	$75,000	5	$15.80
34276	5,000	$60,000	4	$12.00
Top 10 Total	46,510			
All Others	54,000	$450,000	30	$8.33
Total	100,510	$1,500,000	100	$14.92

An index of 100 means the brand sales in that market mirror the population. If the index is less than 100, then the brand is not consumed up to the per capita level; if the BDI is over 100, consumption is greater than the per capita level.

CDI stands for *category development index.* Just like a BDI, a CDI is the percentage of category sales compared to the percentage of the population. You use the CDI as a measure of potential, whereas the BDI is a measure of actual brand strength.

The best way to look at a BDI/CDI analysis is to graph it in a quadrant chart. Exhibit 6.1 shows a quadrant chart with each grid reflecting a different relationship between the brand and the category. In quadrant I, both the brand and category are strong. This is a good area to defend. Quadrant II shows that the BDI is much stronger than the CDI, which means that the only brand growth here would be limited to growing the category. In quadrant III, the category is stronger than the brand. This is the area of opportunity. And quadrant IV shows that both the brand and category are weak. This is an area where you will avoid spending advertising dollars.

One last analysis involves creating your own *brand opportunity index* (BOI). This is done by dividing the CDI by the BDI. For example, you have a brand where Atlanta has a CDI of 120 but a BDI of 80. That would correspond to a BOI of 150 (120 ÷ 80). On the other hand, if Orlando has a CDI of 120 but a BDI of 150, then the BOI of 80 (120 ÷ 150) might make it less attractive as a growth market than Atlanta, even though both the BDI and CDI would put Orlando in the top quadrant (see Table 6.3). Both Nielsen and IRI research show that advertising has the best opportunity to

Exhibit 6.1

Brand Opportunities Analysis

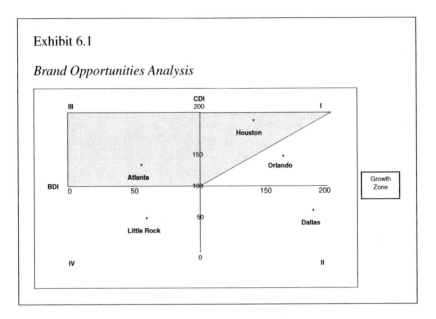

"grow" a brand where it has a strong BOI. So, once you calculate your BDI and CDI and put them in a quadrant chart, calculate your BOI for the final opportunity analysis.

The same BDI/CDI analysis can be done in the retail as well as the business-to-business arena. In retail, you may want to look at BDI/CDI on a market level, not just on a trading area basis. Because the number of stores can determine the strength or weakness of a market, retailers use a sales-per-trading-area analysis to evaluate one store versus another. This can be done by simply calculating the sales of the store and dividing by the number of households within the store's trading area.

Factoring in Distribution

The BDI/CDI analysis is a classic one, but before finalizing your market "heavy-up" decision, you should dig a bit deeper to understand the reason behind the numbers. Suppose that in the Atlanta example, where your BDI is only 80, your brand was in less than 50 percent of the available points of distribution. Now the opportunity market that you thought you had may not be one after all until you gain full distribution.

For packaged-goods products, the term for distribution is *all commodity volume* (ACV). This is a fancy name for the percentage of the distribution channel in which the brand is available.

Table 6.3

Brand Opportunity Index

DMA	BDI	CDI	BOI
Dallas/Ft. Worth	200	80	40
Atlanta	80	120	150
Houston	150	200	133
Little Rock	90	50	55
Orlando	150	120	80

Distribution is an important element when looking at sales by market. Distribution, or the lack thereof, may be one of the reasons why a brand performs the way it does. One way to equalize the effects of spotty distribution is to do a sales-per-distribution-point analysis. This analysis looks at the sales-velocity-per-distribution percentage. It may uncover where a brand is performing well yet has distribution weaknesses. This can be a good tool for the brand manager to use with the sales group to shore up any weaknesses in the distribution area. For example, suppose that your brand has 2 percent of its sales in Dallas/Fort Worth, which has roughly 2 percent of the U.S. population. You would say that Dallas is an average market with a BDI of 100. But if you found that you had your brand in only half the available retail outlets in Dallas, then you would say that Dallas actually has a BDI of 200 in the outlets where your brand is available. Based on this analysis, Dallas looks like a great market, once you gain that crucial missing amount of distribution.

From a media planning perspective, understanding the distribution of the brand is critical in selecting either markets to "heavy-up" or test markets. Before just blindly proceeding with the BDI/CDI analysis, step back and ask about the brand's distribution.

Applying Media to Geography

Now that you and your team understand what markets you want to target and are working from the same market definitions, you can begin to analyze what media to apply to various levels of geography.

Although most media can be purchased nationally, regionally, or locally, each medium has its geographic nuances. Let's review the major media and how they can be purchased at various geographic levels.

Television airtime can be purchased on a DMA basis locally or on a network television basis nationally. The major networks—ABC, CBS, NBC, and Fox—can even offer broad regional coverage based typically on five large regions. The only distinction is that network television uses syndicated programming, which is "cleared" locally. For example, a syndicated program such as *Wheel of Fortune* is actually sold DMA by DMA to a local series of unrelated local stations. In exchange for taking the program, the local station gets a certain amount of commercial inventory to sell, while the syndicator keeps its "national" inventory. Depending upon the syndicator's success, a program might "clear" all 100 percent of the country or just a portion of it.

Cable television airtime can be purchased locally and nationally. Most cable networks do not offer regional opportunities; nevertheless, there are regional cable sports networks available to purchase. Cable is a tricky medium from a geographic perspective. Cable channels are purchased by local cable operators. Each cable network is available in various percentages of the cable universe. Popular networks like CNN and the Discovery Channel are in most cable lineups, whereas a niche network like the Food Network may not be. Of course national cable has its own set of geographic issues, but purchasing cable locally is even more challenging. A local buy must be purchased from individual cable operators in that market. In a market such as Dallas/Fort Worth, that may mean dealing with more than ten different cable companies. This complexity means that executing a local cable buy on a DMA basis can be difficult in some markets.

Radio airtime can be purchased locally, nationally, or on an MSA basis. Locally, radio is similar to television; the only difference is signal strength. Some stations are stronger than others, which can impact listening on the fringes of the MSA. Network radio is fairly similar to network television and syndication. You can purchase commercials that air on stations across the country, and you can purchase what is called long-form programming that is similar to syndication. *The American Top 40,* a radio countdown of the week's most popular songs, is an example of a long-form program.

Magazine space can be purchased locally, regionally, or nationally. It is possible to purchase space in a magazine such as *Good Housekeeping* on a national basis, or just in the Southeast, or just in the Chicago DMA. The smaller the publication's circulation, the less likely it is that you can purchase space in it on a regional or local basis. Obviously, there are regional and local magazines of every shape, topic, and size available to purchase.

With the exception of *USA Today,* the *Wall Street Journal,* and the national edition of the *New York Times,* newspaper space cannot be purchased nationally. Nevertheless, there are products that come within a newspaper that you can purchase. Free-standing inserts (FSIs) run in the Sunday newspaper and carry a wide variety of coupons. The largest purveyor of FSIs is a company called Valassis. You can create a national, regional, or local buy using these inserts. *Parade* magazine is another vehicle that is distributed in the Sunday newspaper and space can be purchased as in any other magazine. Newspapers offer the opportunity to market on a micro level, targeting inserts by zip code; insert-only companies such as ADVO provide the same service.

Online advertising can be purchased on all, including worldwide, geographic levels. A Web portal like Yahoo! offers any level of banner or other program support to the widest or narrowest geography possible. Search engines such as Google also offer these opportunities.

Out-of-home media (OOH)—billboards and signs on subways and buses—are, for the most part, a local medium. Still, you can buy advertising space on a rolling basis, that is, on bus routes that cover much of the country. Beyond these standard OOH media, alternative media such as airplane banners, beach logos, telephone-booth advertisements, and bathroom ads are extremely local.

Economics of Media by Geography

We have had a cursory look at how media can be purchased on various levels of geography. There are economies of scale moving from local to national levels of support. Because each medium is a bit different in its local-versus-national purchase, it is sometimes more efficient to schedule a national advertising placement than to buy a number of markets on a local basis.

The rule of thumb for calculating when network television becomes more cost efficient than buying spot television is when the brand is available in approximately two thirds (66 percent) of the states in the United States. Prime-time and sports programming have the lowest national-to-local breakeven point, which is usually at 66 percent. Morning, daytime, and evening news programs can be slightly higher than this level, but the two-thirds rule is a good one to go by.

Because cable is not as efficient as television on a local basis, its national-to-local breakeven point is very low. If you are in the top five media markets in the United States, it is less expensive to purchase national advertising than to buy just those five markets. The national-to-local breakeven point for cable is around 25 percent of the United States, although it can be even lower if you are comparing some very inefficient local markets.

In Table 6.4, we have radio and magazine at similar breakeven points; both are at 33 percent of the United States. Yet there is a subtle distinction in the radio analysis. Local radio typically comprises 60-second commercial units. Many local radio stations have gone to unit-rate pricing, where it costs the same to purchase a 60- or a 30-second commercial; as a result, 30-second commercial units are becoming less common locally. On the other hand,

Table 6.4

National-to-Local Breakeven Points

Media	Breakeven %
Network TV to spot TV (prime)	66
Network radio (:30) to spot radio (:60)	33
Network cable to local cable	25
National magazine to local edition of national magazine	33

national network radio charges 50 percent of the 60-second commercial rate for a 30-second commercial, making network radio much more likely to have 30-second units. So the breakeven point for radio uses a 60-second commercial locally and a 30-second commercial nationally.

Now that you know it is more efficient to purchase national rather than local advertising for your brand, even if the brand does not have national distribution, should you be concerned that you are advertising where the brand is not available? This decision can be a double-edged sword, but there are certainly more reasons to advertise nationally than not if you have the opportunity.

Beyond the cost implications, national commercials or advertisements get more favorable placement in a given program or publication than local ads; studies have shown that national advertising can have upwards of 25 percent more impact or retention value for your commercial message. From a marketing perspective, this type of advertising can help seed your brand in future expansion areas so you may not have to spend as much once you gain that distribution. In today's retail climate, if you can land distribution in a chain like Wal-Mart, you have a national brand instantly.

Geographic planning is a key element in media planning. The first step in the process is to understand your market-area definitions. From there, you can analyze your brand's strengths and weaknesses. Next, develop your BDI/CDI analysis. Determine how you are going to treat different market groups. Then look for economies of scale as you roll out your brand nationally.

The next chapter deals with another cornerstone of good media planning: the seasonal issues of brand consumption and media costs.

Chapter 7
Seasonality and Timing

What time of year your advertising runs is a critical factor in your advertising campaign. It may not be as critical as your target audience or your geographic selection, but proper timing can still make the difference between an effective campaign outcome and a marginal result. The time of the year affects media costs, media effectiveness, and consumers' buying patterns. Nevertheless, there are lots of other advertising media scheduling factors that you must take into account, including schedule flexibility, the pace or rate of advertising, the share of advertising, and possible scheduling remedies for competitive actions.

Seasons and Quarters

Certainly, advertising makes use of the seasons of the year: winter, spring, summer, and fall. But advertising media seasonality refers to a bit more than the four seasons. It also refers to quarters of the year. The first quarter is January through March, the second quarter is April through June, the third quarter is July through September, and the fourth quarter is October through December. But these four quarters do not line up exactly with the 12 months of the year; rather, because there are 52 weeks in the year, a quarter is 13 weeks long. Therefore, advertising flights, or waves, are often 13 weeks long as well.

The cost and effectiveness of media vary with the time of year, too. Because so much advertising appears during the Christmas shopping season, the fourth quarter has the most advertising—in all media, print as well as broadcast. That means higher levels of competitive advertising during the fourth quarter, which also means that each advertising placement may be less effective during the fourth quarter simply because there are so many competing messages (see Table 7.1). Because of the high demand for advertising during the fourth quarter, the media vehicles may raise their advertising rates then, too, which can make advertising in the fourth quarter not only less effective, but also more expensive (see Table 7.2).

Table 7.1

Media Effectiveness by Quarters of the Year

Network television	Average household rating			
	1st Qtr	2nd Qtr	3rd Qtr	4th Qtr
Daytime	3.4	3.2	4.1	3.3
Early news	8.0	7.1	6.7	7.8
Prime time	8.8	8.3	6.9	8.8
Late fringe	3.4	3.3	3.2	3.3

Source: Advertising Media Services.

Table 7.2

Advertising Costs by Quarter of the Year

Network television	Average cost per :30 commercial ($)			
	1st Qtr	2nd Qtr	3rd Qtr	4th Qtr
Daytime	18,000	21,000	29,000	21,000
Early news	67,000	73,000	49,000	77,000
Prime time	146,000	160,000	132,000	189,000
Late fringe	49,000	54,000	47,000	53,000

Source: Advertising Media Services.

On the other hand, there is comparatively little advertising in the first quarter, not because it is the beginning of the year, but because it follows the highly used fourth quarter. Many advertisers have expended much of their advertising budgets during the fourth quarter, so they pull back during the first quarter of the following year. But it is during the first quarter that consumers' media usage goes up because bad weather keeps many people at home. In broadcast, especially television, there may also be good programming during the February ratings sweeps, because attractive programs build viewership. So the first quarter may be a bargain for television advertisers. Choice of insertion times is broad because fewer advertisers are trying to buy television advertising time, there are fewer competitive advertisements on the air, and viewership is at one of the year's highest levels.

Other media have seasonal patterns, too. For example, newspaper readership is apt to drop during the summer when people go on vacation and suspend their subscriptions. Magazine readership may dwindle during the Christmas shopping season and then increase after the holidays, when the weather is poor for out-of-home activities. Radio usage increases in the summer when school is out. And because in the summer the days are longer, people spend more time outside than they do in the winter, resulting in a good time to schedule out-of-house advertising.

Buying Patterns Affected by the Weather

Consumer purchasing patterns vary during the year, depending on both the product category and the weather. If there is a heavy snowfall at the beginning of winter, consumers may look for snow tires, thinking it will be a long, snowy winter. If snow falls in March, consumers are less likely to shop for snow tires, figuring they have already made it through the worst of the winter without them. Similarly, a heat wave in May will spur sales of air conditioners, but a heat wave in September may not, again because consumers believe that they have already been through the worst that the hot summer season has to offer.

Packaged goods may benefit from weather changes at any time, though. Whether there is a heat wave in May or September, sales of soft drinks will jump. No one is going to refuse a cool drink in September just because most of the summer has already passed. Cold weather in winter typically causes canned soup sales to climb; during the warm summer months hot soup is not nearly as popular.

Weather can be an important advertising strategy. For example, Quaker Oats ran a campaign based on the theme: "Below 50 degrees is oatmeal weather," and the company worked with the media to trigger the message when the local temperatures fell below 50 degrees.

Day of Week and Time of Day

The season or quarter and the annual climate may affect your media selections and insertions. Similarly, the time of day and the day of the week may be important, too. Golf balls may be advertised on daytime television, but likely only on the weekend. Hair products and packaged food items may do well advertised on daytime television during the week. Lawn fertilizer and health items may do better during the early news or on prime time (roughly 8:00 to 11:00 P.M. in the evening).

Other Scheduling Factors

Season, quarter, day, and time are all important, but they may be largely intuitive, and they are among the least complex factors in timing. Several other kinds of timing considerations also come into play in advertising media scheduling, all of importance, yet perhaps not as intuitively obvious.

Susceptibility

Consumers may be more susceptible to a message at certain times. Sylvania focused its advertising for light bulbs on the day when daylight savings time ends and it gets dark earlier. Consumers were more attuned to lights at that time. A classic campaign was conducted for Brinks Security, which ran a radio announcement during work hours that said, "While you are at work, who is watching your home?" These are good examples of exploiting certain times of day, based on consumers' susceptibility.

Flexibility

You may need flexibility in your media buys so you can switch from one media placement to others. Quick tactical maneuvers or other media schedule changes may be needed to meet competitive assaults or to take advantage of such external shifts as economic changes, unusual weather, consumer fads, and real or perceived threats.

When the World Trade Center was brought down by terrorism on September 11, 2001, sales opportunities increased for security products and decreased for vacation packages. When crime rose on one Caribbean island, that locale developed a serious marketing problem; at the same time, other Caribbean islands gained in tourism as they promoted their safety and security. When Vanilla Coca-Cola became a hit, opportunity suddenly opened up for other vanilla-flavored foods and beverages. If the economy takes a dip, sales of packaged goods may remain steady, but consumers may switch to smaller packages that require less cash outlay. A longer-than-normal rainy season in spring may delay purchases of lawn weed killers, making it necessary to extend the advertising flights to match; the same can happen with automotive antifreeze when extended warm weather lasts into autumn.

Rate of Advertising

Even your advertising budget may be a scheduling factor. Low levels of advertising are likely to bring low levels of customer response. High levels of advertising, on the other hand, are extremely and sometimes prohibitively expensive.

We have already seen how advertising expenditures can be ameliorated or leveled out by advertising in waves. High-expenditure flights can be offset by low-advertising hiatus periods. Waves of advertising permit you to gain high visibility when it is needed, followed by reminders during less intense time periods. At the same time, the advertising budget is stretched out so the campaign can cover more of the year.

Share of Advertising

Another type of unanticipated challenge may come from your competitors. If you have more to spend on advertising than any of your competitors do, congratulations! You are in a rare position. But even then you need to turn your dominant share of money into a dominant share of advertising, which is not always as easy as it might seem. It requires at least parity in advertising message strength and competitive efficiency in media selection and buying. Otherwise, the financial advantage will disappear and your firm will be just another part of the competitive pack.

More likely, you do not have as much money to spend on advertising as your largest competitor does. If your competition is spending at a level that you cannot possibly match, then you will probably choose to advertise in waves. Determining when the waves should run depends on a number of factors: the purchase cycle of your brand, the likelihood of brand-switching by your customers, the anticipated levels of competitive activities, and the life cycle of your brand and your product category.

You can also meet a larger competitor by not trying to match dollar-for-dollar and insertion-for-insertion across the board. Instead, you may be able to match the strongest competitor during parts of the year; if so, why waste money by spreading it thinly throughout the entire year? Another approach is to match your largest competitor in certain markets rather than throughout the entire country. Or you may be more selective in your choice of target audiences; this strategy will give you matching advertising weight against the primary target, even though you may have to sacrifice reaching audiences of lesser importance.

Varying Advertising Scheduling Patterns

There are several reasons why you may wish to vary your advertising placement schedule. Sometimes customers can be "unsold" by too much advertising. In broadcast, it is possible to induce an "irritation factor," when potential customers become so tired of seeing your advertising that not only do they flip channels but they actually begin to have a negative reaction to the surplus of advertising. You may not advertise so much that you irritate your audience, but there is no reason to advertise past the optimum point of exposure; going past the optimum advertising level is wasteful, even when it is not irritating.

If you are using the same advertising schedule from day to day, and you have more than one television commercial that you can run, you may want to alternate the commercials so the viewers do not tire of seeing the same message over and over. If you have only one or two similar commercials, then consider varying the times when they appear so you are not always exposing the same audience to the identical message.

Some products have "life cycles." If your goods fall into this pattern, it may be advisable to reduce or quit advertising for a while, allowing for a "gestation period" when the advertising information can sink in and have an effect.

Sometimes short bursts of advertising, such as in a wave pattern, can produce more sales than a steady amount of heavy advertising. Saving money while gaining greater impact would certainly be attractive, and it would make sense to follow through.

These possibilities may be unique to your brand or to your product category. Because of the differences between products and brands, it is not possible to lay out rules or standards for every kind of advertising media operation. Good research, close observation, and insightful common sense will determine which, if any, of these situations applies to you and how you should proceed.

Starting Date

Many advertising campaigns are scheduled for a year at a time. The year may be a fiscal year or a sales year rather than a calendar year. But no matter what kind of year, the advertising starting date need not be the first day of the campaign.

Let's say that your advertising is planned for the calendar year. Should you start your advertising placements on January 1? If you have an item that fits appropriately into New Year's parades and football games, maybe you should start then. Most products and services, however, do not fit that mode. New Year's Day advertising is competitive and thus expensive, yet viewers do not always pay close attention; they are often gathered in groups, talking and eating while the television set is on, and some members of the audience are likely to be recovering from the night before. All these factors make New Year's Day a less attractive advertising opportunity—unless, of course, your item fits in well and you can afford it.

Similarly, if your advertising campaign year begins at any other time during the year, you do not need to begin advertising placements on the very first day. Look at the buying patterns, competitive advertising, your budget, and your preferred waves or other advertising patterns. Base your decisions on your objectives and your strategies, including your scheduling strategies.

Advertising Scheduling

When you plan your campaign schedule, start with a good calendar that includes all the holidays and special events; candy sales increase for Secretaries' Day, an event that is not included on all calendars. Then begin to put together your advertising schedule. Most of the time, the calendar is transferred to a flowchart, which shows the patterns of advertising along with the levels of advertising, all on a sheet or slide that incorporates the proposed advertising schedule, advertising weights, and respective target audiences for the entire campaign period.

In addition to your marketing and advertising objectives, your audience targets, your geographic targets, and your scheduling aims, you will want to take into account the creative needs of your message and their implications for your advertising media plan. That is the subject of Chapter 9.

Political Windows Impact Media Scheduling

By law, political candidates get the lowest media rates offered by a media outlet, along with first rights to that inventory. There are specific times, called political windows, when this law is evoked. Typically, a political window is a six-week period that leads into primary elections (usually in the spring) or a specific election, held in November, for a local, state, or national position. The impact of the political window is particularly relevant to advertisers who use broadcast media where only a limited number of commercial units are available. The risk that an advertiser runs by scheduling advertising during a political window is that the ad may not run as scheduled. For example, there have been times in recent history when more than 50 percent of all news commercials have been aired by various political parties. Meanwhile, advertisers that may have booked that time well in advance are left looking for alternative programs or media.

The second impact of the political window is on media costs. Since broadcast properties must sell political commercials at their lowest unit rate, they are less likely to negotiate low rates with their regular advertisers during these political time periods for fear of losing considerable dollars per unit sold. For these reasons, your role as a savvy advertising media planner becomes even more crucial—and complicated—during an election year.

Chapter 8

Competitive Analysis: Implications in Planning

If all we had to do to succeed in advertising media planning was figure out the right message to send, the right target to receive that message, and the right number of times to send it, advertising planning would be a breeze. But most brands don't live in isolation. Just as we are trying to persuade the consumer to try our brand, some other brand manager is looking to do the same thing.

Competitive analysis is crucial for establishing a point of difference for your brand as well as for developing the competitive attack plan. Using a competitive analysis in a strategic manner can lead to a number of media strategy decisions. For example, suppose you see a trend emerging where all the competitors in your category are moving their money from television to magazines; that might indicate an opportunity to stand out from the pack by increasing your television exposure. Perhaps your spending is not keeping up with the other brands in the category; this may force you to rethink your national strategy and place greater emphasis on key spot markets where you have the greatest volume.

In today's environment, you must be able to react quickly to competitive threats. Most brands have contingency plans that are based on competitive scenarios. Fortunately, there are a number of competitive information tools on the market today that offer a wealth of data about your brand and the brands against which you compete.

Competitive Tools

There are two major national competitive media tracking tools available for assessing media placement. The larger of the two is Competitive Media Reporting (CMR), acquired by TNS Media Intelligence in 2000. The second is Ad*Views, which is owned by Nielsen Media Research. Each service offers a good national overview of media spending. CMR covers a more expansive list of media, whereas Nielsen's Ad*Views is a bit more in line with the packaged-goods industry.

CMR tracks over one million individual brands for 15 media categories. For television, CMR provides actual program-by-program estimated dollars spent and ratings for network and cable. It also offers spending information in the top 100 media markets in the United States, including network and spot radio as well as more than 300 Internet websites. On the print front, CMR tracks consumer magazines, including Sunday magazines (Sunday supplements), and national and international business print media. CMR also monitors outdoor spending for posters and rotary programs.

Ad*Views tracks media similar to CMR; nevertheless, there are some differences. Ad*Views does not cover international print or business-to-business print but does cover free-standing inserts (FSIs), which CMR does not.

Although the usual lag time between gathering data and actually reporting on it is approximately six weeks, both services offer quick "topline" reports. These allow you to see a competitor's broadcast commercial within a week, so the data can be very current.

Both services are extremely accurate with their television and consumer print reporting. Reports on local radio spending are a bit spotty, because much of it is done locally and the services only capture dollars placed through national representatives. Newspaper inserts are also difficult to measure, and there is no measure of direct mail. Even with these caveats the data are relied upon heavily in advertising media planning. Let's take a look at how we can use some of this competitive intelligence.

SWOT

As discussed in Chapter 4, a common approach to analyzing an advertising and marketing competitive situation is the SWOT method, which stands for strengths, weaknesses, opportunities, and threats. The strengths and weaknesses analyze the internal situation as it is now; the opportunities and threats analyze the external situation as it will be in the future, usually three to five years from now. Exhibit 8.1 shows how these analyses work together to cover both good and bad situations, both now and in the future.

The SWOT process is widely used because it is relatively simple and quick to administer. It provides useful information about a firm, a brand, an advertising agency, or any other similar organization. Many advertising managers make use of SWOT or similar techniques because of these advantages.

The outcomes of a SWOT analysis are simply assessed in a combination of visual and written analyses, as Exhibit 8.2 shows.

Exhibit 8.1

SWOT Analysis

	Opportunities Tomorrow	Threats Tomorrow
Strengths Today	You are poised to take advantage	You are strong to defend against threats
Weaknesses Today	You are not positioned well to seize opportunities	Your survivability is threatened

Exhibit 8.2

Sample Advertising SWOT

	Opportunities Targeted ads Partnerships Growing audience High demand for research database Need for information	**Threats** Local economy downturn Aging population Operating expense inflation Competition for employees Audience expectations changing Stagnation
Strengths Financial strength Strong local franchise Ad content Local relationships Autonomy Ads get results	You are poised to take advantage	You are strong to defend against threats
Weaknesses Lack of diverse workforce Only two revenue streams Low understanding of customers Nonresponsive to audience Not tech savvy Cost structure	You are not positioned well to seize opportunity	Your survivability is threatened

Share of Spending versus Share of Voice

The classic way to use competitive information is to understand how much your brand spends in relation to your competitors. Sometimes *share of spending* (SOS) is called *share of voice* (SOV) analysis. Although many media people use these two terms interchangeably, they are different. Share of spending is just that, the percentage of total dollars you spend in the category. So SOS uses absolute dollars as the measuring stick regardless of the medium. In SOS, a dollar is a dollar whether it is spent on television, print, or outdoor advertising. For example, in 2010, Subway was spending at an $80 million level in the fast-food category, which was 6 percent of the total spending. Share of voice, on the other hand, involves the actual impressions delivered as a percentage of the total category impressions. Share of voice then takes into account the delivery for each medium, so it draws a distinction between television and print. For example, whereas Subway represented 6 percent of the total spending, the firm may represent 10 percent of the total impressions in the category because Subway had a more efficient mix of media than did the category as a whole. Because these two measures of competitive spending may yield different results, it is extremely important to clarify which analysis is being performed.

SOS or SOV/SOM Analysis

Once you get a grip on your brand's SOS or SOV, you will want to compare those figures to the market-share (*share of market*, or SOM) levels you and your competitors have. This comparison is called either SOS/SOM or SOV/SOM analysis. For example, if your brand has a 30 percent market share with a 15 percent share of category spending, then you would have a ratio of 50; this figure is found by dividing the 30 percent market share into the 15 percent share of spending (15/30). If you are aggressively trying to gain market share, you may want to spend at a level above your current share. If you are the leader in the market, you may want to maintain a spending level equal to your share so that competitors won't erode your market share. Regardless of your strategy, the SOS/SOM analysis is a good building block to guide you to the proper amount you should invest in your brand.

Many studies correlate these two variables. That is why many brand management teams review these calculations. Table 8.1 shows such an example in the fast-food category. Notice that McDonald's, the category leader, has advertising spending that is very much in line with its market share. The other competitors are spending disproportionately in an effort to take market share from McDonald's.

New Brand Introductions

Suppose you had to introduce a new line of frozen entrées into a very crowded category. How much would you spend to introduce them? Without a market share, it is tough to do the SOV/SOM calculation. But competitive spending is still crucial to your budget plans. Most brands estimate the market share they want to garner in their second year, after the brand is introduced.

Table 8.1

Ratio of SOM to SOS in Quick Service Restaurant Category

Top 10 brands	Share of market (SOM)	Share of spending (SOS)	Ratio
McDonald's	33	30	91
Burger King	14	14	100
Wendy's	10	11	110
Pizza Hut	8	7	88
Taco Bell	8	9	113
Kentucky Fried Chicken (KFC)	7	10	143
Subway	7	8	114
Domino's	5	5	100
Arby's	4	4	100
Dairy Queen	4	2	50
	100	100	100

Source: Brandweek (Technomic Information Services/CMR expenditures).

Then they analyze the competition's spending. New brands typically peg an introductory rate at one-and-a-half to two times that of their Year 2 market share goals. For example, if your goal is to get 5 percent of the frozen entrée market, then you would spend up to 10 percent of the current category spending. This type of analysis is evident in today's marketplace. In 2010, Healthy Choice was spending aggressively at a $17 million level versus market leader Stouffer's at a $10 million level because Healthy Choice was obviously trying to take share from Stouffer's.

Media Strategy

Competitive spending is a good strategic tool for making media decisions. The Heath candy bar was a small brand that faced strong competition in the category. The majority of spending was done leading into Halloween. Heath's sales spiked in October. It had another spike around Easter, when category spending was less pronounced. Heath shifted its spending to emphasize Easter and other key times of the year when the brand could make an impact.

Another strategy decision might be in the media choice itself. If the majority of the category dollars are going to television and you have the opportunity to stand out in radio, then shifting your advertising to radio might be worth considering.

Competitive spending can also be used to determine tactical decisions: In what specific part of the day could your brand make an impact? Is there a creative unit that you might want to use to tell your story? Is there a specific day or days of the week when it may be more beneficial for your brand to run its spot?

All of these questions point to competitive gaps that can be exploited. So, when approaching media strategy, ask yourself if there is something that you can do to stand out from your competitors.

This is certainly the case in the frozen dinner and entrée category shown in Table 8.2. Because Healthy Choice and Stouffer's dominate the spending, other brands are forced to look at alternative media in order to stand out. Weight Watcher Smart Ones puts all its money in magazines to make an impact in a certain medium, while Lean Cuisine Lite Classics allocates a significant amount of its resources to spot television in order to be competitive in selective market areas.

Advertising-to-Sales Ratios

Another use of competitive spending analysis is to determine the advertising-to-sales ratios for your competitors to see what percentage of their revenue they are spending on media advertising. Advertising-to-sales ratio is calculated by dividing the total advertising expenditures by the total amount of brand sales, or revenue. For example, Healthy Choice was a $230 million brand spending $17.2 million on advertising. Healthy Choice's advertising-to-sales ratio was 7.5 percent. Contrast those figures to Stouffer's, a $475 million brand spending at a $10 million level, or an advertising-to-sales ratio of 2.1 percent. Healthy Choice was spending almost twice the amount Stouffer's was spending on an absolute basis, and more than three times that amount on a percent-of-sales basis (see Table 8.3).

Determining Trends in Spending

Another great use of competitive spending information is to calculate trend-line analysis. The media planner should be updating such an analysis every year. You want to see whether spending in the category is increasing or decreasing over time and at what rate. You can compare this result to the sales growth in the category to determine the vitality of the category. If the category is growing at only 2 percent per year in sales, yet advertising is growing at a 10 percent rate, it tells you that a healthy return is going to be tougher to attain. Conversely, if you have a fast-growing category with slower advertising growth, it might suggest that you could step up your own support of the brand.

Trends can be helpful to identify a change in spending patterns over time. Perhaps the category is gradually moving money from television into print,

Table 8.2

Media Mix Comparison: Frozen Dinners and Entrées

Brand	Total media (millions)	Percent allocation		
		Network TV	Spot TV	Magazines
Stouffer's	10.3	50	5	45
Lean Cuisine Lite Classics	5.7	—	50	50
Smart Ones	2.7	—	—	100
Healthy Choice	17.2	60	20	20

Source: Brandweek (CMR expenditures).

Table 8.3

Advertising-to-Sales Ratio

	Healthy Choice	Stouffer's
Sales	$230.0 million	$475.0 million
Advertising expenditures	$17.2 million	$10.0 million
Advertising-to-sales ratio	7.5 percent	2.1 percent

Source: Brandweek (CMR expenditures).

or maybe dollars once funneled into the fourth quarter are now in the third quarter. Over time, you can see how the category is behaving and use this information to help chart your media course.

Marketing-Mix Models

Many brands today are conducting sophisticated marketing-mix modeling. This research is made possible by the availability of a tremendous amount of consumer data. With so many grocery chains using loyalty programs that capture individual purchase behavior, the ability to track purchases and relate them to various marketing elements is a ready-made laboratory. Both Nielsen and IRI use these purchase data and work with manufacturers on developing marketing-mix models. They combine this robust information with powerful multivariate statistical analysis to determine what aspects of the marketing mix are most effective. One element of designing a marketing-mix model is the brand's media spending and the competitors' spending. Marketing-mix models can help brand managers understand the impact of all their marketing elements, as well as how individual media perform.

For example, in Table 8.4 we see that our fictitious brand, Bob's Beans, is extremely sensitive to advertising. For every dollar that Bob's Beans spends on media advertising, the brand receives a return of $1.50. This return is much higher than the return from using an FSI with a coupon or using trade promotions. So, based on this analysis, Bob's Beans should be an aggressive advertiser.

Each brand is going to have its own set of dynamics. One brand may be especially sensitive to advertising, whereas another may respond well only to trade promotion or couponing. With the power of these customer databases, much of what works and what doesn't work can be explained. Competitive media spending plays a crucial role in this sophisticated analysis.

Competitive spending information is a powerful tool for media planning. It can lead to breakout strategies, help determine specific spending levels, and be trended and analyzed within sophisticated marketing models. Competitive spending can be significant in setting communication goals.

Online Competitive Analysis

As more and more advertisers use interactive marketing strategies, keeping up to date on your competitor's online strategy is crucial in the case of most brands. Whereas certain online spending is similar to other media, the aspect of *search engine marketing* (SEM) is not.

All other competitive media spending reports contain the media schedules and the estimated media costs of that schedule for a given competitor. Because SEM is based on bidding, it is impossible for a service to truly estimate the amount of dollars allocated to SEM by a competitor. Table 8.5 shows an example of both SEM and banner advertising for the athletic shoe category. SEM competitive spending is reported in the number of SEM impressions. There is no estimated spending for those impressions. Still, you can get a deep understanding of the SEM strategy as these competitive reports also include the specific keywords that a competitor has included in their SEM campaign.

For banner advertising, there is an estimated media spending amount provided for these impressions. Banner advertising in this case can mean anything from static banners to rich media. The specific creative unit is detailed in the media planning report so you can understand the mix of creative elements being deployed in a competitor's online campaign, as well as the specific sites where they advertise.

Table 8.4

Marketing-Mix Model: Bob's Beans

Item	Incremental profit per $1 spent
Media advertising	$1.50
FSI coupons	$1.00
Trade promotions	$0.85

Table 8.5

Nielsen/NetRatings Ad Relevance
Impressions and Estimated Spending by Category for Custom Advertiser
"Athletic Shoes"

Company	SEM impressions (000)	Banner impressions (000)	Estimated banner spending
Nike, Inc.	17,282	789,315	$4,704,400
Adidas-Salomon Ltd.	13,485	425,898	$2,164,700
Reebok International Ltd.	7,356	177,366	$731,500
Skechers USA, Inc.	11,185	101,642	$329,500
New Balance Athletic Shoe, Inc.	12,128	471,930	$262,700
ASICS Corporation		4	$0
Total	61,436	1,966,155	$8,192,800

Source: NetRatings, Inc.

Chapter 9

Creative Strategy: Implications in Planning

In many advertising agencies, the term *creative department* is used to describe the function whereby the actual advertisements are thought up and illustrated. Sometimes the term *creative* applies only to copywriting; other times, to both copy and layout, which includes art and may involve the art department as well. Even though we are talking about the creative implications for the media portion of the advertising campaign, don't think that creative work occurs only when dealing with copy, layout, and art. There can be creativity involved in media selection and planning, in research, and in other phases of the advertising effort, too; creativity is not limited just to those who write and illustrate the actual advertisements. Perhaps a better term would be *message strategies* or *message functions,* like media functions, research functions, production functions, and management functions.

In this discussion we use the terms *creative* and *message* interchangeably, to reflect their use in the advertising industry, while recognizing that there can still be creativity in other advertising functions.

Creative Wants

"We've got to use television. It's the only thing that is able to handle our message," says the copywriting team, while the media team looks at the advertising budget and replies, "Television is completely out of the question. We can't afford it."

Many times, the creative people working on the advertising account will have definite needs that impact the media selection; other times, they have preferences that may not be absolute requirements but that match their initial campaign approaches. For example, if a new shaving cream lends itself well to demonstration, there may be a concomitant need for such media as television, cinema, and the Internet, all of which offer forms of demonstration. Similarly, if vivid color is needed, that requirement may preclude the use of newspapers and nonvisual media such as radio, whereas television and the Internet may remain under consideration, and other print media with good color capabilities, such as outdoor billboards and magazines, would be strong candidates for the media campaign.

At other times, though, the creative department may have a preconception about the creative approach that may or may not deserve control over media choices. A copywriter may say, "I envision a television commercial with a woman in a flowing gown, walking through a series of video montages." That may be a nice image, but it is essential to determine whether or not there is a real marketing-, product-, or service-related circumstance that actually requires the use of television or other visual media. It is simply an idea, one that may be accommodated by the media plan if it can be afforded.

In still other instances, the creative department may want to use certain media that are simply not good media choices because they do not reach the target audience. If a creative person indicates that newspapers should be used to distribute coupons for an acne cream, it may be a poor media choice because the likely targets—teenagers—do not usually read newspapers, either regularly or closely. If you need to reach teens and teens are exposed to radio, cable television, and the Internet, then those are the media that should be considered for the media buys. Don't get locked into preconceptions of how certain media work; for example, coupons and similar offers can be distributed through many kinds of media, not just print.

Creative Necessities

As we just saw, there are some instances when there are creative necessities, as opposed to creative wants, that should or even must be accommodated by the media selection process.

Motion and Demonstration

If demonstration is needed to communicate the selling idea, visual media are a must, most likely the Internet, television, and cinema. Similarly, if other kinds of motion are needed, visual media are again indicated.

Do not limit yourself to the most obvious choices. The human mind has a tremendous capacity for imagination and visualization, even when the visual is not actually present. Tell people to imagine driving a car in the Indianapolis 500, and they may do well providing their own motion pictures in their minds. That approach may not only save media money, but also greatly reduce the cost of production.

Visuals

If other types of visuals are needed, the media choices can expand to include print media, such as newspapers, magazines, and outdoor advertising. Don't think only of television when visuals are required.

And again, do not limit yourself to even those most obvious choices. Imagine yourself on the first tee at Pebble Beach, or lounging in a hot tub while gazing at the Caribbean and sipping a cool drink. You can see the image in your mind, even though you may never have actually experienced it. In the same way, you can suggest visual images to the audience through radio, sometimes at lower cost and with the resultant higher reach and frequency that the budget will provide.

Coupon Distribution

Mention "coupons" and people automatically think of print media: newspapers and magazines. Outdoor advertising is not considered; how can someone climb up and saw out a coupon portion of the billboard and tote it into the store?

Certainly magazines, newspapers, and direct mail are important media choices for distributing coupons. If you use them, place the coupon near the outer edge of the page so readers can tear out the coupon easily and quickly; most people do not have scissors with them when they are reading, and they do not want to destroy the entire issue just to get at your coupon. But Internet users can print out their own coupons. And coupons can be attached to posters, flyers, or an in-store display.

Coupons do not have to be actual items provided by the advertisers. Coupons could be almost anything. Ask consumers to get your product and use it as the coupon: "Bring any Pepsi item to the water park this week and get $4 off a regular admission." You may get both sales and the coupon incentive. Even better, get consumers to make their own coupons. When they write out the name of your product, their memories have an even stronger impression of your brand name than when they simply hear or see it. Ask them to print your product name, service logo, or advertising theme on a piece of paper and bring it along in order to save on their purchases. By couponing in this way you can use almost any advertising medium, including cinema, radio, transit, and outdoor.

Information

When you want to impart specific information to the audience, there may be legitimate media implications. Long passages of detailed wording may not lend themselves to broadcast media but may be handled quite well with some print media and with the Internet.

Exhibit 9.1

Some Thoughts from an Experienced Media Planner

Maybe the point to be made upfront is that the overall media selection is an *advertising* decision. It requires that media and creative work together on the best approach to get the job done. There may be compromise on either side.

For example, when Motel 6 first broke its Tom Bodett radio campaign on network radio, the media group argued for a :30 because it is half the cost of a :60. Stan Richards, the principal of the Richards Group, didn't feel that Tom could pull it off in a :30, so they went to a :60. It has been one of the most successful campaigns in radio.

On the efficiency side, nearly 50 percent of all network television commercials are :15, so media planners have had a real impact there.

What we do is a series of trade-off exercises with the creatives to see what is possible. That brings me to the other point, which is the actual creative unit used; that is the other major trade-off on creative. Do we use a magazine full page or can a 2/3 page do the job? How about :30s versus the cost savings and time for the message in :15s on television?

When providing information in your advertising, your media choices will depend on a number of other factors, such as audience familiarity, message complexity, and legal requirements.

Audience Familiarity

How familiar is the audience with your service or product, or with your advertising theme? They already know what facial tissues do and you do not need to demonstrate them, but they may not understand what a new car-wax wipe does and how it is used, so they may need to see it in action. You need not explain what Dr Pepper is; most already know. But if you have a brand-new soft drink entry, you may need to tell them about it and even show the package.

Message Complexity

A very long or complex message requires adequate space. Sometimes it is possible to read those explanations very rapidly over broadcast media, although nobody will really hear them, or to superimpose passages in small type at the bottom of the screen, although the audience probably will not read them and certainly will not understand them. Billboards do not lend themselves to long passages of body copy, either.

But newspapers and magazines do, as do direct mail and perhaps Internet and in-store displays. Your media choices may be influenced greatly by the complexity and length of the intended message.

Legal Requirements

If you conduct a contest, you must provide certain information about the prizes, odds, entry methods, and purchase requirements and their alternatives. Not all of this information needs to be in the body copy; often, it is presented in small type as a footnote. Still, it must be there, and including it affects your media choices. You may be able to include such footnotes on a television screen, but they will be read and understood by very few and may only marginally meet the legal standards, and radio may not be conducive at all to including lengthy legal language.

The same considerations apply for including loan requirements, prescription medication caveats, and other messages under similar circumstances.

In-Depth Information

Sometimes you want to include information not because you are required to, but because it enhances your selling message.

For example, you may want to tell consumers how they might make use of a new product; for either a new or an existing product, you may indicate how they might benefit from using it. If you are selling a food product, you may want to induce usage by providing recipes. These message requirements will certainly affect your media choices.

Political Advertising

Selling ideas, whether lobbying for charitable support or running political advertising, may lend itself to certain media. Research shows that audience members are most likely to read and listen to media that seems to agree with their own views: Republicans read Republican newspapers and Democrats read Democratic newspapers. Independents would like to read independent newspapers if they could find them. To promote a candidate of a certain political party, advertising in media vehicles that are read primarily by the opposition may not be productive, whereas promoting an independent candidate through those same media vehicles may prove fruitful.

These political considerations take into account the ideas and parties that you are selling, as well as the competing ideas and parties.

Efficiency versus Impact

Advertising media can be used in varying weights and patterns. Spending a lot of money on reach may limit how many advertisements can be included for each medium, as well as the impact that each ad carries. Spending money on large print ads or long broadcast commercials will necessarily limit the size of audience that can be reached. This situation is the classic "efficiency versus impact" dilemma that almost every media plan must face.

Whether emphasizing impact or efficiency, the advertising can be directed at wholesalers and retailers. This method uses a "push" strategy—to force the product or service through the distribution channel. Or the advertising can focus on the eventual consumers, trying to "pull" services and products through the channel.

Only one brand can have the largest budget within any product or service category. Thus, all the remaining competitors must work with budgets that do not match that of the leader. It may be possible to have better advertisements, although there is always the danger that a highly entertaining ad will draw the audience's attention to the wrong elements. Many campaigns that have been recognized for their originality, creativity, or entertainment have failed to impress the brand name on the audiences' minds.

Those trailing brands may be able to match the budget leader in certain areas of the country, or in certain media, or for certain periods during the year, even if they cannot match up in all media for the entire campaign.

Chapter 10

Working with a Communication Budget

All communication plans begin and end with an accounting of the communication budget. The amount of dollars allocated to the communications task will largely dictate the type of communication channels and tactics that are possible. For example, if your communication budget is $1 million, you won't be scheduling a national Super Bowl commercial for $3 million. The budget puts a parameter around what can be done.

Companies develop their communication budgets in a variety of ways. Some develop the budget based on the task or objective. Others update their budget based on last year's efforts. Other companies develop their budget based on the competition. There is no right or wrong way to develop the communication budget. It is up to the company and precision with which they can tie communication dollars to a specific marketing and business outcome.

Communication Budget as a Percentage of Sales

Regardless of the method of developing the communication budget, it will undergo scrutiny from senior management. Every budget is put into the context of the total sales or revenue of the company. The marketing or advertising manager will be asking senior management for money along with other departments such as information technologies, human resources, and operations. No company has unlimited resources, so the CEO must ultimately decide what percentage of his or her company's sales will be devoted to marketing and to communications.

Table 10.1 is a hypothetical example of four companies who compete in the life insurance category. Each brand is detailed in terms of total sales and in terms of how much and the percentage they allocate to communications.

For example, Boston Life allocates $5 million to communications. They have a total annual revenue or sales of $125 million. The percentage they

Table 10.1

Communication Budget as a Percentage of Sales

Brand	Communication budget (million)	Total sales (million)	%
Boston Life	$5.0	$125	4.0
American Life	$7.5	$250	3.0
Great Lakes	$15.0	$250	6.0
Sierra Madre	$20.0	$1,000	2.0
Total	$47.5	$1,625	2.9

allocate to communications is 4 percent of their total sales. This is calculated by dividing $5 million by $125 million (5 / 125 × 100 = 4.0 percent).

From this simple analysis, you can see that the average percentage spent on communications among the four brands is approximately 3 percent of total revenue. The range is from a low of 2 percent for Sierra Madre to a high of 6 percent for Great Lakes.

A CEO would request this type of analysis to understand the context in which her competition is allocating their resources compared to his brand. Based on such an analysis, she may adjust the overall amount of dollars allocated to communications up or down.

Categories of Communication Dollars

Once an overall communication budget has been determined, there are four broad categories that the marketing director or advertising manager reviews. The four categories are as follows:

1. Working Dollars

These are dollars that are allocated to programs that will impact the market. It can be paid media, promotions, publicity, or digital initiatives. It is any activity that is directed outward or is impacting the marketplace.

2. Nonworking Dollars

These are dollars that are allocated to the creation of the programs. It can be production of the creative unit, or message, the talent cost for a spokesperson or celebrity, or other items that facilitate the activity. The nonworking costs are necessary to activate programs, but without a program they will not impact the marketplace.

Table 10.2

Communication Allocation

	% Dollars of Budget				
Company	Paid media	Promotions	Public relations	Digital	Production
Sierra Madre	50	—	20	20	10
American Life	35	—	—	45	20
Great Lakes	30	30	10	15	15
Boston Life	40	20	10	20	10

3. Contingency Dollars

These are dollars that are set aside for a variety of situations. It could be to have a cushion for potential cost overruns. Or it could be a fund to purchase opportunistic media properties or programs that might arise during the course of the year.

4. Agency Compensation

These are the dollars that are allocated to compensate the agency or agencies for their work. This can be done as a fee or a commission or by a hybrid of methods. The budget item is how much the advertiser will compensate their agency partners for their work in devising and activating the programs.

The goal of the marketing director or advertising manager is to optimize the working percentage of the communication budget. More working dollars leads to greater market success. These four areas become discussion items in management meetings regarding the overall use of the communication dollars.

Communication Allocation

The challenge of the communication planner is to allocate the dollars to the appropriate channels. The communication budget may include agency compensation and contingency or it may exclude those items. Regardless, the task is to allocate the dollars across the channels.

At this stage of the process, the communication budget is allocated in broad terms to working areas such as paid media or advertising, promotions, public relations, and digital areas. It is also allocated to nonworking areas such as production. Once this is established, then each respective area is responsible for developing the strategies and tactics from their specific budget.

As stated earlier, Table 10.2 is an example of the communication budget allocation for each of four hypothetical insurance companies. As you can see, each brand has a slightly different weighting of the communication channels. For example, Sierra Madre allocates 50 percent of their budget to paid media whereas American Life allocates just 35 percent. Great Lakes and Sierra Madre allocate resources to promotions while the other two brands do not.

There is no right or wrong way to allocate communication dollars. The allocation is driven by each brand's marketing and communication objectives. As we saw in the chapter on competitive analysis, communication planners do review how budgets are allocated in a competitive context, just as the CEO reviews overall budgets within a competitive context.

Summary

In summary, allocating the communication budget is the key strategic item in meeting the overall communication objective. The overall budget is reviewed by the CEO and the specific allocation of resources is then reviewed by the marketing or advertising manager. The communication planner is responsible for the overall strategy of the budget and works with the marketing and/or advertising director to determine the overall budget.

Chapter 11
Setting Communications Objectives

Once you have determined whom you want to reach, where they are, and when you need to reach them, you must determine how much pressure you need to put behind your message. This is where media communications objectives come into play. Setting communications goals can be a difficult challenge. It is like someone with a weakness for sweets going into an ice cream shop: you want it all, but you have to make some tough choices.

Communications objectives are often reduced to the Big Four dimensions. The first dimension is *reach:* which potential customers do you want to reach? The second dimension is *frequency:* how often do you want to reach them? The third dimension is *continuity:* how many days, weeks, months, and patterns of advertising do you need at the appropriate reach and frequency levels? Another consideration is *impact:* how large do you want print advertisements to be, and how long do you want broadcast commercials to run?

The first data point you need to consider is your brand's purchase cycle.

Product Purchase Cycle

The brand's product purchase cycle is going to be the lead factor in determining how many weeks you need to advertise. Suppose you market a brand of Christmas candy, and 90 percent of your sales are done in the four or five weeks between Thanksgiving and Christmas. You would likely set your communications goals on a weekly basis for that critical period or prior to it to account for the lag effect of advertising.

Conversely, suppose you are marketing a brand of bread. Consumers buy bread every week of the year. You may set a weekly purchase cycle, but then you need to cover a lot of weeks.

Most packaged-goods brands have product purchase cycles of three to four weeks. That means that the consumer is buying the brand about once a month. As a result, many media planners use four weeks as the benchmark for developing reach and frequency estimates. Most reach and frequency models are also built on this four-week curve because one week's advertising may have an unusual pattern, whereas four weeks' worth shows a pattern that is more typical.

It is important to know your brand's purchase cycle. It forms the frame of reference for establishing reach and frequency goals, as well as continuity. Continuity is the pattern of advertising. Obviously, you want the advertising to be active before and during the time periods when people are buying your service or product, whether time of year, season, day of week, or time of day. Yet there is more to continuity; it is an effective pattern where the recall of an advertisement is still in the audience's mind when the next advertisement appears, resulting in a cumulative effect for the campaign.

Many advertisers believe in the theory of recency, that is, that consumers react to purchase opportunities if the message has appeared recently. This concept is an application of the primacy versus recency theory in psychology: some research has found that the first message in a generic category may carry the most impactful recall and sales reactions, whereas other research indicates that the most recent appearance is the most viable. Of late in the advertising industry, the recency theory is winning out, so many advertisers want their message to be the most recent one received before the buyer makes a purchase decision. This theory is discussed again from a different perspective later in this chapter.

Setting Reach Goals

Now that you know your brand's purchase cycle, you are ready to establish reach and frequency goals. Suppose that you are marketing an established frozen-dinner line. The brand's product purchase cycle is four weeks. You want to set your reach and frequency levels to that four-week period.

First, let's tackle the reach dimension. To continue to grow the brand, you want to reach the majority of your consumers with some sort of message within that four-week time frame. Let's set a goal of 80 percent target reach.

How did you get to 80 percent? Media planners can run an analysis of how much it costs to reach your audience. There is a point at which it is difficult to get incremental reach. Typically, that point begins at around 80 percent. So that is why you don't set your goal at 90 percent.

Why not less than 80 percent? Assuming that the brand needs to reach the majority of its consumers, you pick the point at which it is most economical to do just that. Reaching less than 80 percent seems like you would be leaving revenue on the table.

This doesn't mean that you should always set 80 percent as the reach level. There are reasons to set it lower and reasons to set it higher. Most brands rarely set their reach goals at less than 50 percent for the purchase cycle; rather, they stay in the two-thirds to four-fifths range.

Setting Frequency Goals

Now that you have the reach level established, how many times should you reach your potential customers? In the above example, you set your goals based on a four-week purchase cycle. It seems like common sense that you would want to reach your consumer at least one time per week, an average of four times per month.

Most reach and frequency objectives use the average-frequency concept. Whether it is 3, 4, 5, or even 20, that is the average number of times a consumer would see or hear your brand's commercial message in a given time frame.

In this example, we have a reach goal of 80 percent and an average frequency goal of 4.0 within the four-week time frame. But 80 percent of the consumers aren't exposed to your message four times each. Some may see it only once; others may see it eight times or more. Because it is an average, half will likely see it fewer than four times whereas half will see it more than four times.

This dynamic of frequency of exposure has led media planners to set certain levels of effective frequency.

Effective Frequency

Research studies indicate that consumers do not retain an advertising message until they have seen it at least three times. This figure is the basis for effective frequency—that point at which the advertising frequency becomes effective or motivating. Many media planners use 3.0+ as the sacred rule of thumb because this body of research is so compelling.

Media planners then translate effective frequency into effective reach level—the percentage of the audience reached more than three times. In the case of the 80 percent reach at an average frequency of 4.0, the effective reach or percentage of consumers exposed 3.0+ times is 51 percent, which means that half of the consumers have been effectively reached (see Table 11.1).

Setting an effective frequency goal and subsequent reach level can be a good way to establish a delivery goal. In this example, you want to reach at least 50 percent of your audience 3.0+ times within a given four-week purchase cycle.

Table 11.1

Frequency Distribution for 80 Percent Reach, 4.0 Average Frequency Television Schedule

Frequency	Exposed (%)	Exposed at least (%)
1	17.4	80
2	11.9	63
3	8.5	51
4	6.3	42
5	4.7	36
6	3.6	31
7	2.8	28
8	2.2	25
9	1.7	23
10+	5.2	21

Note: Based on women 25 to 54 years old, multiple dayparts.
Source: Telmar.

We have used 3.0+ as the effective frequency level. However, the majority of that research was done in the 1970s with mature brands. So is 3.0+ always the standard for effectiveness? No. Is there value in the first or second impression that a consumer sees? Yes.

Developing the appropriate effective frequency level is as much an art as a science. There are factors that might suggest more frequency or less frequency. Weights can be applied to the first and second impressions ranging from 100 percent effective to 25 percent effective, depending upon message strength and creative approach.

Some advertisers want even higher frequency levels. Research indicates that it may require ten or more messages to result in effective recall of a sales message, so sometimes the 3+ effective frequency is expanded to a 3–10 effective frequency.

Keep in mind that even though this concept is referred to as effective frequency, it is actually a reach level: the percentage of the audience that will be reached at least 3 or more times, or the number of audience members that will be reached 3 to 10 times during the campaign period. Setting the effective frequency level can be a complex process. Let's look at some of the factors that might affect your decision.

Communications Matrix

Obviously, you want to reach your target audience at least once. So the real question becomes, how many more times do you need to reach them with your message before it sinks in and motivates them to act? This is the sixty-four-thousand-dollar question, but there are some commonsense ways to narrow it down.

For example, if you were introducing a new brand, you would need to have more frequency than you would need for an established brand. The same would be true if your brand had very low awareness.

Perhaps you are in a category that has had a number of new entries, and the marketplace is becoming a real dogfight. That may warrant more frequency just to maintain your current position in the category.

The advertising message can also have an impact on the amount of frequency you assign—say, if you have new copy that would warrant more frequency to seed the message. Or if you had a limited-time offer that expires in a week, then you would want more frequency to ensure that it is noticed and remembered.

Table 11.2 shows a frequency planning matrix that takes into account brand maturity, awareness, competition, the newness of the copy, and the type of message that is to be advertised.

Depending upon where your brand falls in relation to these elements, you simply add the outcome to the base level of one. If your brand is more than five years old, totally dominates the category, has over 90 percent awareness with every audience available, faces no competition, and has a brand campaign that is over two years old, then we applaud you. Based on this matrix, you don't need to advertise. We have yet to meet a brand manager who doesn't need to advertise, so until we do, the matrix stands as an example of how to assign values to get effective frequency, that is, the appropriate frequency level.

Just to put the matrix to the test, let's suppose that you are introducing a new product into a heavily advertised category. Because your brand is new and has no awareness, you would add frequency to the base of one. Also, you have a new campaign and a very competitive category, so you add frequency there as well. Although you are using short-term promotional tactics such as coupons and price promotions in-store to gain immediate trial, you have decided that your advertising message will be a brand-differentiation message that is in for the long haul. Using the matrix, you come to the effective frequency level of four, so you would peg your objectives to reaching so many of your target consumers four or more times within a given product purchase cycle.

So those are ways of defining effective frequency solutions to your brand's communications problems. Effective frequency is certainly a viable method for developing communications goals. But it is not the only one. In the past few years, we have seen the rise of a new philosophy called *recency* (see Table 11.3).

Advertising campaigns today are placing increased emphasis on engagement; it is no longer enough simply to inform the audience. Instead, it is essential to engage the audience with interaction, involvement, searches for

Table 11.2

Frequency Planning Matrix

Factor	High (1)	Average (0)	Low (−1)
		Add to base level of 1	
Brand maturity	New	Brand in market 2–5 years	Brand in market 5+ years
Brand awareness	New or low awareness	Average awareness	Strongly established leader
Competitive category	Very aggressive	Some spending but your brand is on par	Little spending. Your brand has over 50 percent share
Advertising campaign	New campaign/ message	In second year	Has run for 2+ years
Type of response	Short-term promotion	Mix of promo/ brand	Long-term brand

additional information, and other methods in conjunction with the product or service. Keep in mind that it may be possible for the audience to be engaged with the medium without being engaged with the item being advertised; for example, the television program *American Idol* which induces millions of viewers to vote for their favorites. The audience is thus engaged with the medium, but not with the item or items being advertised. Actively voting for their favorite performers is not the same as actively searching for where they might purchase the service or product being featured.

Many people are skeptical about advertising, so engagement can help build emotional relationships between audiences and products or services. A communication goal of establishing an emotional link, such as trust, helps overcome the skepticism, and it may lead to more interest in the brand and eventually to greater involvement, engagement, and trust.

Recency

Recency theory suggests that you want to have your advertising impressions as close to the point of sale as possible. So recency theory puts much more emphasis on being constantly in the market with advertising, rather than being in the market only with a higher level of impact or effective frequency. Recency planning has been in vogue in the past several years, particularly with mature brands, where it has proven to be a very effective strategy. Consumers need constant reminders to purchase the mature brands.

In recency planning, the emphasis is on covering as many product purchase cycles as possible. Many recency plans use weekly goals of, say, a

Table 11.3

Recency Planning Matrix, New Product Introduction in Heavily Advertised Category

	Add to base level of 1			
Factor	High (1)	Average (0)	Low (−1)	Comment
Brand awareness	X			New product with no awareness
Competitive category	X			Highly competitive category
Advertising campaign	X			New ad campaign
Type of response			X	Long-term brand
Brand maturity	X			New introductions
	4	0	−1	= 3 incremental + 1 base level = 4+ frequency level

60 percent reach with a once per week frequency but advertise on the air 75 percent or more of the weeks of the year.

Whereas the term *recency* is a relatively new one, the concept of continual advertising is not. As Vernon Baird, the head of Mrs. Baird's Bakeries until his death in 1992, was heard to say, "Advertising is as important an ingredient as flour. People buy my bread every day and I advertise every day." His strategy seems to have paid off: Baird's became the number-one brand of bread sold in Texas, whereas store brands dominated sales in almost every other state.

Continuity versus Impact

We have now discussed *effective frequency,* which determines the desired frequency level at which you want to advertise, and *recency,* which is a lower-level, continuity approach to advertising. So which approach is the best?

Each approach has its own merits. There is no one size that fits all. As we have discussed, it all depends on your brand's situation and relationship to the category in which it competes.

If you have a new brand or are restaging an old brand, then you are more likely to use the effective frequency concept for setting your communications goals. If you are in charge of a mature brand that is consistently purchased and you need that constant contact with a broad target group, then you are more likely to go down the recency path.

As with most strategies, there are hybrid strategies that come from either side. The real trade-off is the amount of media weight in a given purchase cycle versus the number of purchase cycles with media weight.

Let's say that your brand is canned green beans and that you can afford 1,800 target rating points (TRP) a year. Let's assume that canned green beans have a relatively flat seasonal purchase skew and are purchased every four weeks.

For the same budget dollars, you could schedule 60 TRP for 30 weeks and cover nearly 60 percent of the year with your advertising, or you could schedule 120 TRP a week and cover 15 weeks of the year. One schedule offers continuity and the other impact. It is the age-old trade-off.

In this case, being on the air more weeks than not seems like the best course of action, particularly if each week basically represents approximately 2 percent of sales. One schedule covers around 60 percent of sales, while the other covers only 30 percent of sales. So the impact of the second schedule must be worth two times that of the first schedule for it to pay out.

Response Goals for Communications

Throughout this chapter we have discussed setting communications goals based largely on achieving brand awareness. This is a typical approach to media planning, regardless of the type of industry or brand that is being advertised. But reach, frequency, and continuity of exposure are all just different means to the same end. That end can range from an awareness gain to a change in attitude to generating more traffic to a store. Regardless of your situation, you are looking for some form of response from your advertising dollars.

Another way to approach setting communications goals is to start with the response that you are trying to achieve and working backward. For example, if you have an advertising budget of $1,000 and you know that you need to generate $10,000 in incremental sales to be successful, you now have a goal. If you also know that the average customer spends $50 in your store, then your advertising must generate 200 additional customers for you to be successful. Armed with these facts, you now know that you have a ceiling of $5 per new customer, or your advertising will not pay out. (This rate was calculated by dividing the $1,000 ad budget by 200 new customers.)

So, if your media plan has a mix of media that costs 10 cents per person, it would generate 10,000 impressions. If 2 percent of these people respond to your offer, you are home free.

The point of this exercise is that sales response is a crucial component to setting communications goals. Whether it is through sophisticated marketing mix models or just looking at next-day sales, the response to advertising is the barometer for how much advertising you are likely to do. This type of information is vital to media planners as they begin to construct a plan. There is no sense in coming in with a plan that won't deliver the expected results. Over time, most brands have a track record of what works and what doesn't. Using response information in conjunction with reach and frequency analysis is an excellent method of determining how many resources you should allocate toward a campaign.

Response analysis is the core of setting communications goals for online media. Online media have built-in response analysis tools, so online plans are highly measurable. Most online campaigns have specific response goals established as benchmarks prior to the campaign. As the campaign unfolds, the online media professional begins to adjust creative or media strategies to meet these goals.

Conclusion

Setting communications objectives is a complex task. Much of it involves commonsense decisions. The first step in the process is to understand your brand's purchase dynamics. From there you can assess the appropriate levels of reach and frequency necessary to achieve the specific advertising response. It is important to meld reach and frequency information with any sales or other response metrics to build the appropriate communications goals.

Chapter 12
Establishing Media Objectives and Tactics

If media objectives are the "what," then media strategies are the "how." Media strategies are inexplicably linked to media objectives. Media strategies are the answer to how you would achieve the objective.

Media objectives outline where you want to go. Media strategies outline how to get there. Media tactics provide the specific details on how to get there. So, if your objective is to get to Dallas and your strategy is to fly there, the tactic is to take Southwest flight #9 that departs Tuesday at 2 P.M., arrives at 4 P.M. and costs $99.

One simple way to look at objectives is "*to* do something" and at strategies as "*by* doing something." Media strategies, then, are the overall use of media to achieve the media objectives. Media strategies take two overall forms. The first is the media mix. The media mix is what combination of media you recommend to achieve the outlined objectives. The second is media scheduling. Scheduling is when you recommend deploying the various media types to meet the objectives.

Media strategy is often confused with media tactics. Media strategy is the broad strategy of using media whereas tactics are the specific media vehicles. For example, a media objective may be to reach 80 percent of women who are homemakers. The strategy to accomplish this objective is to use a combination of cable television, magazines, and online display. The tactics would be to use Lifetime cable network, *Good Housekeeping* magazine, and Yahoo for online display.

Media strategies, then, are typically using categories of media while media tactics are the specific media vehicles. The only time that this is not the case is when there is no broader umbrella for the category. A sponsorship of the Super Bowl would be an example of this.

Media Strategy Examples

Media strategies should match specifically to media objectives. You shouldn't devise a media strategy in a vacuum. The best way to organize media strategies is to match them to the four overall media objectives. They are target, geography, seasonality/timing, and reach/frequency. Here are examples of media strategies for each of these objectives.

Objective	Strategy
1. To reach 90 percent of teenage boys an average of 1 × per week	By using a mix of television, print, online, and gaming
2. To provide support for all four-week product purchase cycles	By providing continual support with magazines and by flighting the television schedule
3. To provide national support with emphasis in the top 10 DMAs	By using national cable and magazines for national support and by using radio and in-store media within the top 10 DMAs

Media strategies follow media objectives. They are the action plan for how you are recommending allocating the budget. Some media planners use allocation percentages as a part of their media strategies. For example, if the objective is to provide national brand support, a strategy statement could be "By allocating 80 percent of the available dollars to national print and television."

Strategy Alternatives

There is more than one way to meet the objectives outlined. A method that many media planners use when developing a media plan is to review alternative strategies. For example, if the overall goal of the plan is to reach 90 percent of the target an average of four times per month, the media planner may develop three or more alternative plans for review. These plans would have different combinations of media or different weighting of the same media. One plan might be a television only plan. A second plan might be a combination of television and print. And a third plan might be a combination of television, print, online, and radio. Each alternative strategy would be analyzed in terms of how it meets the overall media objectives. This is a routine method that media planners use to justify their specific recommendation.

Media Tactics

Media tactics are the details of your media plan. Tactics become the actual plan. You can't implement strategies without tactics. Media tactics include four components: description, cost, impressions, and the rationale.

1. Description

The description details what you are recommending. In the case of print, it would be the specific publications, the creative unit placed, and the purchase frequency. For example, if your strategy is to schedule women's magazines, a tactic would be to schedule six full-page four-color ads in *Good Housekeeping.*

Descriptions vary by the medium chosen. So, in the case of broadcast, a tactic written in a media plan would include the types of stations, the dayparts to be purchased, and the creative unit to be used. It may or may not include the specific programs at this juncture because they have yet to be negotiated. This is done once the plan is approved. It could be done simultaneously, though, if the marketer has "bought off" on the broad direction of the media strategies.

Outdoor media include the type of unit, the number to be purchased, and the general locations. Specific details are conveyed upon the final purchase.

Online display contains the sites, the creative unit, and the dayparts to be purchased. Search engine marketing would include the pool of keywords to be tested and the geography of the test.

2. Cost

All tactics include costs. Costs are provided at the category level and at the tactic level. For example, you may allocate a budget of $4 million to national magazines. The plan would itemize each publication's cost, which would then be added together to reach the $4 million magazine budget.

The cost for each element in the media plan should reflect the agency compensation agreement. If the agency is working on a commission basis, then the media should contain the appropriate commission. If the agency is working on a fee basis, then the media should be shown in net dollars. At the tactic level, the marketer will want to understand the specific costs that he or she will be billed. The tactical cost aspect of the plan becomes the financial road map for the marketer in working with his internal accounting.

3. Impressions

All tactics will include the amount of the target reached. The amount can be determined in a number of ways. It can be shown by gross rating points (GRPs) or it can be shown by impressions or both. As communication plans contain more of a variety of elements—from paid media to digital media to promotions and more—the planner is moving toward impressions as the measurement standard for reach in tactics. This is the simplest form of showing reach and the easiest to use across any form of communication.

For example, you might show that *Good Housekeeping* cost $750,000 for three ads and generated nine million impressions based on a target of women aged 25 to 54. Showing impressions in the media plan for each tactic helps the marketer understand the target for which the impressions are calculated. It provides a frame of reference for the client to understand the strength of each element.

4. Rationale

There are a number of ways of executing a media strategy. Therefore, the tactics you recommend should contain a detailed rationale. The rationale for a media tactic revolves around how it reaches the target, how cost efficient it is, and how it may benefit the brand through association. For example, your rationale for selecting *Good Housekeeping* could be as follows:

- *Good Housekeeping* has the highest coverage of our target.
- *Good Housekeeping*'s cost per thousand (CPM) is 12 percent below average for the women's service group.
- *Good Housekeeping* will endorse our brand through the *Good Housekeeping* seal of approval.

This is a strong rationale for why *Good Housekeeping* should be a part of the magazine plan. Each media tactic should have a similar rationale. Not all tactics will have all of these components. The important part of writing a rationale is to answer the question, why this specific vehicle instead of another?

Summary

Media strategies should answer the objectives outlined in the media plan. To provide a strong media plan align your strategies specifically with the objectives. If you find that you have strategies that do not match an objective, then you should reconsider those strategies. Once you provide a recommended strategy, consider, or benchmark, alternative plans. This way there can be no argument: your recommendation is the best path to take to meet the objectives.

Media tactics are the backbone of the media plan. It is what the marketer wants to understand, because it is the specifics of what will be in the marketplace. Each tactic should contain a detailed description; include the cost, the number of impressions, and a detailed rationale for why it was selected.

Chapter 13

Learning the Language of Media Planning

Once you understand the strategies you may be using, you need to deal with the media for specific tactics. These can be broadcast programs, magazines, websites, or a myriad of other media and vehicles. Each media category has its own language; nevertheless, there are some terms that are common to most. To understand how any business operates, you must know the language of that business. It is the same in advertising: when you know the terminology of advertising media, you will be well on your way to understanding the process and function of the mass media in your advertising campaign.

Knowing terminology can do even more. By knowing the terms and concepts of advertising media, you can contribute your own ideas and precepts, you can envision how the entire advertising campaign fits together, and you can be accepted as a knowledgeable, contributing partner in the campaign development process.

Advertising media terminology is not difficult or complicated. Nobody tried to create complicated terms to describe how the media work. Instead, the terminology just developed along with the industry, so many of the terms make logical sense in how they are defined and used. But at the same time, nobody wants to stop in the middle of a discussion to define terms for you; everyone assumes that you know the terminology. You must know these terms as well as you know other basic concepts, like "right" or "left," or "up" or "down." You will not have time to stop and figure out the terms in the middle of a meeting; work and ideas move rapidly in advertising, so the terminology must be second nature to you.

Here, then, in simple and direct language, are the basic terms used in advertising media planning.

We can start with the term *media*. The *media* are go-betweens, the facilitators that make it possible to deliver an advertising message. The term *media* is plural; the singular is *medium*. The alternate plural, *mediums,* refers to fortune-tellers and seers, not advertising. A single media outlet, such as a magazine, a broadcast network, a radio station, or a newspaper, is called a *media vehicle*. The specifications of the individual advertisement are the *advertising unit*. For example, if your media choice is magazines, your vehicle might be *Family Circle,* and your advertising unit might be a full-page, four-color bleed advertisement.

The Four Basics

There are four basic concepts that underlie most advertising: *reach, frequency, impact,* and *continuity.* Be sure to master these four basic terms because they are used commonly and serve as a foundation for much of what happens in advertising media planning. For example, many persons think that frequency and repetition are the same thing, but as Exhibit 13.1 explains, they differ.

Reach

There are two kinds of reach: *numerical* and *percentage.* Numerical reach is the number of persons (or households, or adult women, or whatever your target population happens to be) to whom your advertising will be communicated. Numerical reach is usually rounded, so you may try to reach eight million male teens or one and a half million households.

Percentage reach is the percentage of all the persons (or, again, households, or working women, or whatever your target) you will reach with your campaign. If there are 35 million college students in the United States and you reach 10 million of them, you are reaching about 28.6 percent of them. Because percentage reach is often rounded to the nearest integer (whole number), you would have 29 percent reach in this case.

Reach is often abbreviated as "R" in tables and informal reports.

Frequency

There are also two kinds of frequency: *frequency of insertion* and *frequency of exposure.*

Frequency of insertion describes the number of times your advertisement appears in the media. Often, frequency is described on a per week basis, rather than the frequency per year or the frequency during the course of a campaign. So you might be running your advertising 25 times per week on a radio station during your 13-week campaign.

Just because you run advertising insertions frequently does not mean that the audience will see or hear your advertisement every time it runs.

Exhibit 13.1

Frequency and Repetition

Some people believe that frequency and repetition are the same thing, but they are not. Frequency is the number of times you advertise, whether the same message is repeated or not. Repetition is using the same advertising message over and over again, whether it is done frequently or not.

A local store buys 25 spots per week on a local radio station and has the messages delivered impromptu by one of the station's on-air personalities. The advertising is appearing frequently, but it is unlikely that any of the messages is repeated exactly. Here we have frequency without repetition.

A large insurance company runs its Christmas message in magazines every December, using the same message every year. Advertising one time per year is definitely not frequent advertising, so here we have repetition without frequency.

In fact, it is unlikely that any member of your audience will be exposed to your advertising every time it runs. If you have a frequency of insertion of 25 times per week, the average audience member will see or hear that advertisement only three or four times each week, which would be your frequency of exposure.

When scheduling multiple advertisement insertions, you are likely to reach your audience members with varying degrees of frequency. If you schedule, say, 10 advertisements, perhaps only 10 percent of the audience members will see all 10 and 30 percent will see only one. One method a media planner uses to analyze the impact of an advertising media schedule is to look at a frequency distribution of the impressions.

There are different schools of thought on how many times consumers must see or hear an advertisement before it registers in their minds. The concept of effective frequency pegs a specific frequency number, such as 3+ (persons who see or hear the advertisement three or more times), which is when it is believed that a consumer will retain the message.

Frequency is often abbreviated "F" in informal plans and tables. Because no single week may be completely representative or average, we often count up the frequency over a four-week period and then divide the figure by four to come up with the weekly average. That way, a week that is higher or lower than average will not skew the figures.

Impact

The *impact* that an advertisement has on the audience is the result of a number of factors, many of them relating to the message: headline, illustration, body copy, and other message components. The media contribution to impact comes from the size of a print advertisement or the length of a broadcast commercial or from the use of color or "bleed" (print that appears to "bleed" off the edge of the page) or reverse (e.g., white type on black background) printing. These advertising unit specifications, then, define the impact that is derived from the media portion of the campaign.

Continuity

Continuity involves the scheduling of the advertisement. You want to plan the pattern of your advertising so that subsequent messages build on top of the gains made by previous insertions. If the advertisements are scheduled too far apart, you may be starting over with each new ad because the audience has forgotten what you said in previous advertisements. On the other hand, if you schedule your advertising properly, each subsequent ad will appear before the effects have worn off from previous advertising, so you gain a cumulative effect. Proper scheduling can provide continuity. Continuity is the pattern of advertising, with messages scheduled for maximum effect.

Buying more reach in advertising costs more money. Similarly, buying more frequency costs more money. And buying more impact (larger advertisements, longer commercials, color, etc.) costs more money. Continuity, on the other hand, does not necessarily cost more money; it involves scheduling the optimal pattern of advertising, not necessarily buying more advertising.

Audience Measures

Copies Printed versus People in the Audience

Different media accumulate their audiences in different ways. In print media, such as newspapers and magazines, the first part of the statistic is the actual number of publications distributed, or circulation. However, more than one person usually reads each copy of a publication; for example, most newspapers average two readers per copy, while certain magazines, such as *People,* may have upwards of eight readers per copy. So the total audience is the circulation multiplied by the readers per copy. Thus, in print media, such as newspapers and magazines, the circulation is the number of copies printed, whereas the audience is the number of persons who read those copies of the publication. Because you want to attract more than one reader per copy of the publication, the number for the audience will usually be larger than the number for circulation.

Outdoor advertising also has a circulation measure. Each billboard has a daily effective circulation, or DEC, which is the actual number of people who drive by or see that billboard. To get the total audience, you simply multiply by the number of days that particular poster is showing.

Broadcast media, on the other hand, have no circulation measure. The audience is measured by a random sample of viewers or listeners. The Internet also has no circulation figures but is measured in a similar manner as broadcast, with one single measurement.

Accumulative Audience

As we have just seen, numerical reach measures the size of your audience. But confusion can result between the reach for a single advertising insertion and the total reach for a series of advertisements or for an entire campaign. To reduce this confusion, the term *accumulative audience* (also called *cumulative audience,* or *cume*) is used to refer to the audience of a series of advertising placements or of an advertising campaign (see Table 13.1).

If you run a series of advertisements in a single media vehicle, the total number of audience members you have reached is the accumulative audience. For example, let's say you run three advertisements in the *Chicago Tribune.* The accumulative audience is the total number of different people who have been exposed to your campaign in that single media vehicle. Each audience member is counted only once, no matter how many times he or she may have seen the advertising.

Unduplicated Audience

Similarly, if you run your advertising in a combination of vehicles, the total audience size is called the *unduplicated audience.* Again, each audience member is counted only once, no matter how many times he or she may have heard or seen your advertisements; counting a person again would inflate your unduplicated audience figures.

Let's say you are advertising in *Newsweek* magazine and on the *NBC Nightly News.* Whether audience members see your advertising in *Newsweek* or hear it on the nightly news or both, they are each counted only once.

Table 13.1

Accumulative Audience

Insertion #	New readers	
1	500,000	
2	100,000	
3	50,000	
	650,000	Total

Note: New readers are those who have not seen the advertising before.

The unduplicated audience is very much like the accumulative audience. The difference is that the accumulative audience involves the total number of different people who are exposed to your advertising through a combination of advertisements in a *single vehicle,* whereas the unduplicated audience is the total number of different people who are exposed to your advertising through a series of advertisements in a *combination of vehicles.* These terms are often misused in the advertising business, particularly by persons who are not knowledgeable or experienced in the media portion of the business. The most common error is for someone to use *unduplicated audience* for both unduplicated and accumulative audiences. Such an error is not a major sin, but keeping the terms straight can help avoid confusion and add efficiency and accuracy to your media planning.

Audience Percentage Measurements

The terms *rating* and *share* are not difficult to understand once you grasp the basic concepts that underlie them. Because they began as broadcast terms, perhaps using broadcast examples will make them easier to comprehend. Although both terms deal with the percentage of audience members who are exposed to your advertising, each percentage is calculated as a portion of different populations.

First, it will help to understand what is meant by a television household, abbreviated as TVHH in the media business. A household is a group of people who live together, most often a family, but also a single person living alone, persons of the opposite sex sharing living quarters (what the government abbreviates as POSSLQ), or roommates. A television household is a household that has an operating television set; the set may be on or off, because the term *operating* means that the receiving set works, not that it is being used at any particular moment.

Another common term is *households using television,* abbreviated as HUT. It refers to the television households with a set turned on as a percentage of all television households. The major radio ratings service reports on *people using radio,* abbreviated as PUR, which is persons listening to the radio expressed as a percentage of all people with radios.

Rating

In television broadcasting, the rating refers to the persons who see or hear a particular program, station, or network expressed as a percentage of all TVHH, whether they have a set on at that moment or not. The rating can be for a certain region or broadcast area, or it can be for the entire country.

Similarly, a radio rating is those persons tuned to a particular program, station, or network expressed as a percentage of all the households that have operating radio receivers. All radios are counted, including those in use and those turned off at that particular time.

Rating is often abbreviated as "Rtg."

Share

Again using television broadcasting as an example, the share is those persons tuned to a particular program station or network as a percentage of all television households with sets turned on, that is, as a percentage of HUT. The share could be for the entire country or for a particular geographic market. A radio share is those persons tuned in as a percentage of all households that have their radios on at that time (the households using radio, or HUR). Share is often abbreviated as "Shr."

So both rating and share involve the same people, those tuned to a particular program, station, or network at a particular time. Rating is those persons as a percentage of all the households with receiving sets, whether they are on or not at that particular time, and share is those same persons as a percentage of all those with sets on at that moment. (See Exhibit 13.2.)

Let's say that there are 100,000 television households in Erie, Pennsylvania, and that 60,000 of those households have their television sets on at 8 P.M., and that 20,000 of those households are watching a particular station in Erie. The station's rating would be 20 percent and its share would be 33 percent

$$Rating = \frac{20,000}{100,000} = 20 \; percent$$

$$Share = \frac{20,000}{60,000} = 33 \; percent$$

Exhibit 13.2

An Example of Ratings and Shares

Palookaville has four television stations serving its population of 250,000 television households (TVHH). For 8 P.M. on Wednesdays, when 54,000 TVHH have their sets on, here are the ratings and shares for the four stations.

Television station	TVHH sets on	Rtg	Shr
KAAA	12,000	$\frac{12,000}{250,000} = 4.8$	$\frac{12,000}{54,000} = 22$
KBBB	15,000	$\frac{15,000}{250,000} = 6.0$	$\frac{15,000}{54,000} = 28$
KCCC	18,000	$\frac{18,000}{250,000} = 7.2$	$\frac{18,000}{54,000} = 33$
KDDD	9,000	$\frac{9,000}{250,000} = 3.6$	$\frac{9,000}{54,000} = 17$
		21.6 HUT	100%

$$HUT = \frac{54,000}{250,000} = 21.6\%$$

Note that you can quickly check your calculations by adding the ratings to compare with the HUT that you have calculated.

Because the concepts of rating and share are so useful, they have been applied to all types of media: print, outdoor, and new media, as well as broadcast media. In print, we cannot have a publication turned on or off at a particular time, so instead we usually use the entire population or all the households as the size of the potential audience. A newspaper with a circulation of 25,000 in a market of 100,000 households would have a 25 percent rating. In print media, ratings are commonly discussed as *coverage.*

Rating is likely to be applied to all media, because rating is a more useful concept for advertisers than is share. The share tells how well a media vehicle competes with other vehicles in that marketplace, which is most useful to the broadcaster or publisher. Rating, on the other hand, tells how that time or space segment fares with the total potential audience in that marketplace. These terms are applied to the particular time segment when a commercial runs or the particular print segment where an advertisement appears, so the rating or share for an advertisement concentrates on only that time or place where the advertisement is run.

Combining Reach and Frequency for Audience Totals

Because reach and frequency are so important, it makes sense that a figure combining both reach and frequency would also be useful. In fact, we have two such combination figures.

Gross Rating Points and Target Rating Points

The sum of the ratings for a certain period of time is called the *gross rating points,* abbreviated as GRP. Let's say you are running five advertisements a week on a television network, and the ratings look like this.

Spot #	Rtg (%)
1	11
2	8
3	12
4	10
5	9
Total	50 GRP

But also notice that we have run five spots for a total of 50 GRP, which means the average spot pulled a rating of 10 percent. So 5 is the frequency (F) and 10 is the average rating, or the average percentage reach (R). Thus, our 50 GRP gave us averages of 10 percent reach or an average rating of 10 combined with the frequency of 5. As you can see, the GRP gives us a combination of reach (10 percent in this example) and frequency (5 in this example) in a single figure.

$$10R \times 5F = 50 \; GRP$$

So *reach* (as a percentage) multiplied by *frequency* produces *gross rating points.*

$$R\% \times F = GRP$$

Also keep in mind that a single rating, called a rating point, reaches one percent of the audience.

Exhibit 13.3

An Example of Reach, Frequency, GRP, and TAI

A furniture store realizes that it cannot achieve 100 percent reach in its local community of 50,000 population, but it would like to get close to 100 percent. Here are the advertising results from eleven weekly advertising insertions.

Insertion	Reach %	Reach #
1	11	5,500
2	8	4,000
3	9	4,500
4	6	3,000
5	13	6,500
6	5	2,500
7	17	8,500
8	10	5,000
9	8	4,000
10	6	3,000
11	6	3,000
F = 11	99 GRP	49,500 TAI

$$R\% \times F = GRP, \text{ so } \frac{GRP}{F} = R\%, \text{ so } \frac{99GRP}{11F} = 9\%R \text{ (avg.)}$$

$$R\# \times F = TAI, \text{ so } \frac{TAI}{F} = R\#, \text{ so } \frac{49,500 \text{ TAI}}{11\,F} = 4,500\,R \text{ (avg.}$$

$$R\% \times F = GRP, \text{ so } 9\%R \times 11F = 99GRP$$

$$R\# \times F = TAI, \text{ so } 4,500R \times 11F = 49,500 \text{ TAI}$$

With 99 GRP, did the store get close to its goal of 100 percent reach? It is unlikely, unless no audience member was exposed to more than one advertising insertion, which is doubtful. More likely, the average audience member was exposed to perhaps three of eleven insertions, so the percentage reach would be about 33 percent.

$$R\% \times F = GRP, \text{ so } \frac{GRP}{F} = R\%, \text{ so } \frac{99GRP}{3F} = 33\%R$$

As advertising media planners, we are often more concerned about how well we cover our target audience than how well we cover the total audience, which includes people who are not even prospective customers. Thus, we can apply the concept of GRP just to our target audience to figure the *target rating points* (TRP). If we have targeted correctly and selected media that go to those targets, our TRP figures should be higher than our GRP figures, which would include waste coverage; obviously, you do not want much reach or frequency to go to waste coverage.

Total Audience Impressions

Reach and frequency can also be combined into a single figure using *total audience impressions* (TAI), but using numerical reach instead of percentage reach. Let's use our same example with audience numbers instead of ratings.

Spot #	Millions of people
1	27.5
2	20.0
3	30.0
4	25.0
5	22.5
	125.0 TAI

So again we have a frequency of 5 but now with an average of 25 million audience members for each insertion. So our average numerical reach is 25 million. TAI gives us both numerical reach and frequency in a single figure.

$$25 \text{ million } R \times 5F = 125 \text{ million } TAI$$

So *reach* (as a number, not percentage) multiplied by *frequency* produces *total audience impressions*.

$$R\# \times F = TAI$$

Some people get confused by the fact that reach multiplied by frequency can produce both GRP and TAI. The key is to remember that using reach as a percentage produces GRP, whereas using reach as a number produces TAI.

The term *impression* is used to represent every time a piece of advertising is seen or heard. An audience impression is a member of the audience being exposed to your advertising one time, and here we count every time that any member of the audience is exposed to the advertising, whether it is the same person or a new audience member. These impressions are sometimes abbreviated as "IMPs."

Media Cost Comparisons

In addition to selecting media that reach our target, we must judge how efficient the media are, often comparing the cost of one media vehicle with another on the basis of cost efficiency. Because costs vary so much from one medium to another, these cost comparisons are usually made for one vehicle versus another, rather than one medium versus another. Only a person who is highly skilled and experienced selecting and comparing media uses these cost comparisons to compare one medium with another. It is difficult to know whether a full-page, four-color bleed advertisement in a national magazine is equivalent to a 30-second network television commercial (called a :30), or a 60-second commercial (a :60), or perhaps a :15. It is safest, then, not to use these cost comparison figures for intermedia comparisons.

Total Impressions as One Media Standard

We have gone through how we derive total impressions from the dimensions of reach and frequency. When the media landscape was devoid of the Internet, gross impressions were a nice boxcar number that marketers used largely as sales tools. Many brand managers used these terms to sell into the grocery trade to make their media plans bigger than life. "Our media plan reaches over 36 million women," came from one sales sheet for a food brand trying to get space into a grocery chain.

Now, the Internet has made total impressions a more meaningful number, and one that is looked at with greater scrutiny. Search engine marketing is reported by total impressions. Other new media such as video games and cellular phones are sold by total impressions. Most new out-of-home media use some form of total impressions as their measuring stick for reach potential.

Total impressions are one measure that can be used regardless of the medium. As one elevates media alternatives in an ever-fragmented media landscape, total impressions are one way, in a television campaign, say, to compare an online effort with an out-of-home effort.

Online Terminology

The rapid rise in online advertising has added some new terms to the media language. Although the terms are new, the principles behind them are similar to those previously discussed in the text relating to offline media.

The online term for unduplicated audiences is *unique visitors to a site* (see Table 13.2). For example, based on the February 2011 comScore numbers, there were a little over 17 million different online consumers who visited ESPN online. Their total impressions for the month should be higher than 17 million, as many consumers are prone to visit ESPN frequently to catch the scores of their favorite teams.

The online world has some advantages over the offline world in terms of metrics. For those of you who are measuring the offline world, you are getting audience numbers for the medium or program and not specifically for the ad you may have placed there. Although there are new measures coming out that better define commercial ratings, it is certainly not a standard within the industry.

In the online world, on the other hand, commercial ratings are similar to direct-response advertising. An *ad click* is a measurement of a user's response to an ad that causes a redirect to another Web location or another frame or page within the ad. The *click rate* is the number of clicks divided by the total number of ad impressions. Because there are a variety of ad units now available in the online world, an ad click can be defined as a *click-through* (taking action on the ad) or a *mouse-over* (placing the mouse over the ad without clicking on it). So, as the online world evolves, it is important to get operational definitions of some of these terms, because they can have multiple meanings. Once an action has been taken on the ad, you can track this action all the way to its end result. That is called a *conversion* or *response:* people take action based on your ad to fill out an application, or go to your Web site, or purchase an item if you are offering e-commerce (see Table 13.3). This level of detail in terms of response is why online advertising is so popular among advertisers. It is one medium that is certainly highly measurable.

There are many kinds of cyber advertisements, and some of them are listed in Exhibit 13.4.

The Importance of Knowing the Universe

In this chapter we have discussed the measurement of media in terms of reach and frequency as well as total impressions. These concepts on their own are not difficult to understand, but they can become difficult to put into practical practice.

The reason why reach and frequency can be elusive is that each medium can have very different universes upon which they base their information. As one who controls the media budget, it is crucial for you to understand the basis for the numbers that are being sold to you.

Table 13.2

An Example of Unduplicated Audiences Online

Sport sites	Unique visitors (thousands)
ESPN	17,806
FOX Sports on MSN	15,852
Yahoo Sports	13,026
AOL Sports	11,695
NFL Internet Group	8,393

Source: Ad Age Fact Pack; comScore Media Metrics.

Table 13.3

Prototype Online Campaign

Item	Number
Total impressions	10,000,000
Click	200,000
Click rate	.02%
Applications completed	50,000
Applications conversion from click	25.0%

For example, 99.9 percent of all households have a television set. So, if you see a 5 rating for a program, you know that 5 percent of the audience has viewed it. However, cable household penetration is hovering around 80 percent. So, a 5 rating in the cable universe is really only a 4 rating in the broader television universe, because 20 percent of the population doesn't have an opportunity to see the program.

Radio stations are likely to tout their ratings based on a metro or SMSA (standard metropolitan statistical area). Most metros are considerably smaller than a television DMA (designated marketing area), so if you are comparing a rating between these two media, you will need a common ground for a meaningful comparison.

As you review online impressions, it is important to realize that as of 2011, about one quarter of Americans do not have Internet access at home. Nevertheless, more than 85 percent of the population has been online, gaining access through their work or at a public school or library. Again, it is important to understand the base and how the numbers are being used.

The best place to start with understanding the media universe is to understand your consumer universe and convey that universe to the media

---

Exhibit 13.4

Types of Cyber Advertisements

- Banner ads
- Rich-media ads (e.g., animated)
- Pop-up ads
- Interstitials (appear in a separate browser, streamed)
- Superstitials (same as intersticials, but cachéd)
- Extramercials (must scroll sideways to see ad)
- Video banners
- Webmercials
- Advertorials/infomercials

---

team so that everyone is on the same page. If you are a brand manager in charge of a national peanut butter brand, you are likely to have millions of users. But if you are in charge of selling oil rig equipment, chances are you are marketing to fewer than a thousand potential buyers. Whatever the circumstances, in today's ever-changing and expanding media world, understanding the fundamentals of your brand's customers and their media habits will pay dividends.

Chapter 14
Learning about Media Costs

Understanding Media Costs

Once you understand the audience of a medium or a media vehicle, the reckoning of media planning comes about when you assess its value. Media planning and negotiating are based on judging how efficient media are and comparing the cost of one media vehicle with another.

In the advertising industry, there are *absolute costs* and *relative costs.* Absolute costs, sometimes called unit costs or vehicle costs, refer to what you are going to pay for the media placement. A full-page advertisement in the national edition of the *Wall Street Journal* costs approximately $180,000. Running a 30-second commercial during the Super Bowl costs approximately $2 million. Buying a local radio commercial in Sherman, Texas, might cost $40. So, unit costs vary widely and are based largely on the total number of impressions that the individual media vehicle delivers and the value that advertisers place on those impressions.

That brings us to relative costs. It is important to understand the relative efficiency of the Super Bowl and the *Wall Street Journal.* Without such an understanding, how would you know what the best value is? To compare one media vehicle to another and one medium to another, the gold standard in media cost comparison is *cost per thousand,* or CPM.

Cost per Thousand

In advertising, the number 1,000 can be abbreviated as K (*kilo*) or M (*mille*). Most often, K is used for money and M is used for audiences. Because 1,000 × 1,000 equals a million, we use MM to mean a million. (Do not be confused by media headlines, which often abbreviate million using just one M.)

All this is a bit of background to explain the abbreviation of "cost per thousand" as CPM. With that little history lesson under our belt, we can put the CPM term to work. CPM is a mainstay for comparing one media vehicle to another, as well as comparing one medium to another. Let's start off by looking at how to use CPM to compare one media vehicle to another.

It can be difficult to compare one media vehicle to another because you must take into account the advertising unit rates or prices along with the reach or impressions that they deliver. Let's say that you are looking at two different magazines that have different unit rates and different circulations. Say that Magazine A, with a circulation of 2.1 million, charges $23,500 for a full-page advertisement, and that Magazine B, with a circulation of 1.2 million, charges $13,500 for the same full-page ad. You might expect that the magazine with the larger circulation charges more because costs rise as you reach more people, but is it the more economical way to reach your audience?

This is where CPM comes into play. Instead of trying to compare the cost and circulation at the same time, we assume that each magazine has a circulation of only 1,000. We compare the cost for each 1,000 circulation by dividing the advertising rate by the circulation to get the cost of advertising in a single copy of the publication. Then we multiply the answer by 1,000 to compare the cost of a thousand-copy circulation.

Here is the CPM for Magazine A:

$$Magazine\ A = \frac{\$23,500}{2,100,000} \times 1,000 = \$11.19\ CPM$$

Doing the same for the other publication gives a comparison CPM.

$$Magazine\ B = \frac{\$13,500}{1,200,000} \times 1,000 = \$11.25\ CPM$$

So, according to this CPM analysis, Magazine A has a CPM based on its circulation of $11.19, whereas Magazine B has a CPM of $11.25. In this case, the CPMs are virtually identical. Because Magazine A has a 75 percent higher circulation than Magazine B and is priced at relatively the same cost as the smaller circulation publication, Magazine A seems to be the better value of the two.

CPM is used in every media analysis from print to broadcast to online. The only difference between the various media is the method used to calculate the audience. Raw circulation figures are typically used as a point of comparison for print, whereas audience estimates are used for broadcast and online audience figures. Still, the same analysis can be performed whether you are comparing two websites or two television programs.

CPM as an Intermedia Comparison Analysis

It is difficult even for the most seasoned media professional to compare one medium to another. Is a full-page, four-color bleed advertisement in a magazine the equivalent of a 30-second network television commercial? Or is the placement in a video game worth the same as a banner ad on a gaming enthusiast's website? These are difficult questions, and although there is some research in the area of intermedia comparisons, much of it remains proprietary.

In the case of intermedia comparisons, CPM is a standard to review but certainly should not be the last analysis. The following is a general CPM estimate for a wide variety of media.

As you can see in Table 14.1, if you were selecting based on CPM alone, outdoor would be the medium of choice. Yet, of the media listed in Table 14.2, outdoor has the lowest media impact or advertising revenue. So, although outdoor has a low CPM, advertisers are voting with their dollars on other media.

As a brand manager looking at the media landscape, you will work with your media group to determine the impact of each medium for your particular brand. The impact value of each medium can then be compared to the CPM or used to weigh the CPM for a more definitive analysis.

For example, if you feel that an outdoor ad has the same impact as a television commercial, then you can purchase considerably more outdoor impressions for the dollar than television. However, if you feel that television is worth 10 times the value of outdoor ads, then outdoor may not be such a good bargain.

Table 14.2 is an example of weighing CPMs based on an impact score for each medium for a packaged goods brand. The goal of the brand is to convey appetite appeal and to demonstrate how it is used in a wide variety of situations.

The CPM is the standard measure for comparing media, but it should not be used within a vacuum. It provides the basis for determining value but is not the only aspect to assigning value to a medium.

Cost per Point

CPM is the main cost comparison criterion when looking at a variety of media, but planners working with broadcast costs on both a national and local basis use a standard called *cost-per-point* (CPP). A cost-per-point compares broadcast vehicles on the basis of how much it costs to reach one percent of the audience. Remember that one percent reach is the same as a rating point, so we call this comparison cost-per-point.

Table 14.1

Media CPM Based on Adults

Medium	CPM
TV	$25.00
Magazine	$12.50
Radio	$9.50
Newspaper	$35.00
Outdoor	$5.00
Online	$20.00

Source: FKM.

Table 14.2

Delight Salad Dressing
CPM Adjusted by Media Impact Weights

Medium	CPM	Media impact	Adjusted CPM
TV	$20.00	100	$20.00
Magazine	$10.00	70	$14.30
Radio	$8.00	30	$24.00
Newspaper	$30.00	50	$60.00
Outdoor	$5.00	10	$50.00
Online	$20.00	40	$50.00

Note: Media Impact score 1 to 100.

Let's take a look at how you might use a CPP in comparing two radio stations. Radio Station A costs $5,300 per commercial unit and reaches 2.2 percent of our audience (the rating). So we simply divide the cost by the rating to derive the CPP.

$$CPP = \frac{\$5,300}{2.2 \ Rtg} = \$2,409 \ CPP$$

Now look at Radio Station B, which charges $6,200 per unit and achieves a rating of 2.5 percent. Its CPP would be as follows:

$$CPP = \frac{\$6,200}{2.5 \ Rtg} = \$2,480 \ CPP$$

In this example, Radio Station A is slightly more efficient in reaching a rating point (one percent of the audience) than is Radio Station B. When media negotiators are rapidly calculating hundreds of programs and stations, the CPP is a key measure for efficiency. Think of it as the currency for local broadcast negotiations.

The reason CPP is used in broadcast planning instead of CPM is that it is a much simpler method of assessing costs across various markets or across various dayparts. CPM is a great analysis tool to determine value, as is CPP; CPP, though, allows for the quick addition of costs across various markets. If you are planning to advertise in the top five media markets in the United States in daytime television, you would not want to add up all the hundreds of possibilities of unit costs for this television period across all these markets. The CPP allows you to quickly figure costs by taking into account the size of the market, because one percent of the population of New York is a lot bigger than one percent of the population of Boise. Table 14.3 is an example of how media planners use CPP to add up media costs for a local market campaign.

Online Cost Analysis

As we said earlier, the online media world offers some much deeper diagnostics than most other media. CPM is the initial standard for all online analysis whether it is in search engine marketing or in traditional online advertising.

The second layer of cost analysis beyond the CPM is the *cost-per-click* (CPC). The cost-per-click is calculated by simply dividing the media cost by the number of clicks obtained within a certain time frame. Most online media professionals analyze their online plans after a week or two of activity to determine what sites and what creative executions are producing the lowest CPC. Then adjustments are made to the subsequent schedules to (1) add more impressions to proven performers, (2) eliminate costly performing sites, or (3) add contingency sites to the campaign.

Depending upon the category, online media planners negotiate with the websites on a CPC basis or on a *cost-per-lead* basis (CPL). For example, if the advertisers know they will make money if their campaign hits a certain cost-per-lead target (say, $20), then they will negotiate with the Web publishers to pay for that target response and to not pay for leads above that threshold. For established categories with known conversion rates, such as auto insurance, this is a standard method for online placement. It ties in nicely with search engine marketing pricing, which is done on a bid basis for selective keywords. The more popular the keyword, the more it may cost. For example, the insurance business is highly competitive online, so a keyword such as "auto insurance" could command as much as $200 per click. On the other hand, a lower-interest category, such as hazardous waste hauling, may be only $10 per click.

Table 14.3

Daytime TV Local Costs for Bob's Baked Beans

Market	DMA Rank	Women 18–49 Daytime CPP
New York City	1	$798
Dallas/Fort Worth	7	$303
Buffalo, NY	44	$65
Boise, ID	157	$40
Victoria, BC	204	$20
Total		$1,226

Source: Spot Quotations and Data (SQAD).

Some online media planners also use the term *cost-per-action* (CPA) to describe the cost of generating a sale, acquiring a customer, or making some sort of transaction. Again, this is calculated by dividing the online campaign cost by the action that it is designed to generate.

Internet Pricing

Advertising on the Internet uses some of the same pricing approaches, such as cost-per-thousand, as does advertising in other media. . Nevertheless, there are additional systems used with the Internet that do not apply to other advertising media. As Exhibit 14.1 shows, the most common pricing systems include such things as counting the number of click-through searches, where Internet users go beyond a website by clicking on an icon or other connection that takes them to another site. Total time spent on a site is another pricing approach, but it can be misleading because a person may access a website and then leave the room while still connected. That would add up to a large amount of time viewing, even though no viewing is actually occurring. Size-based pricing is dependent upon the size of the advertisement as a portion of the Web page, but many if not most Internet ads are full-page insertions so that measure may not be very reliable. Cost-per-transaction charges only if an actual purchase is made, which would diminish the role of common Internet searches that do not result in buying behavior at that particular time. Most Internet advertisers now use a combination of these other approaches, known as "hybrid deals."

Social Media Pricing

Social media such as Facebook, Twitter, and others often use pricing systems adopted from other media, especially from the Internet. Much advertiser use

---

Exhibit 14.1

Some Systems Used for Internet Advertising Pricing

- Cost per thousand (CPM)
- Click-through rates
- Time spent listening/viewing/visiting
- Size-based pricing (more space or more pages, the higher the cost)
- Cost per transaction
- Hybrid deals (combinations of other approaches)

---

of social media is not actually involved with placing advertising but rather with using the social media to track how often the company and its products and services are discussed and whether such discussions are favorable. Because many advertisers are not skilled in handling these newer media types, they often use a specialized advertising agency or a consulting service that knows these media well, so a fee for that consulting or agency service is often added to the social-media costs.

Production Costs

In addition to the costs of media space and/or time, there is a cost for producing the advertisements. This can involve setting type, art services, broadcast production, Internet development, and similar costs.

Cost-Plus

Many advertising agencies that handle production for their clients simply take the production costs and add a certain percentage, commonly 15 percent or 18 percent or 20 percent, depending on the type of work and the contact in force between the agency and the advertiser. Such an approach can work but there are other approaches that may provide a more realistic reflection of the actual work involved.

Time-Based

With time-based production compensation, some hourly reimbursement rate is established and then simply multiplied times the number of hours spent on this work. This approach reflects the investment by the agency in the production work, but it is easy to spend a lot of time on details that the advertiser may not want. Unexpected problems often arise in advertising work, which makes advance budgeting difficult or inaccurate. Thus, although time-based pricing may be somewhat more reflective of the actual costs than simpler cost-plus pricing, it still has problems.

Performance-Based

This approach tries to measure the outcome of the advertising and then base reimbursement on the performance; simply put, the more sales generated by the advertising, the more the production costs. But such an approach is difficult to establish, and perhaps even more difficult to measure. It may, for example, be difficult if not impossible to measure what role the advertising played in the marketing work, or how much the advertising came into play in swaying the purchase decisions.

Value-Based

The value of the overall work is measured and then the agency reimbursement is calculated. A print advertisement of a certain size is considered to have a certain value, and a television commercial of a certain length is considered to have a certain value. By setting these values in advance, both the agency and the advertiser know what compensation will be accrued. Some productions may take longer, or require more investment than others, which is difficult to predict and to account for using this system. It may encourage agencies to do work rapidly rather than well, or to prepare more versions of an advertisement than might otherwise be warranted.

Other Fees

The costs of public relations work are most often based on the time spent working on the account. However, like advertising costs, some work has more value and some measure of outcome needs to be considered.

Other common fees are for the use of Internet search engines, such as Google, Yahoo, or Bing. There are also fees for all sorts of other services, such as overnight delivery, attending special seminars or training sessions, or even entertaining the top executives of the client company.

Cost Trade-Offs

Going back to the beginning of this chapter, we discussed the two kinds of cost analysis: the initial analysis is absolute costs and the second is relative costs. These two pillars of media value analysis are used by media planners in their ongoing determination of the best media plan for the dollar.

As a brand manager in charge of media dollars, it is important that you ask a variety of questions regarding media costs. The first question is, What can I do effectively for the dollars that I have to invest in media? This is not asking what the best CPM is, but what the best media plan is. Let's take a look at an example for a national packaged goods brand on a $1 million budget. Here are three plans developed for the same product by different media agencies:

1. Plan A was developed by a CPM-driven agency, which said that the brand should schedule national television spots for eight weeks within the daytime television daypart, with approximately 40 target rating points, or TRPs, per week, or 15 to 20 commercials per week.
2. Plan B recommended only magazines as the support plan. Their plan consisted of six months of support using six publications with four insertions per publication or a total of 24 insertions.
3. Plan C recommended allocating the dollars to the six best markets for the brand to develop a television and print support plan that would cover 75 percent of the year with activity.

Based on the question of effectiveness, which of these plans do you feel meets the criteria? Do you get the same answer if you ask the question, Which plan is the most cost efficient?

Common sense would tell you that whereas Plan A might be cost efficient, it may not be very effective. On the other hand, Plan C may be the most effective but it might be too limiting in terms of sales and efficiency. And so, there you have the trade-offs that happen with every media plan and negotiation. There is always a trade-off between what can be done well and what is most efficient for the brand.

As you assess media plans, it is important to understand the fundamentals of cost analysis, but it is even more important to understand the fundamentals of trade-off analysis.

Chapter 15
General Characteristics of Media

There are plenty of factors other than costs by which to compare advertising media. In fact, if you rely solely on advertising rates and costs, you are likely to place your advertising in front of an unresponsive audience. Let's look at some of the most commonly used characteristics in advertising media analysis and selection.

Audience Qualities

What is the audience like? Are the audience members similar to one another (homogeneous), or are they very different from one another (heterogeneous)? It makes sense that it is easier to reach a homogeneous audience than a heterogeneous one; people who are alike usually engage in the same kinds of activities and pay attention to the same kinds of media offerings.

Demographics

Are the audience members rich or poor, employed or idle, well educated or dropouts? Of course, these descriptions are the extremes, but these demographic characteristics are still important. Demography is the study of populations, so demographic characteristics are population factors: age, income, gender, educational level, employment, number of children at home, whether urban or rural, and the like.

It is easier to sell a Lexus 400 to someone with a sizable income than to someone who barely scrapes by each month. The Great Books series is likely to be purchased by someone who has a college education. Sweetened breakfast cereal is sold mostly to households with young children.

Of course, there are other ways to segment a media audience in addition to demographics. These methods include psychographics, based on psychological differences, and sociographics, based on social and cultural differences.

Audiences can also be segmented according to heavy and light users of a product or service, or by lifestyle, which will be discussed later. Other segmentation patterns include such geographic segments as parts of the country or urban versus rural, and a combination of such elements as geodemographics, a combination of geography and demography; for example, the U.S. Navy may find good enlistment prospects in such landlocked states as Montana and North Dakota because of a combination of population factors and geographic factors.

Activities and Habits

Certain media types and vehicles reach certain audiences. Magazines are read mostly by those with good incomes and educations, while television is viewed by almost everyone, although the lower-income groups spend more of their time with broadcast media. Even within a media type, there are differences: all kinds of men watch football games on television, but televised golf matches are viewed mostly by men with good jobs and high incomes.

Audience Involvement

Do members of the audience pay close attention to a particular medium, or are they somewhat remote and removed from media involvement? People may sit down in the evening to watch television with no outside distractions yet have the radio playing in the background, not giving it their full attention. Some people scan a newspaper while others read it carefully. A person driving down a highway may not give much notice to a billboard, but another person caught in a traffic tie-up on the same road has several minutes to read and remember the billboard message.

Along with involvement, a related factor involves distractions. We know that people who view prime-time television in the evening hours pay closer attention than do people who watch daytime television. One reason for this difference is that there are more distractions during the day: telephone calls, children's needs, meal planning, and the like. Another reason may be the increased number of commercial messages during daytime television, which provides more opportunities to leave the television set in order to complete chores.

Influentials versus Followers

Within your circle of family and friends is there someone who always seems to know about the latest movies, someone else who is knowledgeable about politics, and yet another person who keeps up with current clothing style trends or music or current events? If these knowledgeable individuals tell others their opinions, they are considered to be "influentials," whereas those who listen to and heed their advice are considered "followers."

Many advertisers try to select advertising media that reach influentials, in hopes of persuading these individuals to learn about products and services and then tell others about them. Other advertisers want to use media that reach followers, using the media to play the role of influentials to persuade these followers to listen to and obey the advertising message; still other advertisers may avoid using these same media, believing that followers are persuaded more by influentials than by the media.

Lifestyle

Different people have different lifestyles. Some want to acquire physical goods; others want to live in rustic settings with few possessions. Some people read many magazines and watch little television, whereas others do just the opposite.

Lifestyle impacts people's tendency to purchase certain kinds of products. It is useless to try to sell beer to teetotalers, but it is fairly easy to sell electronic gear to those who want the latest computers, sound systems, and telephones. Some media vehicles appeal to one kind of lifestyle while others attract a completely different lifestyle.

Media Attributes

Advertisers use many factors other than the audience in their media analyses and plans. Several of these attributes are characteristics of the mass media themselves.

Cost

Obviously, media costs are a major consideration. Some media are expensive while others are less so; television has high advertising rates for airtime, and the cost of producing a television commercial may also be steep. Radio, on the other hand, is much less expensive. Although costs are important, the costs must be balanced against all the other factors. Does an inexpensive medium have the same audience impact, or is there a trade-off for the less expensive media outlet?

Most advertising media also offer discounts, which can be based on the amount of advertising purchased—a "quantity discount"—or on regular purchases of advertising—a "frequency discount."

Cost Efficiency

As we saw in the previous chapter, there are various measures of cost efficiency, such as cost-per-thousand (CPM) and cost-per-rating-point (CPP). Efficiency in media is usually a solid advertising media goal, and many advertisers try to consider cost efficiencies as well as the basic costs of advertising. Keep in mind that many cost efficiency ratios are used only for comparing one vehicle with another but within the same general media type, and that intermedia comparisons of cost efficiencies require careful limits and provisos as well as much experience and caution (see Exhibit 15.1).

Reach

One major factor is reach. How many parts of the target group are communicated to by a certain medium or vehicle (numerical reach)? Or what part of the target group sees or hears that medium or vehicle (percentage reach)?

A media vehicle that reaches more of the target audience is usually desirable, but that vehicle may also cost more. So many factors must be considered together: reach, cost, cost efficiency, and other factors.

Frequency

Because frequency is often an essential advertising media goal, media that offer frequency at reasonable rates are usually under consideration. Some media offer frequency as an almost natural part of their package; broadcast media are known for advertisements that appear frequently, and the Internet is available every minute of every day. Newspapers appear less frequently, and magazines even less so. Keep in mind, though, that there are two kinds of frequency: frequency of insertion and frequency of exposure. No audience member will be exposed to your advertisement every time it runs.

If you need more information about reach, frequency, cost efficiency, and similar basic media terms, look back at Chapters 13 and 14.

Irritation Factor

Along with high frequency comes the risk of irritating the audience. People who see or hear an advertisement too often may turn it off in their minds or, even worse, develop a negative reaction to that message. Irritation most often occurs with disruptive and annoying advertisements, but it can happen with any advertising message. The Internet, television, and radio

Exhibit 15.1

Intermedia Comparisons

Several references have been made to intermedia comparisons, such as comparing radio with television, or television with magazines.

It should be obvious that a thirty-second (called a :30 in the business) radio commercial does not carry the same impact as a :30 on television. The television medium combines sight and sound and offers motion and, thus, demonstration. Not only does television provide more impact than does radio, but these added dimensions of television also offer more creative breadth.

At some point, however, more radio may be equivalent to television; maybe two or five or eight commercials on radio carry a weight equal to one commercial on television. And radio advertising tends to cost much less than television advertising does, so it might be used to attain more reach and frequency in exchange for the lessened impact.

Similarly, does a :30 on network television equal a full-page advertisement in a national magazine, or a full-page with color, or a full-page with both color and bleed—or what? The problem is that every individual brand's case is unique, and it is difficult to project an answer from past history. Although selective companies may have proprietary research regarding the value of one medium versus another, there is a dearth of published research on the topic. As you see in Table 15.1, most of the published research was in the 1960s and early 1970s. Its historical relevance to today's issues is questionable, and there is no consensus in the research itself.

For all these reasons, it is unwise for novice marketers and media planners to involve themselves with intermedia comparisons. It is far safer to compare one media vehicle with another, say, one radio station with another, or one television network with the others, or one group of magazines with several others. However, more and more companies are using sophisticated marketing-mix analyses to help them judge the value and economic benefits of their advertising media plans.

cause the most advertising irritation because messages may be disruptive, are presented often, and are beyond the audience member's control. If an advertisement were to appear on several pages of a newspaper, the reader would only have to turn the pages to avoid it, and turning pages is a regular

Table 15.1

Summary of Classic Television vs. Print or Radio Advertising Impact Studies

Sponsor/Date	Methodology	Findings
CBS TV Network/1960–61	Teen spies observe TV and magazine ad exposure among adults, ask brand awareness/desire to buy questions before and after exposure	TV ad exposures in prime time generate double the brand awareness gains than magazine ads and 3-4 times the desire to buy
Look/1962–63	Telephone recall studies of *Look* subscribers and prime-time TV viewers	Page 4C ads outscored TV :60s, 24 percent to 18 percent in verified recall for six advertisers
Life/1968–69	Telephone recall studies of *Life* subscribers and prime-time TV viewers	Page 4C ads outscored TV :30s and :60s by 45 percent to 50 percent for seven advertisers
C.E. Hooper, Inc./1968–69	Telephone coincidental studies of persons just exposed to TV, radio, magazines, newspapers; ability to name last brand ad seen/heard	TV outscored radio 19 percent to 14 percent but trailed behind magazines (34 percent) and newspapers (23 percent)
Gallup-Robinson/1960s–70s	Invited viewing and reading copy tests using 24-hour recall	TV scores twice as high as magazines in verified recall
AAAA/1964	Adults claiming ad exposure to TV, radio, magazines, and newspapers rated them on several criteria	TV commercials were rated as predominantly enjoyable (38 percent) and informative (21 percent), but 31 percent found them annoying or offensive. In contrast, only 15 percent of magazines and 18 percent of newspaper ads were rated negatively.
ABC/CBS/NBC/1970–71	Adults exposed to TV commercials and magazine ads. Criterion: Pre-/post-coupon redemption claims (vs. "control") for twelve brands	TV commercials induced 82 percent greater increments in advertised brand coupon redemption than magazine ads

Source: FKM agency research.

part of newspaper reading. But if an advertisement appears several times an evening on a cable network, the viewer would have to switch stations or stop viewing to avoid the commercial.

Color

For some advertisements, color is crucial. Portraying fashion items may need color, and showing a detergent box may require special colors. Color quality is generally good in most magazines, but not so good in many newspapers. Television and Internet color can be good, but color quality also relies on the type of reception and appliance used by the audience members.

Motion and Demonstration

To demonstrate a product or service, motion may be necessary. Media such as television, motion pictures, and the Internet may therefore be required. The choices are limited, because few media can demonstrate or provide motion well.

Scheduling

When your advertisements appear is an important factor, and some media permit more scheduling flexibility than do others. There are several components of scheduling.

Exposure

Running a television advertisement during prime time will bring more audience exposure than will a daytime commercial, because more people watch television at night, and they have fewer distractions then. A print insertion in a building design magazine may reach many architects in February, when they are planning for the coming building season by consulting sources for the newest and best materials, but it will reach fewer architects in August, when they are likely to be out examining the actual construction sites and have little time to read.

Flexibility

An Internet advertisement appears at any time that an audience member calls up that website. A television or radio station can schedule advertising at any hour of the day. Newspapers cannot offer advertising at any particular hour, but daily newspapers can offer advertising any day of the week. Magazines may offer only weekly or monthly schedules, which provide for less flexibility in scheduling the advertising.

Waves

Scheduling in waves can help avoid the irritation factor and can keep an advertising campaign fresher for a longer time. It can also save money by extending the campaign over a longer period.

The high point in the waves is the period of intense advertising, called a "flight saturation," or simply a "flight." A period of low advertising intensity or of no advertising is known as a "hiatus." If there is a level of moderate advertising after a period of waves, it is called a "sustaining period."

Preparation Time

How much time do you have to perfect your campaign before it appears in the media? Magazines often require that advertising placements reach them weeks or even months in advance of publication. On the other hand, it may be possible to call a radio station and have an announcement read on the air within an hour or so, if time is still available for purchase.

Availabilities and Preemptions

In broadcast media, there is only so much time to sell. If another advertiser has already reserved a particular time, it is no longer available; you must choose from the remaining available time slots, which are known as "availabilities," or "avails."

Some broadcast stations offer preemptible time at a discounted rate. If another advertiser comes along and offers the full price, your advertising will be preempted: either it will not run or it will be shifted to another time slot.

Availabilities are not pertinent to print media because there is little limit to the number of advertisements; if more advertisements are purchased, more pages will be printed, resulting in a larger issue. In fact, the number of advertisements in a newspaper or magazine is usually the determining factor in how many pages that issue will comprise.

Coverage

Previously we covered audience factors. Coverage is basically the same kind of consideration but from a media perspective rather than an audience viewpoint. Certain media do a better job of covering certain audiences.

For example, daytime television dramas and talk shows do a good job of covering women who are heads of households, but a relatively poor job of reaching teenage boys who are employed full time. On the other hand, rock music radio formats reach teenage boys but not older, retired persons.

Selectivity

Selectivity is related to coverage. If you desire coverage of a certain demographic group, you may have a wide choice of media options, but some of those will also cover many kinds of people other than your primary target. Selectivity offers coverage without as much waste; you select media that cover your target group well but are without a lot of coverage of groups you are not interested in.

Responsiveness

Some consumers respond to some media types better than they do to others. For example, a coupon may elicit a much greater response from a mother with a large family, who must stretch the family purchasing dollars, than from a mother with a smaller family. In fact, every medium has groups of consumers who respond better to it than others. Many packaged goods marketers are now using a part of their marketing mix analysis to determine the responsiveness for each medium by different target groups.

Relevance

In today's increasingly fragmented media world, there are media that are certainly on target for specific audiences and products. For example, the Food Network is a cable network devoted to making great meals. A product that is marketed to people who like to cook is a likely match. The same can be said for magazines such as *Good Housekeeping* or *Gourmet,* where recipe ideas are a major part of the editorial content. In fact, the media vehicle can actually become a marketplace unto itself. *Vogue* magazine devotes as much as 75 percent of an issue to advertising; consumers look at these advertisements to make their fashion decisions.

Support for Other Media

Certain advertising media are of questionable efficacy when used on their own, but work well in combination with other media.

For example, if demonstration is required, radio might not be an appropriate choice, but radio might well be used to combine with and supplement the demonstrations shown in television commercials. If the same themes, messages, music, and words are used in both media, the radio commercials will extend the impact of the television ads, gaining both reach and frequency at a lesser expense. Similarly, transit and outdoor advertising are generally noticed only in passing, which may not be enough for a complicated message, but which might be quite good to remind audience members of the messages carried through other media.

Audience Portrayal through Media

Another media characteristic combines media and audience factors: how the audience is portrayed through the media. Many television commercials, for example, portray users of the product or service being promoted, and from these portrayals the audience members learn what kinds of people are being targeted and what uses and benefits they might gain from purchasing the service or product. If people see themselves in a commercial, they may feel that they should also use the advertised item. Earlier, we discussed audience involvement, which might also be a combination of audience and media factors.

Slice-of-life commercials, in which the scene shows a part of people's everyday lives, are actually based on portrayals of persons using the advertised product or service. In contrast, a hard sell utilizes strong messages aimed at convincing the audience to consider buying; these strong arguments are likely to be delivered by an announcer or spokesperson, which diminishes the opportunity to portray real users. Both types are also used in other media, but television provides a handy and universal example.

Subsequent chapters give detailed information about each of the major advertising media. As you read those chapters, keep in mind what you have learned from this chapter.

Chapter 16
Broadcast Media

When we refer to television and radio, we generally call them broadcast media, even though today they are not always transmitted by broadcast. Television can be sent by cable or satellite transmissions, and radio is also sent via satellite. Nevertheless, the traditional term *broadcast* still is used when referring to these advertising media.

Television

When all kinds of television advertising are grouped together, television is the largest advertising medium in terms of dollar expenditures. Television's share of the media pie has diminished somewhat over the past few years as newer media take a larger part of the total advertising investment, but television is still number one in advertising sales.

Industry Structure

Many television stations are joined together in chains called networks. Traditionally, networks provide the programming to the stations and pay the stations to carry the programming. That arrangement has been under attack recently, and network support to the stations has declined or disappeared as newer arrangements are being tested.

The Big Four television networks are CBS, NBC, ABC, and Fox, and they usually have affiliated stations in all or most of the U.S. television markets. Smaller networks, such as WB, have chains of fewer stations, usually in the larger cities. Public television, PBS, is a less formal affiliation in which the stations are less obligated to carry network programs and may not air them all at the same time; PBS does not carry advertising, although it does have companies that help underwrite program expenses.

Television stations are not obligated to join a network. Independent stations also are found in the larger television markets.

So-called cable networks are not really broadcast networks in the traditional sense. Instead, a cable network may have only one channel that is distributed via cable and satellite systems.

Networks, stations, satellite companies, and cable operators all sell advertising. The sales representatives are called "reps" in the business, and some broadcast enterprises have attempted to upgrade the roles of the reps by referring to them as "account executives," although they do not fill the same role as do account executives at advertising agencies.

Types of Television Commercials

Commercial announcements within the body of a program are called participating program announcements, often shortened simply to "participations." Commercials between programs are known as "spot advertising." At one time, participations were sold by networks and stations sold spot time. In recent years, though, the differentiations have become muddled as networks also sell commercials outside the program time, called network spots.

Large advertisers once sponsored entire television programs, or alternated with other advertisers. Because television advertising has become more expensive and advertisers want to reach a varied audience, sponsorships have declined and participations are the common pattern. There are many other patterns of television advertising; for example, infomercials are program-type commercials that take up a full 30 or 60 minutes.

Television Advertising Rates

The costs of advertising time on television depend on the size of the audience, which varies by station or program, of course, but also by time of day. The higher the audience rating, the higher the cost of advertising.

In broadcast, there is a limited amount of time available for advertising, so buying broadcast advertising time depends on availabilities (often called "avails"), which is broadcast time still available for purchase. An advertiser can pay a full rate and guarantee having that particular time in which to advertise, or can risk paying a preemptible rate that is cheaper but that can be taken away by an advertiser who is willing to pay more.

Then a strange thing occurs. Time that has been sold at a preemptible rate goes up in price as broadcast time approaches, as other advertisers may be willing to pay more to gain that time slot. But unsold time decreases in price as the station or network tries to sell at bargain prices, rather than have no advertising to run in a particular time slot.

Exhibit 16.1

Television Dayparts

Below are listed the commonly titled parts of the television broadcast day and the times that they refer to. Times for the mountain time zone vary more widely.

	Eastern time	**Central time**
Daytime	Before 5 P.M.	Before 5 P.M.
Early fringe	5–6:30 P.M.	5–6:30 P.M.
Prime access	6:30–8 P.M.	6:30–7 P.M.
Prime time	8–11 P.M.	7–10 P.M.
Late fringe	11–11:35 P.M.	10–10:35 P.M.
Late night	After 11:35 P.M.	After 10:35 P.M.

On networks, the highest-rated time is prime time, in the evenings, with other categories labeled throughout the day, as shown in Exhibit 16.1. Stations use their own labels for time categories, such as letters or numbers. At one time, Class A time was usually the highest rated, but now some stations have 5A or 6A time, ranging down to Class A as the lowest-rated time, So it is not possible to compare advertising costs of different stations by looking at the time classification; it is necessary to check the actual time and the audience ratings.

Cost comparisons are often made using cost-per-thousand (CPM), which compares the costs of reaching 1,000 audience members or 1,000 households or any other measuring unit for which ratings may be available. Cost comparisons also often use cost-per-point (CPP), which compares the costs of reaching one percent of the audience or of a particular target group.

Like other media, discounts are available for most broadcast advertising, either quantity discounts or frequency discounts. A variety of broadcast advertising slots is often referred to as a "scatter package," where the advertiser may be able to specify which spots are to be used and earn a discount for multiple purchases. In broadcast, there is also the additional cost of preparing the commercial itself, and if people appear in the commercial, regular continuing residual payments, called "residuals," may be required in addition to the time cost of running the ads.

Although the seasonality of network television has diminished somewhat and new programs are introduced at any time of year, there still is a season for original programming, starting in mid-September. For network ad buying, the upfront period is well in advance of the new season, followed by what is known as "scatter buying" of programs still available, and then "opportunistic buying" of leftover slots. Smart advertisers ask for an "out" option so that advertising can be canceled if new programs flop.

In spot buying, there is usually about a 90-second period between programs, when a single 60-second commercial (known as a :60) or two 30-second commercials (:30) are available, often followed by one 20-second commercial (a :20), known as a chain-break commercial. The remaining 10 seconds can be for station identification or for a 10-second commercial (a :10), called an ID.

Advantages and disadvantages of television advertising are listed in Exhibit 16.2.

Audience Measures

Broadcast audiences are measured by the ratings services, which in the case of television are primarily provided by Nielsen. Because these audience surveys use a sample of the total audience, the research determines the percentages of the audiences, and most of the audience measures are reported as percentages. Nielsen uses the concept of the designated market area (DMA) to measure individual markets; a DMA is the entire area where most of the households receive their television from a certain market, such as the Chicago DMA, which stretches out into much of northern Illinois as well as part of Indiana, or the Albuquerque DMA, which covers most of New Mexico and a small part of some bordering states. You can see the map of all the DMAs through an Internet search for "Nielsen DMA Map."

Households using television (HUT) is the percentage of all television households that have a television set operating at any given time. If you are more interested in individuals than in households, persons using television (PUT) is the percentage of television viewers who are watching at a given time. Similar concepts are used for radio, where they become households using radio (HUR) and persons using radio (PUR).

The program rating, usually just called "rating" or abbreviated as Rtg, is the percentage of all television households that are viewing a particular station, program, or network. This percentage can be of the entire U.S. television market or of individual DMAs.

The share of audience, usually simply called "share" or abbreviated as Shr, is the percentage of the HUT that are viewing a particular program,

Exhibit 16.2

Television Advertising

Advantages
- ❖ Demonstration
- ❖ Impact; combination of sight and sound
- ❖ Mass coverage
- ❖ Extensive viewer time; people spend a lot of time in front of the television set
- ❖ Repetition; better and easier than for print
- ❖ Flexibility: of coverage, of commercial content
- ❖ Prestige of the medium
- ❖ Versatile: sound effects, color, motion, stills, voices, etc.
- ❖ Hard to tune out a commercial message; broadcaster controls exposure, to some degree
- ❖ Personal involvement of audience members
- ❖ Techniques of television advertising are so effective they are used for educational purposes, e.g., *Sesame Street*

Disadvantages
- ❖ Control in the hands of telecaster and audience, not the advertiser
- ❖ Cost can be very high
- ❖ Mortality rate; commercials get old quickly
- ❖ Distrust of "personal selling"; print advertisements carry more of a stamp of authenticity
- ❖ Lack of selectivity; the mass audience can be a disadvantage as well as an advantage

station, or network. The rating and share actually count the same audience: those with sets on and tuned to a particular program, station, or network. The difference between them is that the share is those households or persons as a percentage of sets that are on, whereas the rating is those same households or persons as a percentage of all television households, whether their sets are on or not.

If you add up all the ratings for all the programs on which you advertise, your total is the gross rating points (GRP). If you do the same for only the ratings of your target group, your total is the target rating points (TRP).

If you take the rating survey percentages and project them onto the total audience numbers to estimate how many households or persons are viewing, it is called the "projected audience": an estimated number, not a percentage. You can also conduct research to show a minute-by-minute tracking of the audience size during a program. And, of course, advertisers are often interested in the composition of the audience, most often in demographic terms.

The ratings surveys occur as many as four times a year in the largest television markets, and perhaps only three or even two times a year in smaller markets. These television ratings survey periods are known as the rating "sweeps," and Nielsen conducts them in November, February, May, and August.

Buying Broadcast Advertising

Running three or more commercials in a row diminishes the amount of attention and recall to each individual commercial, but although advertisers might like to avoid this problem, it is difficult today to be able to purchase in a time slot that has only two commercials back-to-back. The commercial break when commercials are run is called a commercial "pod."

If your commercial is run improperly, such as without sound, or if there is a mechanical problem with your commercial, you will usually be offered a "make-good," which is the opportunity to run the commercial again in an equivalent time slot. You are not obligated to take the make-good and you can cancel the "buy" instead; you will not yet have paid anything for the spot. After all, if you were running a political advertisement on the day of an election, for example, you would not want a make-good at some future date after the election is over.

Radio

In many ways, radio operates similarly to television, although there are some differences that merit discussion. Network programming is less prevalent in radio, with more independent stations than is the case with television. Individual radio personalities (the on-air announcers and hosts) are an important factor in attracting audiences. And terms such as *prime time* and *fringe* do not apply to radio; instead, other time periods dominate the listening periods, with different terminology, as shown in Exhibit 16.3.

Much radio listening occurs during other activities, especially while driving, but also in the background while working or walking or doing homework. People spend more time in their cars during certain seasonal

Exhibit 16.3

Radio Scheduling Terms

Drive time	The highest-rated radio listening times in most markets, during morning and evening commuting periods
Shift time	A high-rated radio listening time in some markets where factory work shifts constitute a large part of the driving commutes
Morning and noon news	News programs when people are preparing to go to work or school and when they drive to lunch; evening news is more highly rated for television than for radio
Sports	Programming at any time when sports programs are aired or during regularly scheduled sports scores and news
Late evening	Listening periods for talk shows, call-in programs, and similar scheduling, often after the television has been turned off for the night

periods, such as summer vacations and winter holiday shopping, which can skew the listenership patterns for radio.

Radio stations try to sell blocks of commercials, such as packages of 30 or 40 or more commercials each week. But for the typical advertiser those patterns may not reflect the best radio advertising opportunities. In retail, for example, if a big sale is planned, the best pattern is to run 60 to 70 percent of the radio commercials for the first big selling day and then save the balance to promote the next biggest selling day. For a sale that runs Wednesday through Sunday, use the bulk of the money to promote the Wednesday opening and the rest on Saturday, which is likely to be the next biggest sales day.

This affords an important lesson: In any advertising medium, buy the times and spaces that best match your needs, not necessarily that which the sales rep is pushing or that has an attractive packaged price.

Advantages and disadvantages of radio advertising are listed in Exhibit 16.4.

Exhibit 16.4

Radio Advertising

Advantages
- ❖ Timely, flexible
- ❖ Can be economical
- ❖ Penetration into all homes and all rooms; dorms, kitchens, etc.
- ❖ Complements other media; can reiterate and supplement campaign
- ❖ Useful for reaching specialized audiences: farm, foreign-language, ethnic, etc.
- ❖ Strong on-air personality can build large audience of listeners
- ❖ Daily continuity, which may be too expensive in other media
- ❖ Penetration into suburbs
- ❖ Can make excellent use of slogans, music, sound effects
- ❖ At the moment of impact, there is no competition; especially good for small retailers
- ❖ Can reach people anywhere: in cars, on picnics, at the beach, while exercising
- ❖ Good for merchandising; can tie in with promotions

Disadvantages
- ❖ Perishable
- ❖ Rate policies not standardized; must deal with each individual station
- ❖ Advertisements can be easily ignored

For all media, including radio and television, there are some media concepts that apply across the board, so some of the discussions in other chapters, about other types of media, also apply to broadcast advertising.

Chapter 17
Print Media

When learning about the various types of media, it is important to keep in mind that many media types overlap with others. For example, newspapers are a traditional print medium, but much newspaper revenue these days comes from Internet sites, and the Internet is considered a different type of medium altogether. Similarly, ethnic newspapers are often considered an ethnic medium, even though such publications are obviously a specialized type of newspaper.

This chapter explores the traditional printed media: newspapers, magazines, and similar publications.

Newspapers

When we think of a newspaper, we usually think of the typical daily newspaper. A daily newspaper is published at least four days each week, but most dailies come out all seven days of the week, or perhaps every weekday, or weekdays plus one weekend day.

A weekly newspaper is a newspaper issued three or fewer days per week. A local newspaper that is published twice a week is still considered a weekly.

There are other types of newspapers, too, such as college newspapers, ethnic newspapers, foreign-language newspapers, and "shoppers," which are often free-distribution papers filled with local classified advertising. Some of these types of newspapers are covered separately in this book; ethnic newspapers are also covered in Chapter 24 on ethnic media.

Kinds of Advertisements

Two kinds of advertising dominate the commercial side of newspapers: display advertising and classified advertising. Perhaps it will be easier to differentiate between the two types if we start with classified advertising.

Classified advertising is so named because it is organized by classification. Also known as "want ads," classified advertisements are the smaller advertisements, usually toward the back of the newspaper, organized so the potential buyers can easily find the category needed, such as used cars, part-time jobs, lost pets, and garage sales.

Display advertising is the regular advertising, marked by larger sizes, found throughout the rest of the newspaper. The boundaries between types of advertising are disappearing, though, and these days most newspapers will accommodate "classified display," which are larger announcements, like other display advertisements, but still in the proper categories with other classified advertising.

One problem with placing advertisements nationally using many newspapers is that there is no uniformity in the page size of newspapers. Some use five columns, some use six or seven or eight, and the lengths of columns vary as well. This wide variety makes it difficult to prepare a single advertisement and have it appear in many newspapers. To help solve this problem, the standard advertising unit (SAU) was developed, listing several standard sizes of newspaper advertisements, so that an announcement of a certain size will fit into most newspapers, although in some newspapers there may be extra space appearing around the advertisement. Using the SAUs, regional and national advertisers can run advertising placements in almost all U.S. newspapers, without the need to re-size the advertisements for each individual paper. (See Exhibit 17.1.)

Newspaper Advertisement Size

Newspaper space is usually sold by the column-inch, which is a space measurement one column wide by one inch high. Thus, an advertisement that is six inches high and three columns wide would total 18 column-inches (6 col. × 3 in. = 18 col.-in.). But remember that newspapers have different column widths, which means that the size of an advertisement may vary from one newspaper to another; that is why the SAU was developed. What the advertiser is buying is space; do not think of the ad size as type, because some of the space may be left blank.

Newspaper advertising can also be purchased in larger quantities, such as quarter-page, half-page, and full-page. Again, these sizes vary from one newspaper to another.

Newspaper Advertising Rates

Most advertising media offer discounts to advertisers, based on a variety of factors. For all media including newspapers, a *flat rate* indicates that no

Exhibit 17.1

Standard Advertising Units (SAUs) for Newspapers

Depth in Inches FD*	1 COL 2-1/16″ 1xFD*	2 COL 4-1/4″ 2xFD*	3 COL 6-7/16″ 3xFD*	4 COL 8-5/8″ 4xFD*	5 COL 10-13/16″ 5xFD*	6 COL 13″ 6xFD*
18″	1x18	2x18	3x18	4x18	5x18	6x18
15.75″	1x15.75	2x15.75	3x15.75	4x15.75	5x15.75	
14″	1x14	2x14	3x14	4x14	5x14	6x14
13″	1x13	2x13	3x13	4x13	5x13	
10.5″	1x10.5	2x10.5	3x10.5	4x10.5	5x10.5	6x10.5
7″	1x7	2x7	3x7	4x7	5x7	6x7
5.25″	1x5.25	2x5.25	3x5.25	4x5.25		
3.5″	1x3.5	2x3.5				
3″	1x3	2x3				
2″	1x2	2x2				
1.5″	1x1.5					
1″	1x1					

* FD=Full depth

discounts are available; no matter how much advertising is purchased, the rates will not change. An *open rate* indicates that discounts are available, although an open rate is not a discounted rate; it is the highest rate charged, before discounts begin to be applied to the cost of an advertisement. When advertisers see an open rate, they know that eventually discounts may be earned.

For all media, the advertising rates are listed on a rate card, whether there is an actual printed card or only an online listing of advertising prices.

A combination rate applies if a single publisher owns more than a single newspaper, offering a lower advertising rate to advertisers who use more than one paper in the chain.

If an advertiser signs a contract for advertising space, the eventual anticipated discount may be figured into the contract. If the advertiser fails to earn the discounted rate in the contract, the advertiser must pay the difference in costs, known as a *short rate,* that is, money paid from the advertiser to the newspaper because the advertiser failed to advertise enough to earn the contract discount rate. Similarly, if the advertiser uses more advertising than anticipated and earns an even better discount than was contracted for, there may be a rebate paid from the newspaper to the advertiser. Short rates and rebates are terms that apply to all media, not only to newspapers.

Types of Discounts

For all media including newspapers, quantity discounts are based on the amount of advertising purchased over time; as an advertiser uses more advertising space or time, larger discounts may be earned, leading to reduced advertising costs. Frequency discounts are earned for advertising often. Continuity discounts may be earned for regular advertising. Frequency and continuity discounts are similar; frequency applies to the total number of ad placements and continuity applies to regular placements, such as every week or every day.

Special Newspaper Rates

In print media, color costs extra because it involves extra steps in the printing process. Black ink is included with the advertising space, and then one or two or three extra colors cost more; full-color printing is black plus three colors, known as a four-color process (even though black is not considered a color in printing). Color can be added in advance, known as a preprint, or during the regular printing process, known as ROP color, for run-of-paper or run-of-press. Spot color is just exactly that: a few spots of color, such as a border or headline. Process color uses tiny dots of color to make a color picture.

Position in the issue may mean an extra charge for an advertiser, who may be willing to pay more to be sure that the ad is in a particular place in the publication, such as in the sports section or the recipe section of the newspaper. Position on the page may also cost extra; most advertisements are on the bottom half of the page, so an advertiser may be willing to pay more to be sure that his or her ad is not "buried" or surrounded by other advertisements.

See Exhibit 17.2 for advantages and disadvantages of newspaper advertising.

Newspaper Circulation

Circulation is the number of copies of the publication that are actually distributed. There will be some extra copies that are returned as unsold, and some free copies that are given to advertisers to prove that the advertising appeared as ordered. Advertisers are usually interested in the paid circulation, that is, the number of copies that were delivered to paying readers. Advertisers are also interested in the size of the audience, which is the number of persons who actually read the publication.

Many large newspapers offer city-zone editions, which are distributed in the central city and any contiguous areas that appear to be the same as the city itself. There may be separate suburban editions for other areas. Many advertisers want to know the circulation within the retail trading zone (RTZ), the entire area where people live who shop for major purchases in the city zone. Other advertisers may want total market coverage (TMC), with advertising reaching every household in the market.

Mechanical Considerations

As mentioned before, an advertiser may sign a contract to indicate how much and how often that advertiser foresees placing advertising with that medium. Whether or not there is a contract, each advertising placement is accompanied by an insertion order, telling how and where and when the ad is to appear. These terms are used with all media, not just print.

Newspapers offer advertisers a tearsheet, which is a page torn from the actual newspaper that contains the particular advertisement that was run. Do not confuse a tearsheet with a proof. A proof is an advance copy either of the advertisement or of the page provided, so the advertiser can check the ad for accuracy.

Exhibit 17.2

Newspaper Advertising

Advantages
  ❖ Timely
  ❖ Contents vital to audience; thus, good readership
  ❖ Broad reach; appeal to all kinds of people
  ❖ Localized circulation; can target geographically
  ❖ Complete coverage; almost everyone reads newspapers
  ❖ Edited for all ages; can reach adults, teens, men, women
  ❖ Frequent publication; daily advertising results in
     continual impressions
  ❖ Can handle emergency situations; short ordering time
  ❖ Can tie in advertisements with news
  ❖ Can direct customers to stores
  ❖ Advertising budgets of all sizes can use newspapers
  ❖ Quick results
  ❖ Can include many different items in a single advertisement
  ❖ Reader controls exposure (as opposed to radio or
     television)

Disadvantages
  ❖ Many differences in sizes, deadlines, etc., so advertiser
     must have separate dealings with each newspaper; can be
     costly to change mechanical specifications for each news-
     paper (however, can utilize standard advertising units)
  ❖ Great variation in production quality
  ❖ Color may be of poor quality or difficult to use
  ❖ Short life
  ❖ Hasty reading

Buying Newspaper Advertising Space

As we have seen previously, *frequency* is advertising often, and *repetition* is using the same ad more than once. It is possible to have frequency without repetition and also to have repetition without frequency. Few advertisements work when run only once or a few times, so frequency is often an important factor. Larger advertisements attract a larger share of the audience than do small ads.

Many advertisers believe that an advertisement on a right-hand page of a publication draws more attention than one on the left-hand page. Similarly, they believe that an advertisement in the front of the publication is better than one in the middle or back sections. Thus, they often specify "right-hand page, far to the front," although research shows that these factors are not significantly better in newspapers.

We have already seen that an ad on the upper half of the page may have less competition from other advertising. Whether or not the advertisement is near the "gutter" (the center of the layout where two pages meet) does not matter with newspapers.

Timing for newspaper advertising depends on the shopping patterns of the audience members. For example, most newspapers can tell you what day is their "best food day," when national food advertisers along with local grocery stores run the most advertising. Auto tires may do best on a Saturday, when readers have time to shop for tires.

Other Considerations

For all local advertising media, cooperative advertising is an important part of the business. Co-op ads share the costs between the local retailer and the manufacturer or wholesaler. In addition, rates for national advertising are often higher than for local advertising, even in the same media vehicle, so co-op ads try to take advantage of this factor by having the local retailer place the ad at his lower local rate.

Consumer Magazines

There are several types of magazines. Consumer magazines are covered in this section. Business publications are also magazines but somewhat different in use and structure from consumer magazines, so they are covered separately. Farm publications are often an amalgam of consumer magazines and business publications, so they have some traits of both categories.

Consumer magazines can be general-interest or special-interest publications. The days of general-interest magazines are largely over, with only a few survivors such as *TV Guide* and *Reader's Digest*. Magazines that are distributed by newspapers, such as *Parade* and *USA Weekend,* are also general-interest magazines. Most magazines today are special-interest publications and there is a magazine to cover almost any interest, from model trains to retirement locations to the history of the Old West, and there are hundreds of magazines about computers.

Subtypes of magazines include regional and metropolitan (metro) editions, which are circulated in limited areas within the wider national circulation of large magazines. International editions of several publications are available, sometimes simply translated and other times completely reedited. Special-audience editions are also published, such as college-student editions of news or sports magazines carrying advertising that might not interest a more general audience.

Circulation and Audience

Circulation of magazines, like newspapers, is the number of copies distributed, either to subscribers or through newsstand sales. The primary audience is defined as those persons who receive the publication because they subscribe to it or buy it, and the secondary audience, also called the "pass-along audience," is defined as those persons who get the publication from someone else.

Several audience concepts apply to all advertising media, but are perhaps easiest to understand when applied to magazines. The accumulative audience (the cumulative audience, or "cume") is the total number of persons who see or hear an advertisement at least once in a single media vehicle (in this case, in a single magazine), even though the campaign may appear in multiple vehicles. The unduplicated audience, also called "net reach," is composed of all the persons who are exposed to an advertisement at least once in a combination of vehicles, say, when four magazines are used in a campaign. The duplicated audience (also called "dupes") is defined as those persons who are exposed more than once to an advertisement in a campaign. If we add up every time the advertisement is seen by the entire audience in all the media vehicles, that figure is called the total audience impressions (TAI), also known as the gross audience or gross impressions. The average number of times that an audience member is exposed to an advertisement from the campaign is called the average frequency or average exposure.

Frequency and Repetition

Like newspapers, frequency is the number of times people see or hear an advertisement during the campaign, whether or not the same advertisement is repeated, and repetition is using the same advertisement more than once, whether or not it is done frequently. In general, frequency is preferable to reach; that is, people need to be exposed more than once to a campaign, so it may be preferable to have more exposures to the same audience rather than expanding the size of the audience. (See Exhibit 17.3.)

Exhibit 17.3

Consumer Magazine Advertising

Advantages
- ❖ Reader lingers over editorial and advertising matter; gives longer time to sell
- ❖ High quality of production and color; can show package
- ❖ Flexible scheduling: weeklies, monthlies, etc.
- ❖ Selective readership; permits market segmentation
- ❖ Prestige of the medium, in many cases
- ❖ Advertising message retained for a long time; has long life
- ❖ Better audience data than from most other media
- ❖ Flexibility in format: size, foldout, insert, color, smell, etc.

Disadvantages
- ❖ Waste circulation, especially in general consumer magazines
- ❖ Advertisements easily ignored, compared to television or radio

Advertisement Position

Again, as with newspapers, many advertisers ask for their ads to be on a right-hand page, far to the front of the publication. In fact, research shows that, in consumer magazines, left-hand or right-hand page makes little difference, and the front, middle, or back of the issue also makes little difference. It does not matter whether the advertising appears in a thin or thick issue of the publication. What determines readership of an advertisement is the subject of the ad, the interests of the audience, and the size and frequency of exposure to the advertising. Remember, these characteristics are for consumer magazines; later in this chapter, we'll see that the outcome differs when business publications are involved.

Cost Considerations

Like all printed media, color advertising in magazines costs extra; of course, color is now expected for television and cinema advertising so there is no extra charge. In magazines, the illustration can go right off the edge of the page, ("bleed"), and costs more than printing a magazine advertisement with an unprinted border.

Sizes of Magazine Advertisements

The largest regular magazine size is the size of the old *Life* magazine, so it is called a *Life*-sized page, about 12 inches × 15 inches. Most magazines are printed in an 8-inch × 11-inch or an 8- or 9-inch × 10-inch format, about the size of *Time* magazine, thus called a *Time*-sized page. Smaller magazines utilize a 5-inch × 8-inch format, the size of *Reader's Digest,* and called a *Digest*-sized page.

If a *Time*-sized advertisement is placed on a *Life*-sized page, it is called a "junior unit," and a *Digest*-sized ad on a *Time*-sized page is a "digest unit." This allows the advertiser to use a printing plate in more than a single size of publication, and permits the magazine to place other advertising or editorial material on the page, so the cost is often less.

Sectional Editions

To test various versions of an advertisement, an advertiser may ask for a *split run,* when different versions of the ad go to various divisions of the audience. By measuring the sales response, the strength of the advertising appeal or message can be gauged. Split runs can be used for various sections of a city through a local newspaper or for different sections of the country through regional editions of magazines.

Magazine Advertising Deadlines

The deadline for placing advertising in a magazine may be months in advance. The publication issue date is when the magazine is printed and distributed, often first to newsstands and then to subscribers. The cover date is often set a few weeks or a month in advance, to tell newsstand operators when to take the issue off sale and to expect a newer edition.

Business Publications

Business publications and farm publications are much like consumer magazines in most respects, so it is not necessary to repeat all the information that applies for all of them. Nevertheless, there are some differences for business publications that should be observed.

Business publications are categorized as vertical publications, those that reach all levels within a single industry, such as *Advertising Age,* and horizontal publications, those intended for a single job function within a cross-section of industries, such as *Sales & Marketing Management.* Sometimes business publications are categorized as industrial publications, those that appeal to a certain industry; institutional publications, intended for those employed in institutions such as prisons, clubs, or colleges; professional publications, aimed at certain professions; and merchandising publications (also called trade papers), to aid in marketing efforts. These categories may not be mutually exclusive; *Advertising Age* is an industrial publication, a professional publication, and a merchandising publication.

Advertising Rates

And like other media, business publications offer quantity discounts, which are often called bulk rates, and frequency discounts, sometimes known as frequency rates. Many business publications are published monthly and offer per-issue rates, based on the number of issues used—not to be confused with frequency rates, based on the number of advertising insertions.

Most advertising media offer rate protection policies, so that advertisers with a contract will not have their rates increased during the term of the contract, although they may benefit if rates are lowered.

Most magazines charge premium prices for the outside front cover (Cover 1), the inside front cover (Cover 2), the inside back cover (Cover 3), and the outside back cover (Cover 4). There are sometimes other preferred positions as well.

An advertisement that is inserted into the publication rather than appearing on a regular page also usually costs more. Inserts can be bound into the publication or can simply be inserted between some of the pages.

Color rates, short rates, and rebates may all apply, as they do with other kinds of publications. (See Exhibit 17.4.)

Circulation

Many business publications are distributed for free, with the income coming solely from advertising, called free circulation; others charge for subscriptions and single copies, called paid circulation. Some publications control who can receive their publication (controlled circulation) while others have uncontrolled circulation. A publication sent to customers by a business may use franchise circulation, or "distribution paid," where a publisher sells the

Exhibit 17.4

Business Publication Advertising

Advantages
- ❖ Appeal to business interests; no frills, thus avid readership
- ❖ Often read during business hours; reader's mind on business
- ❖ No distractions; no other news or entertainment material
- ❖ Produces direct inquiries, from people who have that concern and responsibility
- ❖ Flexibility in timing and format, same as consumer magazines

Disadvantages
- ❖ Lots of other competitive advertising

magazines in bulk to the business, which then provides them free to good customers.

Checking

A checking copy of a magazine serves the same purpose as a tearsheet of a newspaper: to prove that the advertisement ran as ordered. Many publications include reader-service cards, which can also help measure audience response.

Frequency and Repetition

Frequency is essential for successful advertising in business publications, just as it is in newspapers and consumer magazines. Studies have shown that frequent and steady business publication advertising helps increase readership and recognition, produces buyer inquiries, and helps build brand preference.

In addition, business publication advertising can help increase an advertiser's share of voice (SOV), which is the percentage of messages within an industry category that come from a particular advertiser or firm.

Business publications have special patterns of monthly and seasonal response, so advertisers need to be aware of the readership patterns within a certain industry as well as for a particular publication.

Buying Advertising

Unlike the situation with newspapers and consumer magazines, ad placement, or "position," within an issue of a business publication is an important factor. Advertisements are more effective in the front one-quarter of the publication, as well as more effective on a right-hand page and when facing another advertisement, rather than facing news and editorial material.

There are thousands of business publications, making it difficult for a media buyer to be familiar with all of them. Many business publications can provide a media data form that provides insights into the publication, its readership, and its editorial and advertising policies, which can help the media buyer determine how well the publication matches the target group and advertising goals.

Chapter 18
Out-of-Home Media

Many of the major advertising media reach into the home. Television, radio, newspapers, magazines, Internet, and social media can all be delivered to the home. Yet there are several types of media that are available primarily outside the home, commonly known as out-of-home media, reaching consumers when they are traveling, waiting, shopping, or otherwise situated outside their residences.

Outdoor Advertising

Outdoor advertising consists of billboards, which can be changed periodically, and permanent signs, such as those for a nearby motel or business. The standard-sized billboard is called a 24-sheet or 30-sheet poster, because once it required many sheets of printed paper to cover it. Today these billboards can be covered by just six, or even three, sheets of paper or one single large sheet of printed plastic made of flexible polyethylene film. Billboards smaller than the standard size are commonly referred to as "junior panels."

At one time outdoor billboards were purchased in "showings," and even though outdoor advertising has shifted to using gross rating points (GRPs), buys are still often referred to as showings. Billboards are usually purchased within a market zone, and once a year the average daily circulation of cars, buses, trucks, and pedestrians is measured for each billboard location. This information helps formulate how many billboards are required within a market zone to achieve a certain audience level. In outdoor advertising, the standard buy is 100 GRP over a four-week period, which results in the audience levels shown in Exhibit 18.1. Other levels of advertising, such as 25 GRP, 50 GRP, 150 GRP, and so on, are available but only as divisions of multiples of the number of billboards used to achieve 100 GRP; there is no guarantee that a billboard buy of 200 GRP will achieve twice the audience impact as 100 GRP, only that you will be using twice as many billboards.

Billboards near shopping centers can also be purchased through a shopping-center network. (See Exhibit 18.2.)

Of course, there are outdoor advertising signs that are not billboards. Painted bulletins stay up for several months, sometimes for years. Spectacular signs such as those in Times Square in New York City are another specialized type of outdoor advertising. Highway signs can be billboards or painted bulletins. The locations for billboards and other outdoor advertising must be bought or rented.

Other Outdoor Signs

Many stores post signs outside their locations to attract customers. These signs are not usually thought of as outdoor advertising because they are on the establishment's property and are not considered part of the overall advertising campaign plan. Some companies, especially soft-drink and beer vendors, offer free or discounted signs to small businesses with part of the sign space devoted to the name of the business and the remainder of the space used to promote the beverages.

Today many signs are displayed inside the businesses. These are covered in Chapter 21 on in-store media.

Transit Advertising

Transit advertising makes use of both the inside and outside of transit vehicles, as well as transit stations. Inside buses, subway cars, and commuter trains the signs above the windows are called "car cards." These are usually 11 inches high, although signs above doors must be shorter, and the widths vary. The exterior of buses can carry displays on the sides of the vehicles as well as front-end and rear-end posters. Posters inside train or subway stations, and inside airline terminals, can vary a great deal depending on the exact location, the need for illumination, and the pedestrian traffic patterns.

Transit advertising is similar to outdoor advertising, sold by a showing, or a "run." A full showing or full run has one car card inside every vehicle in the transit system; a half showing or half run would allow for one car card in every other vehicle. Because passengers usually stay in one car and often in one seat, double showings (double runs) and triple showings (triple runs) are common, providing two or three—or possibly even more—car cards within every vehicle.

Signs on the exteriors of taxicabs are usually displayed on the rear trunk or perhaps on the roof of the cab. Trucks can also carry advertising, with

Exhibit 18.1

Outdoor Advertising GRP

A purchase of 100 GRP of outdoor advertising is intended to result in an audience that achieves a reach of:

- 90 percent of the local adult population, with a
- frequency of slightly more than once a day
- over a period of 28 days.

Exhibit 18.2

Outdoor Advertising

Advantages
- ❖ Reaches potential customers close to point of sale
- ❖ Communication can be quick and simple
- ❖ Repetition easy in high-traffic areas

Disadvantages
- ❖ Short message may limit creative breadth
- ❖ Despoiling the landscape; may earn public's enmity
- ❖ Legal restrictions

some trucking companies offering vehicles with lighted signs for nighttime viewing. (See Exhibit 18.3.)

Transit advertising offers a huge audience with an approximate cross-section of the area population. Because people are mobile, the opportunities for repeat exposures to an ad are quite possible.

Digital Out-of-Home Media

Like so many other media types, out-of-home media cannot be simply divided into neat categories because there is some overlap. Digital out-of-home media overlap with outdoor advertising as well as with signs.

Exhibit 18.3

Transit Advertising

Advantages
- ❖ Economical; very low cost per thousand
- ❖ High repetition
- ❖ Continuous exposure, day and night
- ❖ Limited number of competitive messages
- ❖ Captive audience

Disadvantages
- ❖ People are not thinking of advertising; hurrying elsewhere
- ❖ Advertisements subject to mutilation and vandalism
- ❖ Some doubts as to quality of the market

Digital media refer to moving or changing advertising, such as video screens, sometimes referred to as "dynamic media." Such displays can be located in stores, sports arenas, shopping centers and restaurants, along roads, and similar public places. Sometimes kiosks and other accessible locations are used for interactive addressable video screens.

Other Out-of-Home Media

By some counts, there are more than 100 format types of out-of-home media. These include such things as skywriting or airplane-towed banners, mobile billboards, benches and other street furniture, signs on gas pumps and at rest areas, and wallscapes, which are very large signs attached to buildings.

More types of out-of-home media are constantly being developed, which may offer better audience selectivity and higher cost efficiencies.

Chapter 19
Digital Media

The Internet is now an integral part of most Americans' lives. According to the website Internet World Stats, about 78 percent of Americans are connected to the Internet on average for about nine hours a day. This usage is remarkably consistent for kids and adults: adults are using the Internet at home and at work, and kids use it both at home and at school. In addition, increased use of smartphones allows the Internet to be accessed from virtually anywhere a signal exists.

Advertising and Online Behaviors

Many people spend time online doing "directed activities" such as searching for information. Advertising comes into play when a search engine like Google displays results and includes digital advertisements on the results pages. Advertising also plays a part when people use the Internet for social reasons or for entertainment. Ads appear at social networks and in online games, providing revenue for the companies providing the content.

The primary purpose of most digital advertising is to direct people to online sites that are of interest and value to them. Some digital ads direct people to branded sites and online storefronts (also known as *etail* sites) where people can purchase goods or learn more about products they are considering purchasing. Other digital ads direct people to websites where they find out information and, in some situations, pay for additional content. On many of these websites, additional digital ads point people to other sites that may be of interest to them.

There are numerous digital advertising options and creative units, and finding a mix that efficiently builds reach and frequency against a specific target can be difficult. Millions of different websites accept advertising, and finding sites where the audience is "sticky" (i.e., they stick around for a while) and thus have time to see your message can be tough. Finally, the different types of rate options can be confusing to some clients (and frankly to some agency people, too). Should you run ads on site- and pay-based impressions or click-throughs, or should you bid on a campaign and see what happens? There is no right or wrong answer, but information in this chapter should help you understand more about the complex world of digital advertising.

Digital advertising spending has increased significantly since the year 2000. Categories representing the highest level of advertising spending include financial services, telecommunications, and automotive.

Measurement

Measurement of online users involves fairly large samples as well as passive technology. Participants in data collection have special software integrated onto their own computers and data are collected whenever the participants use their computers. The data are transmitted daily to the measurement service. Two of the leading services are Nielsen-Net Ratings and comScore. Nielsen-Net Ratings is a division of the same company that does television ratings. ComScore is a newer company that focuses on all types of digital measurement, including search engine optimization and mobile marketing.

Many websites track their own statistics using a system such as Google Analytics, which provides daily counts of visits to the site, and can identify the country of origin of a visitor and whether the visitor is new or returning (based on IP [Internet protocol] addresses). These analytics programs can also indicate amount of time spent on different pages that make up a site. Demographic information is generally not available, though, and as a result, media planners might use multiple data sources for evaluating Web properties.

Types of Digital Media

The biggest challenge to brand planning in the digital sphere is simply keeping up with the opportunities. Software developers are constantly creating new innovations for online users and advertising is a key way to support these new applications. But many advertisers are conservative, and are hesitant to try something new without support for its success. The most popular digital advertising tactics are listed in Table 19.1. Key players in the digital world are found in Table 19.2.

Search Engine Marketing

The tactic known as "search engine marketing," or SEM, promotes websites by increasing their visibility in search engine result pages (SERPs). In the

Table 19.1

Search Engine Marketing Options

	Free or paid?	Advertiser influenced?	Where are they found?	How are they determined?
Organic results	Free	No, advertisers have no influence on these results	The bottom two thirds of a SERP*	How relevant a search engine believes the site is to a search query
Paid results	Paid, often by a bid	Yes, advertisers place bids on search terms	The top of the SERP, or in a right-hand side bar, labeled as "sponsored links"	Highest bidder
Local results	Free, with an option to pay for enhancements	Yes, advertisers provide information	As part of a "map" of local businesses	Advertisers submit information that is brought up on a map whenever a local search is performed

*SERP, search engine result page.

search engine marketing arena, the key player is Google, which accounts for about two thirds of all online searches. Next in line are Yahoo and Bing. Most of these ads are text based, and include a clickable URL to redirect the online user to the selected website.

Display and Banner Ads

Display and banner advertising entails embedding an advertisement into a Web page. The advertisements include both text and images and, like SEM, attract traffic to an advertiser's website by a link to the website. Generally, the online user needs to click somewhere on the ad to be redirected.

Online Classifieds

Similar to traditional classifieds in newspapers, online classifieds are primarily text-based ads (with occasional images included) that connect buyers and sellers. Although used primarily by individuals selling used goods, other businesses have found a place for online classifieds in their media plans. Retailers list good deals, realtors list properties for sale and rent, service providers ranging from garages to lawyers list their services, and companies list available jobs.

Table 19.2

Key Players in the Digital Advertising World

Search engine marketing	Online classified	Mobile	Online advertising networks	Content networks
Google	Craigslist	Google mobile (google.mobi)	Ad mob (www. admob.com)	Google AdWords
Yahoo!	Local newspaper websites	Yahoo mobile (yahoo.mobi)		DoubleClick
Bing		Sky mobile		Zedo
				Tribal Fusion

Rich Media Ads

Rich media ads provide an interactive online experience for the user. For example, some ads expand and provide a new online context when users click or roll over the ads.

Mobile Advertisements

The growth in penetration of smartphones allows for new forms of advertising. Mobile advertisements consist of both display ads (clickable banners, rich media ads) and search ads (text links). Brands are also creating "apps" for smartphones that can be sold and downloaded for a personalized brand experience.

Content Networks

Most advertising online is placed through advertising content networks. These are companies that connect advertisers to websites that want to host advertisements. The key function of an ad network is to aggregate available ad space from online publishers and match it with advertiser demand. There are three types of online advertising networks.

1. Vertical Networks

Vertical networks clearly identify which websites are part of the network, and advertisers always know exactly where their ads will run. These types of networks are priced slightly higher than other networks. The rationale is that they promote high-quality traffic at market prices and are heavily used by brand marketers. In general, vertical networks offer two types of media placement: ROS (run-of-site) advertising across specific channels (e.g., auto or travel) and site-wise advertising in a single website.

2. Blind Networks

Blind networks offer lower costs than vertical networks but do not provide information on where ads will run prior to the flight, hence the media planner is "blind" to the content where the ads will run. Most networks offer a "site opt out" method which allows for certain categories or sites to be excluded. The networks usually run campaigns on an RON, or run-of-network, basis, across a range of different sites that are part of the network. Blind networks achieve their low pricing through large bulk buys of typically remnant space.

3. Targeted Networks

Targeted networks are referred to as the next generation of targeting. This type of content network focuses on specific targeting technologies such as search-based, contextual, or behavioral targeting. Targeted networks specialize in using consumer click stream data to enhance the value of the inventory they purchase. As in traditional media planning, the planner must carefully identify the key target audiences for the digital advertising campaign. To make these decisions, planners determine whether to use search-based targeting, contextual targeting, or behavioral targeting.

Search-based targeting derives from search engine marketing, discussed above. Conducting searches online is a popular activity, and most online users are familiar with these kinds of ads. For that reason, search advertising continues to soar in popularity. Although search has merit as an effective marketing tool, advertisements go unnoticed if they are not appropriately aligned with the interests of the user. This happens frequently with a specific keyword, chosen by the advertiser, which may have more than one meaning. Here is an example: An online user interested in a Toyota Matrix enters the word "matrix" into a search engine. Instead of finding links to sites or ads about the automobile, the user sees ads for the movie or hair care line called Matrix. The end result, due to lack of relevancy, is a lower click-through rate and opportunity to sell.

Contextual targeting provides users with ads about a subject that is of particular interest to them. Instead of basing the ads on what customers are searching for, contextual advertising looks at the content customers look at as they navigate through the Internet. To market to consumers true contextual advertising relies on relationships between online advertisers and Web publishers. The high degree of an ad's content relevancy promises the potential for a higher click-through rate and an increase in sales and profitability.

Behavioral targeting monitors the behavior of an individual as he or she moves from site to site. Ads are then generated to correlate with this behavior. For example, when using behavioral targeting, the online shoe store Zappos can identify users who visit their website. Then, when those users visit other sites that are part of the network where Zappos has purchased ad space, they will see an advertisement enticing them to purchase shoes through Zappos. Behavioral targeting allows advertisers to appeal to consumers with different ads based on their past behavior, even as different consumers view the same Web page; while one consumer is seeing the Zappos ad, another might be seeing an ad for Nordstrom's. The downside is that behavioral targeting has been considered by many to be invasive. Consumers express concerns about the tracking and usage of their browsing habits.

How consumers respond to these tactics is found in Table 19.3.

Other Planning Decisions

In addition to making decisions about targeting, the planner must be involved in two other key decisions. First is the advertising creative format: Will the ad be text only, a clickable image, or rich media? Will it be on a computer, on an iPad, or on a smartphone? Second is the payment method: Will budget decisions be made on an impression (cost per thousand, or CPM) basis, or on a bidding (cost-per-click, or CPC) basis? Digital advertising revenue is generated from both CPM (impression-based) and performance (CPC) measures. Negotiated CPM advertising is analogous to other types of advertising: the planner or buyer estimates the number of impressions that an ad will generate against their target and a cost is assigned to the impressions. With negotiated CPC, the advertiser will only pay for the people who click on the advertisement. For example, one ad might cost 40 cents on a CPM basis or $2 on a CPC basis (Table 19.4). In this case, the advertiser would set a daily budget and once the goals are reached, the ads would stop running for the day.

To add to the pricing complexity, some sites (including Google AdWords and Facebook Ads) use a bid method as opposed to a negotiation method. The bidding process assumes that multiple advertisers want to reach the same group of people (e.g., new-car buyers). Advertisers would then provide a bid on how much they wanted to pay to reach those buyers. With search engine marketing, the higher the advertiser bids on a keyword, the higher in the rankings the ad appears, and the more likely it is that Web searchers

Table 19.3

Consumer Responses to Digital Advertising

Consumers say they best respond to:	Clients believe the best type of targeting is:
Contextual advertising (62%)	Contextual targeting (41%)
Demographic targeting (28%)	Search targeting (30%)
Geographic targeting (24%)	Behavioral targeting (27%)
Behavioral targeting (18%)	

Source: Dawn Anfuso, "Contextual vs. Behavioral Targeting," iMedia Connection, March 31, 2006. http://www.imediaconnection.com/content/8863.asp.

Table 19.4

Cost Comparisons for Digital Advertising

	Impressions: .40 CPM	Clicks: $2 per click
Daily budget: $20	Total daily impressions: 50,000	Total daily clicks: 10 Approximate click-through rate: 10/50,000

will see the ad. Ranking means visibility, though you do not have to be at the top of the rankings or make the highest bid in order for prospects to see your ad and click on it. Your goal is to get the lowest cost-per-click and the highest quality clicks (sales and leads) for your budget.

With any bidding method, it can be helpful to test different bids and targeting opportunities to track the level at which bids can come in.

The Migration from Offline to Online

Digital advertising is often part of a traditional medium's migration from offline to online, as different media channels recognize that a large portion of their audiences spend their daily media time on the Internet. Traditional media has addressed this in different ways.

TV Advertisements

The established television networks, such as NBC and CBS, now offer much of their programming via streaming video directly from their websites. These streaming programs include advertisements during the established commercial breaks, and most breaks are significantly shorter than the over-the-air breaks (:30 or :60 as opposed to 120 seconds or more). Placements are negotiated as some of network television packages. Additionally, websites like Hulu.com offer the same programs as are on the network sites, plus a range of older programs. Like spots on network websites, ads run before, during, and after programs, and unlike the networks include a billboard ad as well. Rates are CPM based.

Yellow Pages and Other Directories

Internet Yellow Pages (IYP) offer online advertising in a way that is different from that of standard search engines or traditional yellow pages. Whereas search engines return results based on relevancy to the true search term, IYP returns results based on a geographic area. Yellow pages publishers or their agents sell the right to place advertisements within the same category, next to the basic listings (which are free). Costs for premium placement on the website range from $41 per month in small markets to $150 per month and more in larger markets. Studies by independent companies such as Nielsen and comScore have shown that IYPs have a very slim percentage of total Internet searches. Additionally, most of the larger search engines provide similar services for free to small businesses (one example is Google Places).

Direct Mail

E-mail marketing is a form of direct marketing that uses electronic mail as a means of communicating commercial or fund-raising messages to an audience. In its broadest sense, every e-mail sent to a potential or current customer could be considered e-mail marketing. Marketers develop programs on their own using existing customer lists, or contract with a larger company (such as Constant Contact) to manage the program for them.

The Future of Digital

Wired magazine has suggested that most Internet activity will be shifting over to the use of apps: computer software designed to help the user perform singular or multiple related specific tasks. Marketers are developing brand-specific apps for computers as well as for smartphones and iPads; examples include apps developed by restaurant chains that allow users to locate restaurants (with maps) in any city. Sunglass brand Oakley has a customizable "Surf Report" app, delivering a value to its key target. Sherwin-Williams paints allows users to take photographs of colors they love and receive a recommendation on the best paint match. AAMCO has a transmission troubleshooting app; if your car breaks down, you answer a few questions and the app suggests what the trouble is (and also tells you where the closest AAMCO dealer is).

Many online and computer video games now include advertising in the content of the game, and this usage is expected to grow. Ads can be static (programmed into game content) and dynamic (ads that are personalized to the individual, who must be playing the game online or connected to the Internet via a gaming system).

A new technology called Augmented Reality adds digital imagery to real-time media content. For example, during the World Cup soccer tournament, advertisers' brands were digitally inserted onto the soccer pitch and rotated regularly. *Esquire* magazine has experimented with augmented reality by allowing magazine purchasers to download software and hold up the magazine to the computer's webcam in order to access additional content from *Esquire*'s website.

Finally, pricing is evolving from CPM and CPC pricing to engagement pricing, which is based on attention delivered rather than impressions and pay-per-click. A brand provides a number of branded experiences on a website (such as a sponsored game) and pays for the amount of time an individual spends on the experience.

The digital world is constantly changing, and the best brand and media planners devote a bit of time each day to keeping up with these changes and leveraging new opportunities for their clients.

Chapter 20

Social Media

Social media advertising is an emerging field that represents a blending of traditional and digital media with a dose of word-of-mouth thrown in for good measure.

Social media include most types of Internet-based applications that focus on interactivity and that allow the creation and exchange of content created by both users and brands. Social media sites not only support but also encourage interaction. Marketing messages on social media sites no longer focus on one-way, top-down messages from a brand but rather become dialogues between a brand and a customer.

This idea of interactivity differs from that of other types of digital advertisements. Digital messages such as banner advertisements want the online user to click on the ad and be directed to a branded website. Social media messaging can be used for that kind of directional interactivity and to provide purchase incentives, too. But social media advertising is also used to build communities of users focused around the brand. These communities develop positive word-of-mouth for brands.

Social Networking Services Defined

When we think of social media, we specifically think of social networking services (SNS). An SNS has a goal to build and encourage social networks or social relations among people, often people who share interests, activities, or off-line relationships (see Table 20.1.). When your business is part of one person's network, your interactions with that individual can be seen by everyone in that network. What this means is that one individual's conversation can start a chain of conversations within that individual's social group or network, leading to positive word-of-mouth for your business.

Many large and small brands have an SNS presence because large numbers of consumers spend time online. Facebook has over 500 million active users and half of those visit the site daily. The average Facebook network size is 80 people (meaning each time a user posts a message at Facebook, it is seen by 80 others). Twitter has 200 million users, and YouTube reports more than 20 million unique visitors each month. A word of caution: Social media success can be fleeting, with new applications coming in to existence regularly, all focused on providing new, fun, and involving ways for people to engage with each other, and with brands. The top social networking site in 2007, MySpace, now only counts 100 million users, with only about 18 percent of those being active users.

Types of SNS

SNS allow users to share ideas, activities, events, and interests within their individual networks. What this means for a media planner and a brand is that the campaign is not just planned, negotiated, and left to run. The campaign must have consistent involvement with someone (either at the agency or at the client) monitoring and participating in the activities at the social network site. Without this level of commitment, any type of social network campaign will fail.

There are several different categories of SNS (see Table 20.2). The major sites for media planners to be familiar with (and which we focus on in this chapter) include:

- Social networking sites, which allow for multiple forms of communication between a user and his or her network.
- Micro-blogging sites, which provide short messages in primarily a text format. Microblogs often limit entries to fewer than 300 characters, resulting in brief messages. Microblogging applications also allow links to other websites.
- Multimedia sites, which allow for sharing of photographic and video images. Users can tag and arrange content so others can search and find images.

Other types of social media that media planners should know about include:

- Blogs: the term *blog* comes from the term *web log,* which is a website that is generally created and maintained by an individual and which includes regular entries of commentary, descriptions of events, or other material such as graphics or video. Many blogs focus on commentary or news on a particular subject. Others more closely resemble personal online diaries.
- Review and opinion sites: these types of sites allow online users to rate products, services, and businesses (although currently retail stores

Table 20.1

What Is a Social Networking Service?

Component	Explanation
Profile	A representation of the user including name, image, and list of interests
Social links	A way for users to connect with each other, such as "follow" on Twitter and "friend" on Facebook
Channel of communication	Method of sharing information (text, video, image, audio)

Table 20.2

Major Types of Social Network Services

SNS portals	Micro blogging	Photo sharing	Video sharing	Blogging	Review sites	Geo-social
Facebook	Twitter	deviantARt	YouTube	Wordpress	Yelp	Foursquare
MySpace	Jaiku	Flickr	Viddler	Blogger	Insider pages	Gowalla
Friendster	Plurk	Photobucket	Vimeo	Typepad	Angie's list	Bright kite
LinkedIn	Tumblr	Picasa	sevenload	Livejournal		
Ning		Smugmug	Zide			

and services represent the bulk of the reviews). Although these rarely accept advertising, brands can set up branded accounts to respond to user reviews and provide information about the brand.

- Geo-social networks: these are tools that use geographic services such as GPS to engage users who submit their location data to a service either through their computer or, more likely, through their mobile phones. Users can see where their friends are frequenting, and businesses can reward frequent visitors who "check in" at their location.

Within a single category, some sites offer simple and streamlined tools and applications; others offer ones that are more complex. Some appeal to younger people, some to older. Some are brand new, and some have been around for quite a while. Most of these sites have their own analytics systems modeled after Google Analytics. At a minimum, these sites will track followers (different sites have different names, such as friends or fans) and give some indication of the level of engagement (i.e., interactions between the brand and the followers). We focus the discussion in this book on the most used and most popular services in 2010, including Facebook, Twitter, and YouTube.

Social Advertising and Media Planning

Because this type of media is changing every day, one role of the media planner is to be aware of the different social media offerings available, to track their popularity and their demographics, and to assess how well the medium would match the consumers. Working with others in the agency, the media planner also needs to assess whether there is a commitment to consistently providing content for the social networking site as well as a commitment to responding to online interactions. Because there are multiple levels of involvement with social media, the media planner may also be responsible for negotiating media placements in the new media.

Initial Level of Involvement: A SNS Presence

Many brands jump into social media by setting up a simple site and populating it with some content. Examples include a Facebook page dedicated to the Wendy's Frosty Brand, a Twitter feed that outlines new offerings from the Barnes and Noble Bookstore, or a YouTube Video Channel for the sports giant Nike. The key to success is to have a large number of people following the SNS. Many online users will search for brands that they like and choose to join those social networks. Other online users will see that their friends in the SNS like certain brands and will choose to follow those brands at the SNS as well. What this suggests is that a social network site can be set up with no cash outlay as long as some content is available to populate the site. The media planner, then, will be tracking the increases in followers and monitoring the effects of different content.

Second Level of Involvement: SNS Advertising

The established SNS allow advertising on their sites. These ads work similarly to different types of digital advertising, discussed in Chapter 19. An overview of how the sites work is next.

Facebook

Advertisers can create highly targeted advertisements and present them to Facebook audiences. Facebook users provide information about themselves, not only demographics but psychographics. Using the Facebook advertising tool, a media planner can select demographic characteristics for the advertisement including age, gender, and geographic location; advertisers can even choose to target people on their birthdays. Additionally, target audiences can be segmented based on what types of other Facebook sites they have affiliated with, that is, ads can target people who like *The Rachel Ray Show* or "fly fishing." Ads on Facebook can direct people to a site on the Facebook network or to a site off the network.

Twitter

"Promoted Tweets" are paid tweets from advertisers that appear at the top of a Twitter search results page. "Promoted Trends" are updates of the most popular twitter topics that are promoted by advertisers. These Promoted Trends initially appear at the bottom of the Trending Topics list on Twitter and are clearly marked as "Promoted." Users who click on a Promoted Trend will see Twitter search results for that topic, with a related Promoted Tweet from the advertiser appearing at the top of the page. Rates are impression based.

YouTube

YouTube's direct advertising plan includes video clips that begin 15 seconds after a viewer starts watching a video. Another option is placing Google AdWords, where advertisers can select keywords or categories where their ads appear, or can target based on geography, interests, and demographics. Costs are based on CPC bids (see Chapter 19 for more information on bidding).

Third Level of Involvement: Social Ads

Innovative marketers are looking for new and different ways to integrate a traditional type of advertisement with a social network, termed a *social ad*. According to the Internet Advertising Bureau, a social ad is an online ad that incorporates user interactions that the consumer has agreed to display and to share. With this definition, then, a social ad is an ad that contains information about the user (such as a picture or name) associated with some ad content. As a result, this can be seen as a personal endorsement, almost like a word-of-mouth message. Such ads generally appear on social network sites such as MySpace and Facebook (with MySpace being the dominant place for them to appear). Examples include display ads with polls. Ads for feature films, for example, will ask, "will you see this movie this weekend?"

along with response options such as "yes," "no," and "not sure." Once the individual votes, the responses will appear to him or her in a new box, along with a number of names of friends who have also voted in the poll.

Social advertising is currently evolving to generate new and interesting ways of consumer engagement. In the summer of 2010 one of the most talked about ads was that for Old Spice, featuring former NFL player Isaiah Mustafa. Ads ran on network and cable television, but also on YouTube and Facebook sites. As people began to interact with the ads, the agency listened to comments and questions, and created new content where Mustafa responded to questions. And in a final (and what some critics call brilliant) move, the ads spoke to people directly, beginning with a "get well soon" message to Digg founder Kevin Rose and other personalized messages to online celebrities such as Perez Hilton, as well as to movie and sports stars. When the campaign ended in mid-July fans were disappointed to see it go, and a key challenge to social advertisements was identified: the ability to sustain the community around them.

As most media planners will quickly see, social ads are similar to viral videos and other types of video messages: messages that speed through Internet channels very quickly with minimal traditional advertising support (although in the Old Spice case, the traditional television advertisements did not hurt in getting the viral element started). Integrating the content with the social media sites, and measuring and monitoring the effects, would be a key element in the media planner's job.

Pricing Options

In addition to the traditional cost-per-click (CPC) and cost-per-thousand (CPM) pricing, discussed earlier in this book, some other pricing options are being considered and occasionally implemented by some advertisers. These include:

- Cost-per-install: with this option, which is similar to cost-per-click, the advertiser pays each time a user downloads and installs a widget or application on a computer or smartphone. This guarantees distribution of content, but does not guarantee the user will interact with the content.
- Cost-per-action: the advertiser pays each time a user takes a specific action, such as becoming a fan or friend, posting to a profile, looking at a video, or playing a game. This works best when a single, specific action is desired.
- Cost-per-engagement: the advertiser pays each time an engagement takes place over a given time period, such as submitting branded, user-generated content, interaction with such content, votes, and reviews and ratings.

Future of Social Media

With new applications being invented all the time, it is difficult to capture the future of social media. One application mentioned earlier in this chapter, geo-social networking, also known as "lo-so" for "location social," seems poised to become a key advertising vehicle. Applications like Foursquare and Gowalla blend social networking, digital advertising, direct marketing, and games. Users "check in" when they visit physical locations such as restaurants, bars, and retail stores, and their status is sent to people in their own networks. When they check in, they receive incentives such as badges and awards based on visit frequency, and also offers from nearby businesses.

Another emerging SNS are sites that want to serve as portals. Social networks like Facebook and Twitter don't like to think of themselves as websites; instead, they see themselves as stand-alone applications that can organize a user's entire Web experience. Facebook, in particular, is moving toward becoming a "hub"—given the fact that Facebook usage dominates online time for many individuals. One way Facebook is doing this is through a program called Facebook Connect, which is not a media channel but rather software that integrates the Facebook experience into a branded website. At its basic level, a user could log in to branded sites via Facebook, saving them the need to have multiple log-ins and user names. At a more effective level, users indicate their preferences for specific brands using the Facebook "like" feature at the branded website, and the brand uses this information to send the user specific branded messages via Facebook. A cosmetics etailer like Sephora, for example, would notice that one individual likes two specific brands and buys a lot of mascara, and ads and other messages delivered via Facebook would be focused on those purchases.

There is also a growth in social network product placement. Integrating brands into social experiences is a challenge, but one that certain companies are attempting to address. One Facebook feature used by many users is the "poke" feature, which is basically just a text nudge, a way to say a quick hello. Now a company is branding pokes into a program called SuperPoke, so instead of one friend just "nudging" another, the friend could spritz another with virtual perfume, or pass them a virtual bottle of soda.

Instead of interrupting a user experience, brands need to find ways to be part of a user experience when they participate on SNS. The evolving digital landscape is a challenging yet fascinating environment that can allow for creative brands and for media planners to reach new levels of engagement with consumers.

Chapter 21

In-Store Media

In grocery store chains across the country shoppers see brand messages from the moment they park their cars until they complete their purchases at the cash register. And it isn't just in grocery stores any longer; "big box" chain stores like Wal-Mart, Target, and Best Buy now embrace in-store advertising. These messages are valued because they reach consumers close to the point of purchase. According to research by Cisco Systems, about 75 percent of brand choices are made in the store. For example, a shopper may have a list with "butter" written on it, but she will not decide on the specific brand of butter until she is in the store. In-store advertising also can encourage impulse buys: those unplanned purchases that are stimulated by seeing the brand (or an ad for the brand) in the store.

Another value of in-store media is that consumers often buy on impulse, and some estimates show that about half of the total purchase at the grocery is spent on items consumers were not planning to purchase. Younger consumers, in particular, respond to in-store marketing. One study found that they were more willing to consider and purchase brands that they learned about via in-store marketing.

Given the amount of decision making going on in a store, it is not surprising that advertisers are trying to get their messages in front of consumers when they are making these decisions. From a simple "shelf talker" (a small sign on a shelf pointing the shopper to a product) to digital opportunities, in-store advertising has become a key element of many media plans. In addition, individual stores advertise loyalty programs to make sure their store is the one most visited by customers. (See Table 21.1.)

Types of Messages

Three broad categories of in-store advertising are mass messages, personal messages, and loyalty programs. "Mass" in-store messages display the same information to all customers, whereas "personal" messages provide an

Table 21.1

Pros and Cons of In-Store Media

Pros	Cons
• Recency: brand message appears very close to point of purchase • Capitalizes on impulse buys • Register sales data available to connect exposures to sales • Ad can be located anywhere— in stores, next to merchandise, on shopping bags, on ceilings	• Limited space: finite space for messages; may be blocked by other shoppers, employees, etc. • Limited effects on new users, primarily reminds current users • Message exposure time very short • Relatively expensive compared to other media

interactive experience where the consumer can get information appropriate for an individual purchase decision. On average, about 10 percent of U.S. advertising budgets are spent on in-store media. In-store advertising space is managed by many different companies, most with a specialty in one or two types of messages. (See Table 21.2.)

Mass In-Store Messages

In-store signs promote a single product (such as Kraft Miracle Whip) or a group of products from the same manufacturer (such as Post cereals). These messages are placed in aisles near to the product(s) being promoted, providing a persuasive message close to the purchase decision. Within this category are:

- Shelf talkers: small signs that point customers to products on shelves.
- Banners: larger vertical signs that span two or three shelves.
- Floor signs: large graphics placed on the aisle floor to point customers to products on lower shelves. Today, you might even catch a 3-D graphic on a grocery floor: a soda or snack that looks like it is placed on the floor, or a plane ready for take-off.

Ads on shopping carts used by consumers as they shop provide messages on the cart. The ads are exposed both to the shopper with the cart and to the other shoppers as they roam the store. These include:

- A small sign on the child seat of the cart
- A larger ad on the side of the cart
- A complete wrap of the cart in an advertisement

Table 21.2

Players in the In-Store Industry

Type of media	Key companies
In-store signage	Vallassis, CBS, Floorgraphics, Inverted Media
In-store coupons	Smartsource and Catalina Marketing
Shopping carts	Cart America
In-store video	PRN, Target Inhouse Video

Video advertisements provide messages on large screens near the checkout aisles or at other key locations in the store. The screens feature content from cable channels such as the *Food Network, Discovery, Entertainment Tonight,* and *Inside Edition,* and content is updated regularly. Advertisements are embedded into the programming. Whereas the screens near the checkout counters get a higher level of attention, screens throughout the store may be more influential on purchases.

Personal In-Store Messages

Digital Out-of-Home

Digital out-of-home advertising provides targeted messages at specific locations in the store at specific times. For example, prepared meals can be advertised at a grocery store after 5 P.M. to attract after-work shoppers. Digital signs also allow a store to sell ads to other businesses (a grocery store, for example, could sell a digital sign to the local dry cleaner and the local liquor store, changing these throughout the day). Newer types of digital ads include interactive displays on walls and floors that use motion control technology. This allows the images to change when shoppers wave their hands or move their bodies in other ways near the displays. Coors beer, for example, projects life-sized games like foosball onto floors of beverage aisles in grocery stores, and shoppers can play a game of foosball by moving their legs near the projection. The foosball "table" features the Coors logo.

Interactive Kiosks

Interactive kiosks are stand-alone structures that allow consumers to access product information, recipes, and coupons. Kiosks can be placed near the front of the store or the promoted department to maximize customer exposure. Types of kiosks include:

- Leaflet dispensers that provide nutrition and recipe leaflets to customers, often including shopping lists and meal-planning ideas to cross-promote products.
- On-shelf coupons, a small device attached to a shelf near a product allows a customer to obtain a coupon for that product that can be used at the checkout.
- Self-service gift cards, a credit-card-based device to vend gift cards to customers, freeing up sales associates for other tasks.

Register Coupons

Personalized register coupons are based on an individual's purchases. Checkout terminals can be programmed to print out price coupons on customer register receipts. The coupon can be either for a future purchase of a product just purchased or for a competitor product. For example, the purchase of Iams dog food might generate a coupon for Kal Kan dog food.

Loyalty Programs

Loyalty programs encourage loyal buying behavior by rewarding custom-ers for their purchases. Loyalty programs issue a "membership card" to an individual shopper. These are also called rewards cards, points cards, or club cards. Cards typically have a bar code or magnetic strip that can be easily scanned in order to track an individual's purchases. After a cer-tain number of purchases (such as the purchase of 10 cups of coffee) or a certain amount of purchases (such as purchasing $200 worth of books at a bookstore), the shopper receives a reward such as a free product, a discount, or some other benefit on a future purchase. To join a loyalty program, a customer provides a certain level of demographic information which is then compared with his or her purchases, allowing for the col-lection of data that can be used to make marketing decisions. One store, for example, uses frequent shopper data to program handheld scanners that shoppers carry on their shopping trips, accessing special deals and promotions targeted just for them.

Measurement

Measurement of in-store media involves an assessment of both exposure to the message and reaction to the message. Three types of measurements can assess customer activity and thus exposure to messages:

- Traffic counters measure the actual number of people who enter a store. This can be done through technology such as a laser beam across a store entrance. The number can then help to generate the potential "reach" of an in-store vehicle, given that reach is defined as the opportunity to see the advertising in a given time frame.
- Video recognition systems such as wall-mounted cameras count the number of people who walk past a certain place in the store (generally the location of the in-store advertisement). This type of system can also track whether or not customers stopped to look at the message, and for how long, and can generate the total exposures, or impressions, for a specific media vehicle during a defined time period.
- Ceiling-based cameras can assign a unique numerical ID to each customer who enters the store and track the movements of each customer through the store, creating a log of the customer's activity and exposure to advertisements.

Data provided by the Point of Purchase Advertising Institute allow reach and frequency to be calculated. The average supermarket in the United States hosts 6,000 trips per week and the average trip has 1.25 people doing the shopping. Thus, the average exposure of an in-store sign per week is 7,500. The average household shops 1.5 times per week, and the number of unique visitors to the average supermarket is 5,000 per week with an average frequency of 1.5.

Therefore, the average frequency for an in-store campaign can be calculated by multiplying 1.5 times the number of weeks the campaign runs.

Like gross rating points, in-store rating points are calculated by multiplying reach by frequency. This can be used to compare cost measures as well on both a CPP and CPM basis.

Future of In-Store Media

It is highly likely that you'll be seeing more "personal" and less "mass" media in your local grocery store in the years to come. One technology being developed is a shopping cart with a small computer attached to the handle. The computers have cell-phone-style navigation buttons on the handle and a self-scanning feature to use at checkout.

GPS systems can direct you from your house to the store, and now technology is allowing for "in-store" GPS. One supermarket chain launched a mobile app that provides a database of the entire store's offerings, shows customers where restrooms and customer services kiosks are located, and directs consumers to the supermarket's most enticing promotional offers and sale items. It also reminds customers where they parked. The app takes advantage of multiple Wi-Fi hotspots in each store, since GPS does not work indoors.

The Innovation Lab at the international agency IPG has developed a device that transforms the front window of a store into a giant touch screen. Designed for use at retail clothing boutiques, it allows customers to interact with a screen to select outfits for a virtual avatar instead of looking at an outfit on a mannequin. A similar device developed by IPG is a mirror that enables a shopper to scan a dress and then project that clothing onto her body before going to the dressing room. The interactive screen allows the shopper to examine different colors of the clothing and find matching accessories. An image of the outfit can be posted on the shopper's Facebook page.

The retail floor is becoming a battlefield, and smart media planners will look for interesting and new ways to break through clutter to showcase products in the store aisles.

Chapter 22
Direct Response

Every piece of advertising should elicit a response. So, what is the difference between direct response media and just media? That is a question that the industry is wrestling with. There are many different views of it.

The Direct Marketing Association (DMA) has defined direct marketing as "any direct communication that is designed to generate a response in the form of an order, a request for further information and/or a visit to a store or other place of business for purchase of a specific product or service." Others view it as a measurable system of marketing that uses one or more advertising media to build transactions and a relationship database.

Direct response is different from other media in two areas. The first is that direct response media is an interactive marketing system. It links the buyer and the seller directly. Most advertising campaigns use media to help persuade consumers to take action. Direct response media is the conduit for action. Instead of asking you to go to a store to buy something, direct response media is a store where you can buy something.

The second area where direct response is different from other media is in how it is measured. Media are typically measured by how many people are reached. The advertising measurement is gauged in the form of brand measures as well as sales measures. But it assumes that advertising is one element of a broad array of tools for generating sales. Direct response media has an immediate and measurable response. This response can take many forms, from responding to a mail offer, to calling on the phone, or going to an online website. The point is that direct response media is measured based on the transaction rather than the reach.

Landscape of Direct Response

Is it any wonder that direct response media is a favorite among marketing directors? Unlike much of the advertising world, direct response is accountable. Managers know what their return on investment is. In a world where return on investment reigns supreme, direct response media is king.

That is why direct response is such a big business. As *Ad Age* reported in 2009, the CRM/direct marketing slice of the advertising agency pie is approximately $5 billion. It is 17.4 percent of the total advertising revenue ahead of digital, public relations, and promotion.

In fact, as Table 22.1 shows, the top-ranking CRM/direct response advertising agencies all have over $100 million in individual revenue. To put this in perspective, the top two agencies, Acxiom and Epsilon, are larger than the top two general market advertising agencies in the United States. The top revenue advertising agency in the United States is McCann Erickson with $450 million in revenue. Acxiom is nearly 50 percent larger than McCann Erickson while Epsilon is comparable in size.

The other fact is that direct response has been an increasingly growing part of the advertising mix. It has made steady gains while other media have shrunk. Direct response, once the bastion of mail order or interesting late-night television products, has now moved mainstream. Large national advertisers such as Proctor and Gamble have used direct response to market some of their larger brands.

Role of Database Marketing

The rise of direct response is tied to the use of database marketing. Database marketers build and maintain a vast amount of information on current and prospective customers. With the increase of available personal information and the ability to aggregate this information via computer technology, marketers can communicate with individuals in a personal manner using a variety of media.

A good database enables marketers to profile and segment their customers and prospects. It provides them with the knowledge of who their customers and prospects are, when they have purchased, how much they have purchased, and how to best communicate with them.

This leads to the CRM, or customer relationship management programs that direct response campaigns are tied to. Direct response is associated with generating an initial sale whereas a CRM program is associated with subsequent sales. In building more and more sales from the same customer, the marketer begins to build a relationship with that customer. The more purchase history, the more the marketer can anticipate what the customer needs or wants. This is why direct response and CRM play such a large role in many integrated marketing communication programs.

By properly profiling or segmenting the database, the marketer can gain efficiencies of the marketing dollar that are difficult to achieve any other way. One of the basic ways that database marketers segment their custom-

Table 22.1

Top 100 CRM/Direct Marketing Agencies by Revenue

Rank	Agency	U.S. revenue (millions)
1	Acxiom Corp	$632
2	Epsilon	$488
3	Rapp	$340
4	OgilvyOne	$300
5	DraftFCB	$297
6	Wunderman	$262
7	Merkle	$233
8	Aspen Marketing Service	$156
9	Rosetta	$152
10	The Agency Inside Haute-Hearnes	$141

ers is through the RFM method. RFM stands for recency, frequency, and monetary. It is used to identify the best customers and the ones most likely to buy again. Those best customers are typically those who have bought recently and frequently, and spend the most money. Through this type of segmentation, a marketer can elect to serve the most profitable customers.

By using the database as a learning tool, markets can constantly test different media, offers, and creative messages (creatives) to constantly improve their return on investment.

Types of Direct Response

Advertising that asks the consumer to provide feedback directly to the sender is termed *direct response advertising*. Any medium can be used for direct response advertising. Whereas the most commonly used direct response media are direct mail, catalogs, and television, there is a growing array of digital media that correspond to each of their traditional counterparts.

Table 22.2 shows the traditional and digital direct response media for the broadcast, print, mail, out-of-home, and directory categories. Let's discuss each category and how digital media have expanded the direct response universe.

Broadcast

Who hasn't seen an infomercial? Infomercials are those 30- or 60-minute paid programs on television that are selling everything from fitness equipment to kitchen appliances to get-rich-quick schemes. Direct response television is largely associated with the Ron Propeils of the world (think Veggiematic, pocket fisherman, etc.). Still, many brands use direct response television as

Table 22.2

Traditional and Digital Media of Direct Response

Category	Traditional	Digital
Broadcast	DRTV & radio	Video/Audio podcasts
Print	FSI	iPad
Mail	Direct mail	E-mail
	Catalogs	E-commerce
Out-of-Home	Take one's	Interactive kiosks
Directory	Telephone book	Search engine marketing

a key part of their marketing mix. Some recent large brands that use direct response (DR) television include Dell, Allstate, and Tide.

Radio is also a large direct response medium. Like television, radio has paid programming that provides content and then sells a product. Radio is also the home of radio announcers or commentators such as Dave Ramsey who pitches a wide variety of products.

On the digital side, video and audio podcasts are popular ways to gain traction in the marketplace. A number of media outlets provide free content in video or audio podcasts as a means of enticing consumers to subscribe to their paid content. The *Wall Street Journal, Barron's,* and other media outlets regularly provide podcasts as a marketing means to gain future subscribers.

Print

Print has always had a number of direct response advertisers that feature coupons or toll-free numbers as response mechanisms. Print is also the delivery mechanism for large-scale couponing efforts and product inserts.

The recent introduction of the iPad and similar devices takes print into a new realm of direct response. Traditional one-dimensional print ads can now be dynamic, where consumers can click on a website on the ad to purchase the product directly. The iPad is a convergent media delivery system that combines the best of brand media with direct response.

Mail

Direct mail is the grandfather of direct response advertising. Nearly a quarter of all direct response advertising is spent on some form of direct mail. Next to direct mail, catalogs are the next largest category of direct response. Catalogs are a huge business with nearly 10 billion catalogs hitting the mail every year.

As paper and postal costs increase, marketers are turning more to digital alternatives for mail activity. E-mail marketing is a growing category of direct response. E-mail is easy to execute and extremely cost efficient. However, with the increase in spam and more sophisticated spam filters, nonpermission-based e-mail is rapidly falling out of favor with marketers. However, permission e-mail is one of the staples of a multiple-channel direct response plan. Just like mail moving to e-mail, catalogs are moving to digital catalogs and sophisticated e-commerce websites. Many retailers have an e-tail component to their business, which is driven by direct response media.

Out-of-Home

Most people think of billboards when they think of out-of-home media. But there are a number of direct response mechanisms that are outside the home. The simple "take-ones" that are omnipresent at retailers and other public venues is an example of an out-of-home tactic. Billboards that feature a text response can be made into an effective direct response vehicle.

Digitally, interactive kiosks found in shopping malls or at ballparks are examples of how electronic forms of an old medium can breathe new life into a response vehicle.

Directory

Direct response is not always the most glamorous media. That is so true of the directory category. Telephone yellow pages are an old but still effective direct response vehicle. Whereas paper directories are on the wane, their electronic counterparts such as Internet Yellow Pages and Mobile Search are rapidly gaining traction. Obviously, the most used direct response vehicle today is search engine marketing. Business searches on Google alone are a dominant form of direct response.

Measurement and Cost

Unlike other media, direct response media has its own measurement system and currency. Most media are purchased based on cost-per-thousand. The media audience has a certain cost-per-thousand (CPM) value. Multiplying the audience by the CPM yields the media unit cost. The measure of efficiency, then, is how low the CPM is. The idea of a media plan is to reach the most consumers for the least amount of money.

Direct response media, on the other hand, is not based on CPM. It is based on a cost-per-response. That cost-per-response can be a cost-per-lead or it can be a cost-per-sale. The key concept, though, is that every media vehicle purchased is based on a behavioral cost.

Success in the direct response world is based on driving down the cost per lead or sale. Unlike other media, the idea of direct response is to get the most leads or sales for the least amount of money. This may actually mean reaching fewer consumers overall but reaching more active consumers.

To understand what those costs are, most direct response campaigns have a test phase where the media buyer allocates funds to a variety of media or vehicles within a specific medium. Based on this initial investment, the media buyer then determines the optimum cost-per-lead or sale from which to bench-mark future costs. Rather than negotiate with the media based on a CPM, the media buyer will negotiate based on a cost-per-lead or sale. The media partner is rewarded based on sales or activity rather than on total audience.

Table 22.3 provides an example of a direct response direct television analysis for a fictitious product, Hypo Exercise, priced at $50. As you can see, the media buyer purchased programs in a variety of dayparts. Each program in those dayparts has a specific unit cost. For example, the M–F 9a–7p daypart has a unit cost of $300. The balance of the analysis is the response. Just reading across, the M–F 9a–7p program generated 30 leads. By dividing the leads by the unit cost of $300, you get a cost-per-lead (CPL) of $10. The next column shows the percentage of those 30 consumers who purchased the product. In this case, it is 40 percent or 12 customers. Those 12 customers each bought a $50 Hypo Exercise product so that the total sale for this commercial in this daypart is $600. The return on investment (ROI) is 100 percent. A commercial was purchased for $300 that generated $600 of sales. Another way to evaluate it is that it cost $25 for every sale made.

So, this particular daypart was very successful. Contrast this with the next daypart, M–Su 5p–12a. Here the buyer paid $600 for a commercial yet only generated $625 of sales. In this case, the sales barely covered the cost of the media purchased. This particular media placement was not nearly as effective as the prior one.

Armed with this information, the media buyer knows that the average cost-per-lead is $15. Forty-two percent of those leads convert to sales with the average cost-per-sale at $35. The media buyer may work with the media to set a benchmark on the cost-per-lead to be no greater than $15 or even lower. And the media buyer may tell the television media partner that because certain dayparts work much better than others he or she will purchase more commercials in the better-performing dayparts.

This type of analysis and concept can be used with every medium. So, in the interactive area, it may be a cost-per-click and then a cost-per-sale. In the print area, it would be a cost-per-lead and then a cost-per-sale. Other

Table 22.3

Direct Response Direct TV Analysis
HYPO Exercise Product $50

Daypart		Cost	Leads	CPL	Conversion (%)	Sales*	ROI (%)	Cost per sale
M–F	9a–7p	$300	30	$10	40	$600	100	$25.00
M–Su	5p–12a	$600	25	$24	50	$625	4	$48.00
M–Su	12a–12p	$200	25	$8	30	$375	88	$26.67
S/S	10a–5p	$400	20	$20	50	$500	25	$40.00
		$1,500	100	$15	42	$2,100	40	$34.90

Source: Advertising Age, April 26, 2010.
   *Conversion × $50

media would also be the same. Direct response advertisers view each media purchase in two ways. The first is, how much did they make for each advertisement? The second is the learning gained from each media placement. Each placement opportunity is one step closer to optimizing their investment.

The push and pull of purchasing direct response advertising is different from a brand or promotional message. In the case of the latter, the media placement is done at a specific time when the message is most relevant. For direct response, the placement is done based on making the most money regardless of the time. If that means scheduling all your broadcast ads after midnight, then so be it.

The direct response media buyer is evaluating media based on cost and response. If prices get too high on a highly responsive media vehicle, the media buyer will not agree to place the schedule. It is better to save the dollars rather than to purchase media inventory where you will not make a profit.

This type of media purchase strategy is the opposite of a brand strategy. In the brand strategy, you look to purchase media that is popular with consumers. This may be high-demand media where lots of advertisers are supporting the media vehicle. In direct response, you look to purchase media that has weak advertising demand. The weaker the demand, the more likely you are to gain a favorable rate where you can make the most profit.

Creative Units

As we have discussed, direct response advertising is different from brand advertising. Brand advertising is designed to continue to build goodwill over time. It is a cumulative effect. Direct response advertising needs to pay out each time it runs.

Because of these differences, direct response creative units are more involving than brand messages. It is unlikely that a direct response advertiser can develop a compelling story and a call to action in a 15-second television commercial. Yet brand advertisers regularly use this length of unit to communicate brand differences.

Size may not necessarily make a difference in print advertising. A small space ad with a phone number or mailing address that is properly targeted may elicit as much response as a large full-page advertisement. Or a quarter-page ad with a coupon may generate as many takers as a full-page advertisement. Every brand and offer is unique.

Determining the optimum creative message, offer and size or length are key variables that direct response advertisers continually test. Combined with the media placement, these become the test cells for a direct response campaign.

Where there are key creative unit implications for the media team is in the broadcast category. There are three types of creative units. There are short-form units, long-form units, and paid programming. Short-form units are commercials that are 30 or 60 seconds in length. These are commercial units that are also popular with brand messages. Long-form units are commercials that are 2 minutes, 5 minutes, or other lengths of time. They are longer than standard lengths but they are not paid programming. Paid programming is purchasing a 30-minute or an hour program of time.

The logical extension of long-form commercials is an entire network devoted to direct selling. The *Home Shopping Network* and *QVC* are the two dominant networks that have provided a forum for product sales of all types over the past decade. Everything from jewelry to collectibles to general merchandise is sold on the airwaves.

The tenet of direct response is to continually look for opportunities where you can maximize the return on investment. This means that the media team as well as the creative team is constantly seeking ways to improve performance.

Future of Direct Response

Direct response has moved from a specialty advertising area to a mainstream one. The growth of direct response should outpace that of brand advertising in the coming years. There are a few trends that are fueling that growth.

Convergence of Media

There is no doubt that we are in the midst of a convergent media revolution. With new devices that combine the emersion of print, the emotion of broadcast, and the response of the Internet, all media types can be interactive. Print ads can be opened up directly to buy products on a website. Television programs will offer point-and-click technology for deeper dives and product purchase. Radio will have voice-activated purchasing opportunities. So, direct response will morph into the call to action for much of what was traditional brand advertising.

Mobile Media

The rise of mobile media will greatly enhance direct response capabilities. By triangulating your location through your cell phone, marketers will be able to push offers to you as you drive or walk by a store. With greater access to media content via mobile phones, the ability to add this geo-targeting dimension to existing content is a marketer's dream come true.

Mobile Payment

The ability for consumers to pay for goods and services whenever or wherever they want is another boon to the direct response world. As technology accelerates the accessibility coupled with safety and privacy of electronic payments, the opportunity to make a sale is greatly enhanced.

In summary, direct response media is very different from other media. Whereas all media can become direct response, in the way it is bought, sold, and measured direct response is very different from other media types. Direct response is rapidly moving forward as a mainstream marketing method. As technology advances, there is no doubt that direct response will be a crucial part of every marketer's planning arsenal.

Chapter 23

Alternative Media

"Alternative Media" is in some ways a catchall term for various types of media opportunities that don't fit easily into other categories discussed in this book. A better definition, though, is that alternative media are those opportunities that are generally not part of the primary targeted campaign but are used:

- for a special, one-time promotion such as a product launch
- to reach a specific (and generally hard-to-reach) audience
- to deliver a message through a nontraditional media channel

The term *alternative media* is now used interchangeably with the term *guerilla marketing,* which was invented as an unconventional system of promotions that relies on time, energy, and imagination rather than a big marketing budget. These messages, appearing in unexpected places, may surprise the viewer (in a positive way) and thus form a positive impression. They may also get public relations and press coverage. Today, though, alternative campaigns may cost as much as traditional media. Many types of media vehicles start out as alternative vehicles but then move into the mainstream as they gain in popularity. Advertising in video games, for example, started out as an alternative medium and now is considered a mainstream vehicle.

The brand team often works directly with the organization that creates the alternative media opportunity. Both planning and gaining approval for alternative media require some creativity on the part of the planner. Specifically, the planner must be able to compare the pros, cons, and the media value, of an alternative medium to a traditional medium that the client understands (and likely utilizes). Often, this type of comparison must be done in the absence of any strong metrics other than those provided by the medium itself—third-party measurement of alternative media is rare.

Types of Alternative Media

Companies are coming up with new ideas on where to place advertisements all the time. These innovative practices do fall into some clear categories, though, which we discuss here.

Ambient Media

Ambient media messages are delivered via an object. In some ways, ambient media are the next step in the evolution of outdoor advertising, where messages are provided to consumers outside of the home at a microlevel (see Tables 23.1 and 23.2). Instead of being exposed to a passing message on a billboard, consumers are exposed to the message while they are using the object that is carrying the message. In general, the object (such as a coffee cup sleeve) serves some primary purpose other than providing a media channel. For some ambient media, customers carry the object and the message with them as they move through their day. This allows for message exposure to others whom they meet as they walk down the street or ride the elevator to their job. A coffee sleeve, for example, is viewed by one primary user (the coffee drinker) and up to six secondary users.

Ambient media opportunities are found in the following locations.

Restaurants and Coffee Shops

These messages are often for local businesses other than the coffee shop or restaurant where the object was distributed, but can also be used for national campaigns. Because these objects are often carried away from the establishment, the messages on them may include URLs or phone numbers so people can act on the message. Often people are surprised to see a message for a brand other than the one at the place where the food was purchased, which increases interest and involvement. Placements don't stop at paper objects, though; one company sells sponsored messages in fortune cookies.

Nightclubs and Bars

These messages reach younger consumers in a social setting, and are often taken from the venue as a memento of the evening.

Table 23.1

Alternative Media Opportunities

	Ambient media	Public space marketing	Wait marketing
Restaurants/coffee shops	Nightclubs and bars		
Coffee sleeves	Drink coasters	Stenciled messages	Gas station pump video
Napkins	Swizzle sticks	Painted messages with nonpermanent paints	Doctor's office video
Napkin dispensers	Bar glasses	Removable stickers	Vet office video
Carry-out containers	Matchbooks		Post office video
Pizza boxes	Mints		
	Condom sleeves		

Pharmacies

Messages are placed on the bags that hold prescription drugs purchased in pharmacies. The benefits are similar to those of ambient media in restaurants, with the added benefit of having an implied endorsement from the pharmacy. If the prescription is picked up inside the pharmacy, the customer will be carrying a personal billboard serving as a reminder message as he or she walks to the front door. Pharmacy bag advertising has been seen as particularly effective when advertising pharmaceutical products or promoting brands related to health care and welfare.

Schools

Messages can be placed on book covers teachers provide students in libraries and classrooms. Messages are exposed to students every time they pick up their texts.

Clothing

Although brands have been putting their names on clothing they sell for decades, a new twist has emerged where brands are paying people to wear their branded clothing. KFC, for example, paid college women to wear sweatpants with the logo for the Double Down sandwich product on the seat of the sweatpants.

Public Space Marketing

Similar to outdoor advertising, public space marketing provides a message in an outdoor, public location. The difference is that instead of using a preprinted poster, messages are placed on sidewalks using nonpermanent techniques. Placed at high-traffic locations, they receive a high level of attention and can generate buzz. *Allure* magazine, for example, used stickers to announce the availability of a new issue; placed near newsstands, they direct customers to purchase.

Wait Marketing

Building on the popularity of in-store advertising at the checkout counter, several companies have developed media channels to reach people while they are waiting in line. This captive audience is usually receptive to messages, most likely because there is nothing else to do while waiting. Ad messages are integrated into existing content (such as ESPN and CNN reports), and often ads are for products sold at nearby stores (such as the store affiliated with a gas station).

Word-of-Mouth Advertising

Whereas word of mouth (WOM) is not new, the action of providing messages delivered from one person to another person is growing in popularity. This can happen either in person (when one individual delivers a message to a friend, colleague, or family member) or electronically, when it is known as eWOM.

Word of mouth marketing can happen organically. When customers are very happy with a product, service, or retail establishment, they tell people they know about it, and that endorsement is a positive motivation for others to consider that purchase or store as well. Paid WOM involves recruiting individuals to use and promote the product to their families, friends, and colleagues, or perhaps even to strangers. Depending on the type of campaign, the individuals may or may not disclose that they are part of the promotion.

The firm BzzAgent, for example, solicits individuals to become "buzz agents" for different products. The buzz agents are sent new products (such as a new book release) and tell friends and family about the product, and/ or write a review at the buzz agent website. Agents write reports covering who they told and what they said, and receive incentives and prizes for their participation.

Table 23.2

Key Players in Alternative Media

Ambient media	Public space marketing/Street marketing	Wait marketing	Word-of-mouth
GoGorilla	GoGorilla	Gas station TV	BzzAgent
Street Factory Media, and Attack!	Massive Media	MediaLife networks and Norvision	Avenue A/ Razorfish

The key elements of a word of mouth campaign involve finding the appropriate people to talk about the product, that is, people who are good communicators and who, in general, have large networks of acquaintances. Providing these people not only with products but also with product information allows them to create a review or a recommendation that is persuasive. Monitoring the activities, such as the reports that are written for BzzAgent, is also important. You want to be able to track how the WOM is moving through the networks. As a result, these types of campaigns are not inexpensive, with campaigns using 1,000 agents priced at a minimum of $150,000.

Street Marketing

This new type of alternative media delivers messages to a specific audience via a team either performing a service or distributing product at a specific venue. This differs from traditional sampling (where one individual passes out free samples to passersby) in that consumers are encouraged to spend time engaged in the marketing experience to receive the branded messages. These events usually occur at high-traffic shopping districts, parks and beaches, busy downtown work areas, and nightclubs and bars.

Street marketing is, in a way, the sponsored version of something known as a "flash mob," which is a large group of people who assemble suddenly in a public place, perform an unusual and pointless act for a brief time, then disperse. The term *flash mob* is generally applied only to gatherings organized via telecommunications, social media, or viral e-mails, not advertisers.

To promote a new drink, the beverage marketer Fuze worked with their agency to send costumed street teams throughout New York on a double-decker bus. The bus advertised the drink, and dropped the teams off at various sites around the city where they put on a performance showing how two things come together (green and black tea).

Table 23.3

Comparing Alternative Media to Other Media

Medium	Compare to
Ambient media	Specialty outdoor, such as taxi tops
Public space marketing	Outdoor, such as transit shelters
Wait marketing	In-store media such as video at checkout, outdoor media such as video at airports
Word-of-mouth marketing	Direct response
Street marketing	Direct response, outdoor

Measurement

These alternative vehicles are rarely part of any third-party monitoring program, and so the firm itself must generate the data you receive. Look closely at their estimates and see if they seem to make sense to you, and then look for comparable media to make CPM comparisons (see Table 23.3 for some places to start).

What is the future of alternative media? Stated simply, anything goes. Brands and agencies will work together to find unique and interesting user experiences, to introduce new brands, and to strengthen customer loyalty. Creativity is key, and creative media planners can blaze the trail in this area.

Chapter 24
Ethnic Media

Although advertisers talk about ethnic media, the types of media used are the same as for all other advertising: broadcast, print, Internet, social media, and so on. The term *ethnic media* refers to media vehicles that target particular subgroups of the population such as members of ethnic groups, speakers of foreign languages, members of certain religions, and similar specialized audiences.

Television

Television is usually considered a mass medium, that is, one that reaches a broad cross-section of the population, which it does, but there are specialized programs aiming at certain audiences as well as specialized networks. Spanish-language television networks include Univision and Telemundo, along with several others, and there are networks with specialized programming such as ESPN Deportes. Some specialized television programs are also aimed at the Spanish-speaking audience, particularly on local channels in certain markets. Table 24.1 displays the top Spanish television markets. Los Angeles is the largest Hispanic or Latino market, and several other markets are listed that are not ranked as high in terms of general-audience size as they are in ranking as Hispanic markets.

Table 24.2 shows the top 25 African American markets in the United States, and as you can see, New York tops the list of the largest African American market as well as the largest market overall; but the number-two African American market is Atlanta, which ranks only eighth overall. Because of the predominance of the African American population in some markets, programming aimed at this group is only natural.

In addition, there are a few television stations in the United States that broadcast in a foreign language, such as Korean, Japanese, and some Chinese dialects, in markets where there are many residents who have emigrated from

Table 24.1

Hispanic Markets

Total U.S. Hispanic TV households number 12,950,000, or 11.27% of all U.S. TV households (HH), which total 114,900,000.

Rank	DMA rank	Market	Hispanic TV HH	DMAs % of total U.S. Hispanic TV HH	Cumulative % total U.S. Hispanic TV HH	Hispanic TV HH % of DMA HH
1	2	Los Angeles, CA	1,868,200	14.426	14.43	33.01
2	1	New York, NY	1,251,460	9.663	24.09	16.70
3	17	Miami–Fort Lauderdale, FL	666,230	5.144	29.23	43.32
4	10	Houston, TX	561,390	4.335	33.57	26.44
5	5	Dallas–Ft. Worth, TX	506,020	3.907	37.48	19.89
6	3	Chicago, IL	492,170	3.800	41.28	14.06
7	12	Phoenix, AZ	391,770	3.025	44.30	20.91
8	37	San Antonio, TX	388,800	3.002	47.30	46.84
9	6	San Francisco–Oakland–San Jose, CA	382,460	2.953	50.26	15.28
10	87	Harlingen–Weslaco–Brownsville–McAllen, TX	294,640	2.275	52.53	83.20
11	20	Sacramento–Stockton–Modesto, CA	264,100	2.039	54.57	18.80
12	44	Albuquerque–Santa Fe, NM	248,590	1.920	56.49	35.82
13	55	Fresno–Visalia, CA	240,950	1.861	58.35	41.60
14	28	San Diego, CA	239,520	1.850	60.20	22.31
15	16	Denver, CO	234,750	1.813	62.01	15.25
16	98	El Paso, TX	222,800	1.720	63.73	71.70
17	19	Orlando–Daytona Beach–Melbourne, FL	202,710	1.565	65.30	13.93
18	14	Tampa–St. Petersburg (Sarasota), FL	194,490	1.502	66.80	10.77
19	4	Philadelphia, PA	189,490	1.463	68.26	6.41
20	9	Washington, DC (Hagerstown, MD)	184,970	1.428	69.69	7.92

Source: Television Bureau of Advertising.

Table 24.2

Top 25 African American (A-A) Markets and Their Television Consumption

Rank	DMA rank	Market	A-A TV HH	DMAs % of total U.S. A-A TV HH	Cumulative % total U.S. A-A TV HH
1	1	New York	1,257,450	9.2	9.2
2	8	Atlanta	634,820	4.7	13.9
3	3	Chicago	599,620	4.4	18.3
4	9	Washington, DC (Hagerstown)	557,930	4.1	22.3
5	4	Philadelphia	527,930	3.9	26.2
6	2	Los Angeles	487,590	3.6	29.8
7	11	Detroit	391,600	2.9	32.6
8	10	Houston	350,360	2.6	35.2
9	5	Dallas–Ft. Worth	341,800	2.5	37.7
10	16	Miami–Ft. Lauderdale	297,580	2.2	39.9
11	24	Baltimore	294,390	2.2	42.1
12	28	Raleigh–Durham (Fayetteville)	281,090	2.1	44.1
13	47	Memphis	261,000	1.9	46.0
14	42	Norfolk–Portsmouth–Newport News	223,170	1.6	47.7
15	17	Cleveland–Akron (Canton)	214,170	1.6	49.2
16	25	Charlotte	204,140	1.5	50.7
17	21	St. Louis	194,030	1.4	52.1
18	40	Birmingham (Anniston, Tuscaloosa)	176,240	1.3	53.4
19	6	San Francisco–Oakland–San Jose	175,400	1.3	54.7
20	19	Orlando–Daytona Beach–Melbourne	168,630	1.2	56.0
21	13	Tampa–St. Petersburg (Sarasota)	163,940	1.2	57.2
22	59	Richmond–Petersburg	155,240	1.1	58.3
23	53	New Orleans	154,930	1.1	59.4
24	90	Jackson, MS	147,020	1.1	60.5
25	81	Columbia, SC			

Source: Media Information Center.

those countries. There are also television stations that rebroadcast programs that originate in other countries.

Radio

Because it is less expensive to operate a radio station than it is to run a television station, and because there are many more radio stations in the United States than there are television stations, there are quite a few radio stations that program in a foreign language. Table 24.3 shows how many radio stations operate in each language.

Radio stations can also be owned by groups who wish to promote certain views or values, such as labor unions, religious groups, political contributors, and others.

Newspapers

Foreign-language newspapers have been around since the earliest days of settling the Western Hemisphere. Still today, newspapers in this country are published in a wide variety of languages, including Arabic, Chinese, Danish, Dutch, French, German, Italian, Japanese, Korean, Norwegian, Portuguese, Russian, Spanish, Swedish, and even Urdu.

Of course, there are also newspapers aimed at certain ethnic groups, such as African Americans. By some estimates, there are more than 250 such newspapers and similar publications, and there are even groups or chains of African American newspapers.

As was the case with radio, some newspapers are also owned by and aimed at certain political affiliations, labor unions, and religious groups. Newspapers published in other countries are also shipped to and sold in the United States.

Magazines

Some magazines, like other mass media, are also intended for certain ethnic groups. Several large magazines are aimed at or owned by African American interests, and as you can see in Table 24.4, not all of these magazines are edited with only the African American audience in mind, such as *Soap Opera Weekly, Soap Opera Digest,* and *O, The Oprah Magazine.*

There are also several magazines published in the United States in foreign languages, but many magazines published in other countries are also shipped to the United States. With newspapers, the coverage is usually timely, but

Table 24.3

Number of Foreign-Language Radio Stations in the United States

Hispanic	1,339
Chinese	9
Polish	7
Korean	6
Greek	4
Italian	4
Russian	3
Hindi	2
Japanese	2
German	1
Hungarian	1
Iranian	1
Pakistani	1
Punjabi	1
Romanian	1
Slovak/Czech	1
Slovenian	1
Ukrainian	1
Vietnamese	1

Source: Station programming descriptions.

Table 24.4

Top Magazines by African American Audience Composition

	Percentage of total readership that is African American
Jet	95.1
Black Enterprise	92.8
Ebony	89.7
Essence	87.0
Vibe	68.8
Source	54.0
Soap Opera Weekly	34.3
Entrepreneur	33.2
GQ (Gentlemen's Quarterly)	27.0
Soap Opera Digest	26.1
Esquire	25.7
O, The Oprah Magazine	23.4

Source: Publication claims and U.S. Census data.

with magazines, the coverage may be less timely or may use feature stories that have little time relevance, so the importation of magazines is more widespread than it is for newspapers.

Other Media

In regions or neighborhoods with large populations of foreign-language speakers, there are business signs in those languages. Certainly there are thousands of Internet sites originating in the United States that use languages other than English, and because the Internet is so easy to access throughout the world, foreign-language websites are readily available to U.S. residents. Religious groups, political parties, labor unions, local political-action groups, interest groups, and every other imaginable kind of interest or view also has Internet information available. With the growth of new media and social media, these ethnic interests are likely to be served even better and more specifically in the future.

Chapter 25

Sponsorships

As the presence of advertising messages on all types of media continues to grow, advertisers look for ways to break through the clutter and have their brand stand out from other advertisers. One way that brands can do this is through a sponsorship, defined as a unique marketing relationship between an advertiser (or a brand) and an event or organization. The brand provides funds, resources, or services to the event or organization and in return, the brand is provided with an association to the event or organization. This association generally includes some type of advertising as well as other types of promotional considerations.

Sponsorships are different from other media purchases in several ways:

- Sponsorships are a marketing as well as an advertising activity. A brand sponsors an event, say, a football team or a performer, because it is more interested in furthering the brand/business goals than it is in finding an efficient media purchase. For example, a brand may wish to show commitment and support for the city the brand is located in by sponsoring a local professional sports team. For that reason, many marketers make these commitments on their own instead of through their agency.
- Sponsorships may contain a media schedule or they may not. Media may or may not be the most important aspect of the sponsorship.
- Sponsorships are single focused: If you want your brand associated with the Academy Awards, for example, you have only one option. This is unlike other media where there are plenty of options to consider.
- Sponsorships are big commitments in terms of time and dollars. Many sponsorships involve multiyear commitments. Sponsorships of sports teams or leagues can be in the tens of millions of dollars.

The Sponsorship Landscape

Sponsorships are integral parts of many brands' promotional strategies. The term *sponsorship* can cover many types of marketing activities. In

2009, *Product Placement News* reported that U.S. consumers' events spending, including event sponsorship and event marketing, totaled $21 billion. Sports sponsorships totaled an additional $28 billion, making the sponsorship market almost a third of the size of the advertising market. These budget numbers are not surprising because there are many different types of sponsorships. When you hear the word sponsorship, you may think of NASCAR race car drivers with their logo-laden fire suits. But sponsorships go far beyond that. For example, a single brand can sponsor an event, such as the Budweiser Boxing Series. A sponsorship can be for a company or for a brand. Kraft Foods, for example, sponsors the Kraft Nabisco Championship on the Ladies' PGA Tour. A Kraft brand, Crystal Light, is one of several brands that sponsor the Lilith Fair musical tour. Brands can also sponsor major league sports teams, charitable causes (like the Susan G. Komen Race for the Cure), individual performers and athletes (such as skateboarder Tony Hawk), and award shows (such as the Grammy Awards), conferences (like South by Southwest, or SXSW), and a range of local and regional events like parades, street fairs, and school events.

Types of Sponsorships

Sponsorship possibilities are virtually unlimited, and there are numerous ways to think about sponsorships.

Team Sponsorships

With a team sponsorship (see Exhibit 25.1), brands sponsor professional or amateur teams over the course of the teams' seasons. These sponsorships include a mix of messages for the brand, such as television and radio advertisements, sponsor logo on printed matter such as newspaper ads and programs, signs inside the stadium, and uniform logos. Brands receive continuous exposure over a specific period of time which may increase involvement in the brand. If the audience likes the event (and end up with positive feelings toward the event), they are more likely to have positive feelings toward the sponsoring brand. A winning team can also promote positive feelings toward a brand, but the converse is also true: When a team does badly over a season and fans are upset, the brand could experience similar negative feelings. Additionally, indiscretions among individuals on the team may also damage the sponsoring brand.

Exhibit 25.1

Regional Network Radio Sponsorship Example: Bi-Mart/Oregon Ducks Football

Advertisers in the Pacific Northwest such as Bi-Mart purchase sponsorship of the Oregon Ducks on the Oregon Sports Network. This includes:

- Sports on all live football broadcasts on 21 station networks in both regular and post season
- Spots rotated through play-by-play, pre-game, and post-game
- Up to 10 live reads and billboards throughout the game, about 10 seconds each
- Sponsorship mention in game-day football program
- Sponsorship mention in stadium

League Sponsorships

Similar to a team sponsorship, a brand can sponsor an entire league such as Major League Baseball. League sponsors are allowed to refer to themselves as the "official" brand of that sports league in their category, and receive on-site signage and advertising during high-profile events with high ratings such as playoffs, all-star games, and championship games (see Exhibit 25.2).

Event Sponsorship

Brands also sponsor events of short duration, such as an awards show or a music festival. These events build awareness quickly, and can have a high level of impact as there is often significant promotion of the event before it occurs. Factors such as bad weather, for example, can hurt attendance at events, which minimizes the effectiveness of the sponsorship (see Exhibit 25.3).

Performer Sponsorships

Brands sponsor an individual performer or a group of performers, such as singers or actors (see Exhibit 25.4). For example, the brand helps to fund performances and is recognized at events for that support.

Exhibit 25.2

League Sponsorship: Everlast/Budweiser Boxing Series

Everlast is a sporting goods manufacturer which produces products such as boxing gloves, shoes, and apparel. Everlast sponsored the Budweiser Boxing Series, live professional boxing league broadcasts airing on three consecutive Saturday afternoons in May. For their sponsorship, Everlast received:

- 30 spots on broadcasts on both NBC and Telemundo networks
- Virtual, in-arena, and ring signage
- Guarantee that Everlast equipment, fight gloves, and apparel would be worn during the bouts

The broadcasts received ratings from 1.4 to 1.6, higher than expected, and performed especially well in Hispanic and African American markets.

Exhibit 25.3

Local Event Sponsorship Example: Columbia Sportswear/Portland Rose Festival

Columbia Sportswear, located in Portland, Oregon, sponsored the Portland Rose Festival, a four-day festival of arts and entertainment held over Memorial Day weekend on the Portland riverfront. Rose Festival sponsors receive:

- Thirty-second spots on broadcasts of events including the Rose Parade
- On-site sponsor mentions on banners and other signage
- Access to hospitality tents and VIP chalets
- Corporate tale sponsorship at auction event
- Event tickets to fireworks show and parade
- Website and program mentions

Exhibit 25.4

Performer Sponsorship Example: State Farm Insurance/OK Go

Indy pop band OK Go produced a video for their song "This Too Shall Pass" which featured a single-shot, Rube Goldberg machine storyline. The video took many months and 60 engineers to fully execute. Released on March 1, the video was streamed six million times within six days. The cost to State Farm was $150,000, and for that:

- A toy truck at the start of the video has a State Farm logo on it.
- At the end of the video, State Farm gets a wholly transparent "Thank You" screenshot from the band.
- Numerous mentions to appear in articles and press releases.

The sponsorship is part of State Farm's efforts to connect the brand with younger consumers; they have also sponsored a Spanish language band called Conjunto Raza Pedorosa.

Sponsorships within an Overall Media Buy

Brands spending specified amounts in certain programs may receive sponsorship credit. For example, a brand that runs a regular schedule on a television program may receive sponsorship identification (as in "this show is brought to you by . . ."), in that program (see Exhibit 25.5).

Measurement and Cost

Sponsorship costs vary greatly, depending on whether they are national, regional, or local, long term or short term, and whether they contain a media schedule or not. Additionally, an exclusive sponsorship (such as soft drink exclusivity for the entire broadcast of the Super Bowl) will cost more than partial exclusivity (sharing soft drink exclusivity with another soft drink). To say this another way: The overall value of a sponsorship is often based on factors other than the direct media cost. So even though the media team may be asked to weigh in on the media value of a sponsorship, the client and their marketing team often consider additional factors in deciding whether to commit to a sponsorship.

How should a media planner evaluate the sponsorship? First, assess the appropriateness of the target audience for the brand. Whereas sporting events

Exhibit 25.5

Network Prime Time Sponsorship Example: Subway/Chuck

The NBC prime time show *Chuck* was on the verge of cancellation in
2009 when NBC reached a sponsorship deal with the fast-food chain
Subway. As part of the agreement:

- 30 Subway ads ran on *Chuck*.
- Subway received product placement mentions on *Chuck*, including
  having characters sing the "Five Dollar Footlong" jingle and eat
  Subway sandwiches.
- Subway promoted the show in-store and in print ads.

usually skew toward men, some events may skew older and some may skew
younger. Community events most likely reach both men and women, often
with families and often upscale.

Next, track the popularity of the event over time. Is this an event that
is growing in popularity, is declining, or has remained static over time? A
growing audience means that the brand has the opportunity to be the start
of something that may continue to build and may result in a very strong
and impactful partnership. Look at the timing of the event to determine
how the sponsorship fit into existing (or planned) media schedules. Can
(and should) other planned media be cut back to utilize the media weight
from the sponsorship? Are there appropriate executions available for the
sponsorship?

Evaluate the other sponsors for the event. Are these sponsors ones
with similar targets and images comparable to your brand's image? Said
another way, will the other sponsors enhance your brand or detract from
your brand?

The next step is to evaluate each element in the sponsorship package in
order to estimate a media cost based on existing cost per thousand, or CPM,
estimates. Ways to do this include the following:

- Television and radio spot values can be estimated using either daypart
  CPMs for the network or local dayparts and ratings estimates.
- Television and radio "billboards," or sponsorship mentions, can be
  estimated at 25 percent to 33 percent of the CPM of a full 30-second
  ad, depending on the length of the sponsorship message.

- Print program costs can be estimated based on CPMs of comparable print vehicles (such as city magazines) and using the circulation and readership information provided by the sponsoring organization.
- Website mentions can be calculated using exposure metrics provided by the sponsoring organization.
- Stadium signage value can be estimated using CPMs for local outdoor and stadium attendance estimates.
- Ticket costs for various events can be provided by the sponsoring organization.

It is likely that the brand will pay a premium and such a premium should ensure some type of exclusivity for the sponsorship. Sponsorship premiums can range from 10 percent to 50 percent over the direct media estimates.

Future of Sponsorships

The sponsorship landscape is experiencing some changes, probably because of extended economic problems in the United States and the proliferation of sponsorship opportunities that have become available. Recently, some large brands have dropped some long-held sponsorships (such as FedEx and the Orange Bowl). Will a brand step up to replace FedEx? If not, we may see fewer "marquee" sponsorships like the FedEx Orange Bowl and more smaller, shared sponsorship opportunities. It is also likely that more sponsorship opportunities, like the *Chuck*/Subway sponsorship, will begin to come up in order to provide funding for television programming in the product placement model. There is likely to be a move to more global sponsorship opportunities as more brands become truly global brands. Also, the roles that social and mobile media will play in sponsorship are yet to be explored.

Many brands believe that the future of sponsorships is creating your own. Red Bull created its own art event. Budweiser creates its own network. So, there is a push by the marketer to really own these events. But because they are not efficient media buys, sponsorships must pay out in other ways. Determining these benefits, that is the real challenge.

Chapter 26
Sales Promotion

Sales promotion isn't a medium. Nor is it a special method of buying a medium such as direct response. Sales promotion is an activity to stimulate short demand for a product. Because most brands are under short-term pressure to perform, sales promotion activity is a large part of many brand's integrated marketing plans.

As a communication planner, you will be faced with planning, developing, and analyzing sales promotion activity. Even if you are not directly involved in that activity, the marketing director or brand manager will be weighing sales promotion activity and dollars versus that of alternative approaches to communication.

So what is the world of sales promotion? The term *sales promotion* can be misunderstood. Sometimes it is associated with advertising. Other times it is associated with publicity. Other times it is seen as a sales responsibility. The truth is that sales promotion can fall into a number of camps. Let's define what sales promotion is and how we treat it in the context of media planning.

Sales promotion is a direct inducement that offers extra incentives anywhere along the marketing route to accelerate the product's movement. There are two types of sales promotion, trade and consumer.

Trade Promotion

Trade promotion is called "push marketing." It is activities primarily designed to secure the cooperation of the retailer by the manufacturer. These activities may impact the consumer but they are aimed at the distribution channel.

Trade promotion is where the manufacturer provides an incentive to the retailer to feature its products. This can be as simple as discounts or other dollar incentives to stock or sell the product. Many times retailers will pass either all or part of this savings onto the consumer through a short-term sale or special.

Other trade incentives include advertising allowances either as a percentage of gross costs or as a fee where the retailer can purchase advertising that features the brand as well as other retailer private-label products.

Another popular trade promotion is a display allowance where the manufacturer pays a fee for in-store floor displays to promote the product.

Consumer Promotion

Consumer promotion is called "pull marketing." It is activities aimed at the consumer to persuade them to buy or request your brand now.

Consumer incentives can take a variety of forms. Normally they involve a direct incentive to buy now or buy more, visit a store, request literature, or take some form of action. The incentives can be money, prizes, gifts, or special information.

The idea behind a consumer promotion is to get the product off the shelf now. From a marketing standpoint, the idea behind consumer promotions is to accelerate the purchase process. This acceleration can be by incenting current customers to stock up or by trying to incent new customers to try the brand.

Of course you need to be aware of trade promotions because they do compete for your integrated marketing dollars. Nevertheless, the focus of this chapter is on consumer promotions. Consumer promotions can involve traditional media as well as alternative media channels. Regardless of the type of promotion, the goal of sales promotion is to make sales happen in the short term. That is the measure of success.

Landscape of Sales Promotion

Although most advertising and public relations agencies do sales promotion activity, there are specialists in this area. The agencies that specialize in sales promotion take this activity to a very high level.

Table 26.1 shows the top 10 sales promotion agencies in the United States based on revenue. These agencies are not as dominant as the direct response specialty agencies, but they are extremely large. Carlson Marketing, Mosaic Sales Solutions, and Integer Group all would be ranked in the top 20 advertising agencies in the United States.

Each of these agencies takes a bit of a different view on what sales promotion is. In the case of George P. Johnson, they view themselves as helping marketing create an experience. Their experiential marketing approach combines large-scale events with short-term promotional strategies. Carlson Marketing, on the other hand, combines customer relationship management with sales promotion activities so that they move into "brand engagement."

Table 26.1

Top Promotion Agencies by Revenue

Rank	Agency	Revenue (million)
1	Carlson Marketing	$166,400
2	Mosaic Sales Solutions	$133,000
3	Integer Group	$127,000
4	George P. Johnson	$123,460
5	Momentum Marketing	$114,000
6	Tracy Locke	$104,000
7	Marketing Arm	$100,000
8	Jack Morton	$80,000
9	GMR Marketing	$78,000
10	Octagon	$76,500

Source: Advertising Age, April 26, 2010.

Mosaic Sales Solutions specializes in the human resource side of sales promotion. They hire, train, and develop promotional solutions that require an extensive field force. This can be to man promotional booths, go door to door, or be an extension of a company's sales force for a short period of time.

The Integer Group is probably what most people think of when they think of sales promotion agencies. The Integer Group is an advertising agency that focuses on "the intersection between brand and sales." They develop retail promotions for manufacturers to move product off the shelf. They function as a marketing partner within a brand organization.

As you look at others on this top 10 list, you will find that sales promotion is a catchall for a variety of marketing communication activities. Every company defines their specific niche in their own way. Sales promotion does overlap with direct response advertising and event marketing. Because promotions are designed to elicit a response, there are elements of direct response used in sales promotion. Many times these responses yield customer names, so there can be a database component to sales promotion. And because promotions can take on large-scale events as a catalyst for consumer interaction, there can be an event component to sales promotion as well.

These varied companies are a reflection of the wide array of sales promotion activities available to today's marketer. Let's examine the most popular sales promotion types.

Types of Sales Promotion

The types of sales promotions available to a marketer are based on fulfilling several distinctive objectives. The more common objectives are: to gain consumer trial of the product, to reward brand loyalty, to encourage a consumer to trade up and to stimulate the consumer to buy more of the brand. These are all offensive marketing strategies. Defensively, a marketer might use promotional tactics so that other brands don't steal share when they are also implementing promotions. The sections below cover the key promotional strategies that fulfill these objectives.

The role of media planning in sales promotion strategies may be to find the best medium to deliver the strategy or to find a media partner to best execute a strategy. Much of the sales promotion media strategy is to determine the role of in-store versus outside media.

Couponing

Sales promotion is sometimes defined by couponing. A coupon is a certificate that provides a value that when presented to a retailer will offer a discount on the specific product purchased. There are approximately 300 billion coupons in distribution in the United States, yet only about one percent are actually redeemed.

The media role in providing coupon support is to find the most effective means of distributing the coupons. This may be through a wide variety of media. Newspapers, magazines, door to door, on packages, and direct mail are all options for coupon distribution. There are specific media vehicles whose sole function is to provide coupons. One of the largest is Valassis Corporation, which provides the free-standing insert (FSI) that contains coupons found in your Sunday newspaper.

A rapidly growing distribution point for coupons is online. Online shopping sites such as coupon.com, couponmom.com, and yahooshopping.com are but a few of the large number of websites where consumers can get coupons.

There are a number of coupon methods that involve in-store media. Many supermarkets have interactive touch-screen kiosks where consumers can load up their store membership card with electronic coupons. Coupon dispensers can be put at the point of purchase so that consumers can simply hit a button and a coupon will be available as they buy the product.

To incent consumers to switch brands, Catalina Marketing offers a coupon method where you receive coupons at the checkout stand. Coupons are dispensed based on the category you purchased but for a brand you didn't purchase. For example, suppose you bought Crest toothpaste. You may then get a coupon at the cashier for Colgate once you have checked out.

Mobile couponing is a burgeoning area where you use your mobile phone to scan the bar code of the products you are purchasing. Based on your purchase habits, you may be rewarded with a coupon that you can then scan at the cashier's, all by using your mobile phone.

Coupon incentives are a large and complex part of sales promotion. There are media specialists who just focus on this area of media planning and buying. Each coupon method has its pros and cons. And each has a number of cost components, which we discuss later in this chapter.

Sampling

Who of you hasn't been in a store where you were accosted by a salesperson offering you a free sample of their goods? You can't make it through the cosmetics department of a department store or the aisles of the grocery store without running into someone offering you a smell or taste of something.

Sampling can be a very costly way to incent someone to use your brand. However, sampling is one of the most effective methods for new products because it offers consumers a free trial in hopes of converting them to become loyal customers.

Just like coupons, samples can be distributed by mail, door to door, via coupon advertising, or in person at the store. Because sampling is so expensive, marketers are always looking for targeted methods to ensure that their samples reach their specific target market.

One method of doing this is through "polybagging" in selected print media. In polybagging, samples are delivered in a plastic bag along with the specific newspaper or magazine. This allows marketers to target their audience either by the type of reader or geographically or both. It is also a benefit to the newspaper or magazine because it is giving that reader something of value at no charge.

Another method of sampling is to develop sampling events that are promoted by the media. This could be by sponsoring a concert where you provide free samples to the audience. Or it could be at a race or a community event. Sampling events involve organizing a relevant event for your audience and then promoting it through the media. Tied to the event, then, is the sampling opportunity. This type of sampling promotion can be complex logistically. But it offers the brand exposure through media along with the opportunity to convert consumers to loyalists via a sampling program.

Event sampling programs are many times driven by the media themselves. To encourage advertisers to buy their media, many media brands extend their reach by developing events. For example, *Southern Living* has a cooking school event that moves from city to city within their dominant circulation area. In the school, they feature the brands that advertise with them along with recipes for these brands and samples. Programs like this are offered by many different media companies. They can be a part of the paid media program for the sponsoring brand.

Sampling, like couponing, can be simple or complex. It can be done in-store or through the media or by developing an event.

Media Celebrity Tie-In

Just as the media are looking to extend their brand through events, they offer an advertiser the opportunity to leverage their on-air or editorial talent. Giving you the opportunity to tie into a media property and to use their talent to promote your brand is an attractive method of sales promotion.

One common local way that retailers or auto dealers develop short-term promotional excitement is by having a radio station schedule an on-site promotional event. In radio parlance, this is called "scheduling a radio remote." This remote, or event, features one of the station's on-air personalities who provides prizes and other incentives to get his or her listeners to come to the local retailer for a limited-time event. The remote usually has a short time limit so there is an incentive for consumers to act quickly.

Another variation on this theme is sponsoring a tour that features, for example, a key editorial person from the print media. For example, a financial institution sponsors a traveling event where the publisher of the *Wall Street Journal* speaks. This may be an invitation-only event through which the marketer is using the media personality as an inducement for customers to sample his or her brand.

As media planners work with a media vehicle, they are on the lookout for not only how to find the proper advertising fit, but also how to use personalities within the media to further promote the brand.

Sweepstakes

Sweepstakes offer prizes based on a chance drawing of an entrant's name. What a great opportunity for an advertiser to stimulate some excitement about the brand and to build a database of prospective buyers. *Sweepstakes* is a catchall term for games, contests, and sweepstakes. Games are similar to sweepstakes with the difference being that games are usually conducted over longer periods of time. A sweepstake is a one-time event, whereas a game may be played out over the course of months. The advantage of a game is that consumers must continue to engage with the brand or the retailer, so it leads to repeat purchases or visits. A contest technically offers prizes based on an entrant's skill. Contests are another way that customers engage with the brand.

Media play a huge role in sweepstakes, games, and contests. One example of a sweepstakes is the partnership between a marketer, Cost Plus World

Market, and a media outlet, Home & Garden Television (HGTV). The idea was to create a partnership where HGTV would promote the "Cost Plus World Market and HGTV Spooktacular Sweepstakes" as an incentive to drive traffic to Cost Plus World Market during Halloween. Viewers would register at Cost Plus World Market and win prizes such as a room makeover, free in-home consultation with an HGTV celebrity designer, and a personalized Cost Plus World Market shopping experience. This is a great example of how the retailer and the media worked together to benefit each other.

Contests are a popular way to engage with loyal consumers. Doritos held a contest for its consumers to make a Super Bowl commercial. The winning entry actually got to produce their television commercial, which aired during the Super Bowl. All of the entries posted their commercials to Doritos as well as the YouTube online video site. This generated millions of page views which enhanced the brand's popularity. Each entry received a coupon for Doritos which stimulated short-term sales.

Sweepstakes must be promoted aggressively by advertising to be effective. And a sweepstake program must be well thought out from a retail perspective. It is important that the manufacturer and the retailer and the media work together to ensure success.

Cost and Measurement

There is nothing like a successful promotion to stimulate short-term sales of a brand. However, the more successful you are with sales promotion, typically the more money you spend. So sales promotion can become a double-edged sword. You want it to be successful yet you want to ensure that you don't make it so successful that you can't afford it.

It seems counterintuitive to question success. However, with sales promotion tactics, you are offering a discount incentive to consumers to buy your product. That means you are not selling it at full price. If you discount too much, you erode your profit margin. And you must pay incentive dollars at the time of purchase. You may not get all your money from the retailer or the consumer until later, so sales promotion can impact short-term cash flow.

All this means that when you plan sales promotion media, you need to take into account more than just the media cost. You need to understand the impact of the discount as well. Table 26.2 provides an example of a sales promotion cost analysis for Bob's Baked Beans.

In this example, there was a media support for a $1.00 coupon incentive. The media total included broadcast media, print media, and online media. The total paid media was $4.5 million. Two million consumers used the $1.00 discount, so the cost of the coupon redemption was $2 million. To

Table 26.2

Bob's Baked Beans

Sales Promotion Cost Analysis

Item promotional media	Percentage of cost ($ million)
Broadcast	3.0
Print	1.0
Online	0.5
TTL Media	4.5
Incentive redemption	
$1.00 incentive at 1% redemption rate	2.0
Processing fee	0.2
Misredemption contingency	0.4
Total redemption cost	2.6
Total cost	7.1

process the coupons from the retailer to the manufacturer is another cost of $200,000. The marketer also budgeted $400,000 for the possibility of misredemption of coupons. All told, this program cost $7.1 million yet the media total was only $4.5 million.

The lesson in this example is that if the media planner had only factored in the paid media for the budget instead of estimating the outcome of the promotion, there would be a $2.6 million budget discrepancy.

As sales promotion programs are developed, the media team not only must budget for media but must estimate the success rate of the promotion. Success for the promotion is usually measured by the number of consumers who take advantage of the offer. Future success of the promotion is based on those consumers who return to buy the brand without the offer.

Sales promotion costs include a number of items outside that of traditional paid media. We have just mentioned that one big aspect is the actual redemption or consumer response. Other costs that may be included are talent charges if the plan uses a celebrity from the media. There also can be legal charges for developing the rules of a contest to ensure that it meets federal guidelines. And there can be a myriad of processing and handling or logistics charges.

Future of Sales Promotion

It is safe to say that marketers will always have a need to drive short-term sales. It is equally as safe to say that consumers are always receptive to a discount or a deal. Those two factors combine to make sales promotion a growing force for the future.

Just like direct response, sales promotion has been impacted by digital media and the growing sophistication of database marketing. The future of sales promotion will be impacted by the following trends.

Paper Coupon to Digital Coupon

Even with the rapid rise of online couponing, 90 percent of all coupons are paper based. The key hurdle for online couponing has been the redemption security for the manufacturer. As online couponing becomes safer, it will certainly grow at a much faster rate than has print couponing.

Mobile Incentives

Mobile couponing is the wave of the future. Imagine that while shopping you present a coupon at the checkout without having done a prior online search or cut the coupon out of the newspaper. That will be possible in the mobile coupon arena where your cell phone becomes an incentive magnet.

Convergence

Just as you see with the leading sales promotion agencies, there is convergence in terms of direct response and sales promotion. The ability to link incentives to store-loyalty programs is rapidly gaining steam. Developing incentives that are both new customer and loyal customer centric, and that are tied to an ongoing program, is the wave of the future.

Mega-events

With over 50 percent of the United States using some form of coupon and more than 80 percent involved in at least one store-loyalty program, it is difficult for marketers to break established purchase cycles. This leads to mega-events, where marketers go over the top to provide an experience that leads to trial. For example, J.C. Penney has experimented with pop-up retail stores. These are short-term lease stores that generate excitement and trial in the marketplace. Large-scale events such as this will be the norm.

In summary, sales promotion is more than just a media purchase. It is an inducement to buy a product based on a time-limited incentive. These sales promotion incentive programs can take many shapes and forms from simple couponing to elaborate sweepstakes. Sales promotion is a crucial part of the marketing and media mix.

Chapter 27
Publicity

Advertisers who make use of advertising media will often also utilize several other avenues to spread the message and, perhaps, to reach the widest audience or, contrarily, to reach a specialized audience that may be difficult to address through standard mass media. One of the channels used most often is publicity, which is usually intended to supplement the regular advertising campaign.

Promotion and Publicity

Promotion encompasses most publicity and advertising activities. Advertising, public relations, sales promotion, personal selling, and publicity efforts all can fall under the rubric of promotion.

Promotion is usually referred to as a specialized activity utilizing unpaid mass media outlets as well as other channels to spread favorable news about a company, product or service, candidate, industry, or other entity. If the publicity can be distributed through a regular news outlet, such as a newspaper, magazine, or broadcast news program, the media environment can lend credibility and believability to the news item, thus building confidence in the entity being promoted. Whereas advertising, sales promotion, and personal selling all involve a good deal of financial investment, public relations and publicity can sometimes be gained for free or for a low cost.

There are many avenues for publicity outlets, as shown in Exhibit 27.1. Some of these activities can be carried out individually, although a coordinated publicity campaign often makes use of a combination of these outlets. Such campaigns can continue over long periods of time, perhaps for many years, as opposed to the more finalized time segments usually planned for advertising and public relations campaigns.

Of course, because the media space and time are not purchased, there is little control of how the news will be used by the media in a publicity

Exhibit 27.1

Some Important Publicity Outlets

- Analyst relations
- Awards receipt of proferring
- Columnist contributions
- Contributed articles
- Editorial calendars
- Editorial onsite visits
- Expert sourcing
- Internet distributors
- Letters to the editor
- Lists
- News stories
- Press releases
- Press tours
- Product reviews
- Speaking engagements
- Trade shows

Source: Adapted from Dovetail Public Relations.

effort. As you can imagine, there are literally thousands of companies and persons trying to gain publicity all at the same time, and the individual media vehicles can use only a small number of the news items provided to them, so the chances of getting your news in an appropriate medium and vehicle are small indeed.

Publicists

One can manage a publicity campaign alone or one may wish to engage the professional services of a publicist. A publicist often has built up personal contacts with certain media outlets, helping to improve the chances that a news item will be used. In addition, experienced publicists often know which outlets are most appropriate for certain types of news and information, again improving the odds of getting a news item included in the media vehicles while reducing the expense of contacting inappropriate media outlets.

If the publicity effort is intended to support an ongoing advertising campaign, then the publicity will often be handled by the advertising agency, either by people who are particularly skilled in this area or, in the case of very large agencies, a specialized media department or subsidiary.

Web Distribution

New media technologies have made it easier to distribute news and information, utilizing the Internet for quick communication and possibly for two-way communication. There are also several Web news distribution companies that can assist in spreading the story to a wide variety of media outlets. Some of these web distributors are listed in Exhibit 27.2.

Using these kinds of Web-distribution services does not necessarily make the publicity task easier or less complicated. Instead, it now becomes critical to know where these stories are being disseminated. Sending out stories to wide distribution lists often involves waste, and repeatedly contacting the wrong media may actually build up animosity, making it even more difficult to place a later story when that medium or vehicle might be more appropriate.

Special Events

A newsworthy event is often covered in the media. Publicists often actually create an event, just to generate publicity and gain media space and time. Special events are complicated, and those that are established for little reason other than publicity may lead to failure and again may generate animosity on the part of news reporters who attend. Many times, the news reporters are treated to a meal or given a special gift to help attract their attendance and to offer a bit of compensation for their time and effort in participating.

Conventions and meetings are large special events in which many advertisers participate on a regular basis. Planning, arranging, and carrying out such a large event can be complicated, so using an experienced person or a special meeting organizer or firm can be helpful. Many times the host site, such as a municipal convention center, a large hotel, or other venue can be helpful with suggestions, arrangements, staff, and space. Exhibit 27.3 is a list of suggested activities in planning for a large meeting or convention. As you peruse this list, note the many opportunities for involving media for publicity efforts, not just the listed publicity activities but also other possibilities in which the media might be interested.

Exhibit 27.2

A Sampling of Publicity Web Outlets

PRWeb
PRNewswire
Presswire
Pitchengine
Massmediadistribution
eReleases
Ambosmedia

Advertising Uses of Publicity

As mentioned above, publicity is often used to supplement an advertising campaign. In these cases, it is critical that the publicity use the same themes and message content as does the advertising, so that there is continuity from the advertising to the publicity and back again.

Here again, the media can be helpful. Large activities such as conventions and trade shows often recruit media participation and sponsorship, thus gaining some additional media publicity while possibly gaining financial support as well. If a media personality can be enticed to speak at an event or to act as the spokesperson for a product, imagine the credibility that immediately is attached to the publicity. Such a spokesperson need not be in the news every day; in fact, retired news personalities, politicians, celebrities, and similar people can often be hired for less money than would be needed for a person currently in the news. If a celebrity provides a testimonial in the advertising, it is only natural to include that person in the publicity efforts as well. In these ways, publicity can extend and enhance the advertising effort, often at a lower cost while reaching a wider audience.

Too often, publicity campaigns will operate in a sort of vacuum, separate from the advertising, public relations, and other promotional activities. Not only is that a poor strategy but it also wastes the synergistic effect that can be gained from a combination of complementary activities. Also, it is necessary to measure the outcomes of the publicity campaign, not just by counting the number of stories placed but also in measuring the changes in knowledge and opinion on the part of the media audiences.

Exhibit 27.3

Meeting Promotion and Publicity Checklist

- Review previous years' promotional budgets.
- Determine objectives and scope of program.
- Determine audience(s): membership, potential exhibitors, an industry or trade, general public.
- Develop theme and corresponding graphics.
- Considerations should include purposes of individual pieces: who will receive them, tone to be conveyed, how they will be produced, how many colors will be needed, what layout is required at each stage (from rough to comprehensive), and how much is budgeted for them.
- Develop a schedule for the campaign.
- Set promotional budget based on characteristics of membership, features of the venue, time of year, strength of program, and costs of attendance.
- Develop promotional materials according to tested criteria: short and forceful sentences, convincing explanation of benefits to attendees, clear emphasis on important elements of meeting, and easy means of registering.
- Plan for all campaign items to carry theme forward, taking into account costs of special effects like embossing or die-cutting; quality, grade, weight, and finish of paper; number of ink colors used; time for production; and quantity required:
  - ❖ Premeeting letters and announcements
  - ❖ Preliminary programs
  - ❖ Registration and housing forms
  - ❖ Promotional pieces for both exhibitors and attendees
  - ❖ Invitations
  - ❖ Follow-up mailings
  - ❖ Final agendas/program books
  - ❖ Badge inserts
  - ❖ Tickets
  - ❖ On-site registration materials
  - ❖ Signage
  - ❖ Newsletters
  - ❖ Lists of registered attendees

(continued)

Exhibit 27.3 *(continued)*

- Solicit a minimum of three competitive bids for all printing, checking samples of paper stock, samples of work for other meetings, references, and explanation of other services each firm can provide.
- Select printer(s), taking into account whether need is for "quick" or commercial quality, demonstrated ability of a single printer to handle all needs, availability of necessary equipment for jobs, and ability to meet deadlines.
- Agree with printer on schedule into which extra time is built, and monitor deadlines for rough layout, submission of copy, preliminary approval, completed layout, final approval of blueline, and delivery of job.
- Promote at previous year's meeting.
- Release promotional pieces, press releases, and related materials in accordance with schedule, with news releases preceding membership promotional mailings.
- Target local, national, international media as appropriate by type: trade papers, newspapers and periodicals of general interest, radio and television tailored to market.
- Control promotional costs through the following measures:
  - ❖ Obtain firm written bids for services.
  - ❖ Provide clean, competently proofread copy to printers.
  - ❖ Use standard paper sizes when possible.
  - ❖ Use same paper stock for many pieces.
  - ❖ Piggyback print items using same color.
  - ❖ Use standard PMS ink colors.
  - ❖ Re-use graphics.
  - ❖ Avoid unnecessary special effects.
  - ❖ Avoid perforations in favor of dotted-line cutting guides.
  - ❖ Coordinate printing times.
  - ❖ Set and enforce firm policy on overtime.
  - ❖ Minimize number of copy changes.

Note: This list is used by Marriott hotels to assist meeting planners.

Chapter 28
Preparing an Advertising Media Plan

When you propose an advertising media plan, you need to keep several things in mind: logic throughout the plan, sensible progression from one stage of the plan to another, fully explaining and justifying every recommended decision, and meeting the stated objectives.

The steps in a media plan are fairly straightforward. Most plans use a format similar to the one illustrated in Exhibit 28.1.

Overview or Executive Summary

As we do with most business reports and proposals, we start with an overview, often called an executive summary, in which major recommendations are summarized. This summary should not be used to tell you, the advertiser, things you already know about yourself, your company, and your brand. Instead, this section should be a summary of the media recommendations that are contained in the body of the report.

Use the executive summary to preview what is to come. With this advance knowledge, you can read and make more sense of the actual proposed media plan. Some top executives may read only this summary, but the brand manager needs to read and study the entire proposal, using the overview to provide background information and expectations before getting into the heart of the media plan.

Ironically, even though the executive summary is the first section of the media plan, it cannot be written until the rest of the plan is completed because it provides a review of the entire proposal.

Competitive Analysis

Complete analysis of your major competitors should be detailed in your media plan, along with the competitors' marketing and advertising efforts

Exhibit 28.1

Outline of a Media Plan

An advertising media plan may take more than one approach and there is no industry-wide outline that is always used. The organization below includes the necessary topics and can serve as a guide to prepare a media proposal for an advertising campaign.

Overview/executive summary
Competitive analysis
Market situation
Objectives and goals
    Marketing objectives
    Communication objectives
    Advertising objectives
    Media objectives
Media strategies
    Targets
        Markets
        Groups
        Audiences
    Media types
Media tactics
    Media vehicles
    Media units
    Media schedule
Media promotions
Media logistics
Continuity plans
Calendar
Budget
Integrated marketing and media

and their targets and media used. It is essential that the competition be analyzed thoroughly and completely before getting into the objectives. Because some of the objectives will likely deal with meeting the competition, the competitive analysis is an important input to those objectives.

Market Situation

If the marketplace is complex and its analysis cannot be covered in the competitive analysis, it will require a separate section. Again, information needs to be analyzed prior to the formation of objectives.

Objectives and Goals

Next come the actual objectives, what you will try to accomplish with your advertising media plan. There are usually at least three categories of objectives: overall marketing objectives, advertising objectives, and media objectives.

Marketing Objectives and Communication Objectives

The marketing objectives deal with the overall selling goals. They may be established at the corporate or company level, or at the marketing level. The advertising staff may be involved in establishing the marketing objectives, but oftentimes the objectives have already been set by the time the advertising media planner gets them, leaving little chance for input or adjustment to these goals. Communication objectives support the marketing objectives as discussed in Chapter 11.

Advertising Objectives

Similarly, the advertising objectives are essential. They must support the overall marketing objectives and focus on the overall advertising effort, including the research, message, visual, and media phases of the advertising campaign. Again, the media planner may be given these advertising objectives and told to follow them; fortunate is the media planner who has a chance to provide input and to influence the advertising objectives.

As is the case for all objectives, the advertising objectives need to be spelled out in detail, with thorough justification of each one.

Media Objectives

The media objectives must be consistent with the overall advertising objectives, which in turn must complement the overriding marketing objectives. In fact, sometimes the marketing objectives and advertising objectives are summarized here, providing lead-ins to and references for the media objectives. Look back at Chapter 3 for examples of the various topics that might be included under each type of objective.

Media Strategies

Remember that strategies are plans, so this section contains the actual plans that are proposed to meet the media objectives.

Targets

Although some media planners include the targets in their objectives, in many ways the targets are part of the planning to meet the objectives, rather than objectives in themselves. Therefore, it often makes more sense to place the targets in the strategic phase of the plan.

Targets should be fully described and their selection should be justified. There are at least three types of targets that may be considered.

Target Markets

If the term *markets* is limited to geographic areas, then the geographic planning for the media campaign is spelled out here.

Target Groups

The kinds of people that the media plan attempts to reach, usually outlined in demographic terms, are given here.

Target Audiences

Because there is no advertising medium that reaches all of a target market or target group and only that target market or group, the media audiences are often defined separately.

Media Types

Remember that advertising media are ways of achieving ends, they are not objectives in and of themselves. That is why the media to be used are included as strategies rather than goals. The selection of each advertising medium proposed for a campaign must be fully justified. In addition, other advertising media that were considered and not selected should also be listed, along with the reasons for not using them.

Media Tactics

The tactics are the implementation of the plan—the actual advertising campaign being carried out. Even though the tactics do not come into play until the proposed media plan is approved, there still should be some discussion at this point of the tactics to be used and complete justification of each.

Media Vehicles

It is likely that the media types will be spelled out in the strategies section, but the individual media vehicles to be used might not be. Under *tactics,* each specific media vehicle selection should be discussed and then justified.

Media Units

The length of broadcast commercials, size of print advertisements, and specifications such as the use of bleed, color, and the like should be presented here, again with justification.

Media Schedule

The advertising campaign schedule may be discussed in the advertising objectives, or it may be set earlier. Still, there should be some detail on the proposed timing of the advertising, including starting and stopping dates, flight and hiatus plans, levels of advertising, coordination of scheduling across the various media, and recognition of the selling calendar and other timing factors. Again, justification is required.

Media Promotions

If the use of nonadvertising promotions is not discussed anywhere else, it should be included here. Although its proposed use may come in an earlier section, it is most likely to appear in the tactical stage.

Media Logistics

Support activities such as special media research, photography, print and broadcast production, and similar concerns may need to be treated, discussed, and justified.

Contingency Plans

The contingency plans should be complete enough to be used if they are actually needed. If something in the original campaign must be changed, it will likely be on short notice, leaving little opportunity to develop complete plans in a high-pressure situation.

See the detailed discussion of contingency plans back in Chapter 3.

Calendar

The scheduling may be discussed elsewhere in your media plan, but it is a good idea to have one central place where the media and promotion schedules can be included. This schedule is often presented in the form of a flowchart. See Exhibit 28.2 for an example of a flowchart.

Budget

The advertising media budget needs to be presented, with allocations shown for each major type of medium and other major uses, along with any necessary explanation and complete rationale.

Integrated Marketing

Because so many firms make use of integrated marketing, the integration of the advertising media plan into the overall marketing picture may need to be disclosed. The use of integrated marketing communications and of integrated media, if used, can also be included here.

Conclusion

You can see, then, that a media plan needs justification and rationale at every stage, along with a logical progression from objectives through strategies to tactics and outcomes. Check back to make sure that all the media objectives are being dealt with and can be accomplished.

A solid media plan is vital to bringing a successful conclusion to your advertising and marketing efforts.

Exhibit 28.2

Brand Planning Calendar for Magic Beans

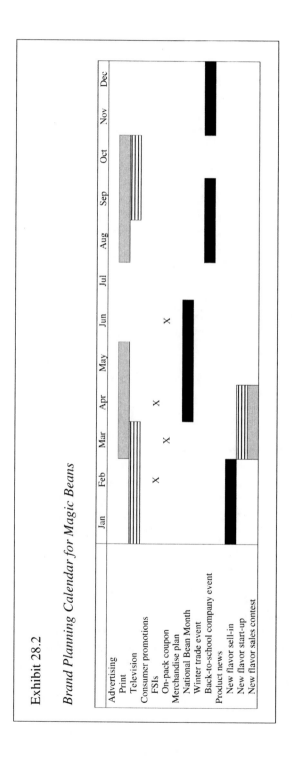

Chapter 29

Evaluating an Advertising Media Plan

Like so many professional tasks, evaluating a proposed advertising media plan requires experience and knowledge. Such evaluations are much easier after you have seen a few others, and even better once you have been exposed to dozens of them.

Even if you do not have a high degree of experience, there are still some major and minor factors to watch for, examine carefully, and use to determine whether the media plan seems to be "on track" or is just a random collection of haphazard ideas.

Format

The format of a good media plan should be clear, logical, and easy to read and follow. The format should take you through the entire process, from the background information on which the plan was based to the current situation and on through the hoped-for goals and objectives. Then it should move from objectives into strategies and plans, the methods that will be used to achieve the goals and objectives, including the types of media to be used. Next are the tactics to implement the plans, which might include media vehicles and units. There may also be a final section that involves the necessary support activities, such as research, production, and checking.

Any media plan will be judged more favorably if it looks good; as in real estate or in meeting new people, first impressions are important, and a sloppy plan that is not carefully crafted and assembled will likely receive a poor evaluation.

Is there a table of contents, with page numbers, included in the plan? Does that table of contents make logical sense, and does it match up with the actual pages on which the corresponding materials appear?

Are the pages numbered and assembled in proper order? An upside-down or backwards page creates the impression of poor planning and hurried thinking.

Starting each new section of the plan on a new page, using double-spacing, including graphics and tables, and providing full explanations will also create a better impression in the evaluation.

Overview

The overview or executive summary should be the first element in the media plan, even though it cannot be written until all the other sections have been completed. The overview lets the reader see what is coming, so that he or she is not forced to read through it all twice. For the senior executive, the overview gives the essential information and answers the questions: who are the targets, where are they located, and what media will be used to reach them?

It is important not to give too much information in the overview. For example, including the history of the client firm is unnecessary; after all, the client will know this history better than the media planner ever could.

Current Situation and Competition

There should be some treatment of the current marketing situation—the problem that this media plan is attempting to overcome.

In addition, there must be detailed information about the competition. It is not possible to establish the advertising and media objective without first considering the competition. This section should include not just general competitive information but also detailed insights into the competitors' uses of advertising and media. And all competitors should be included, not just the major ones.

Objectives

It is essential that objectives are set early and followed throughout the rest of the media plan. The objectives and goals must be explained, with complete rationale and justification.

Too often, strategies such as the types of media to be used are included in the objectives. It is important that this section include only what is to be accomplished—the goals—and that the strategies to achieve them be held back. Media, after all, are strategies, not objectives. Using television or magazines is not a goal; the goal is to sell, to convince, to change opinions, to inform, and to communicate, and the media are strategies that will be used in the plans to achieve these ends.

Media planning objectives should be specific rather than vague. The best objectives will be quantified with actual goal numbers stated, so it is clear at the end of the campaign whether the objectives have been reached.

Targets

There should be three kinds of targets: *target markets,* which are the geographic areas and cities where advertising will be focused; *target groups,* which are the kinds of people the advertising will reach, usually given in demographic terms; and *target audiences,* which are the people who can actually be reached through advertising in the mass media.

For example, the advertising for the Hyundai Accent automobile may be aimed at lower-income persons in some large metropolitan areas, but there is no advertising medium that reaches those persons, only those persons, and all of those persons; therefore, the target audience may be slightly different from the target group and target market.

Targets are sometimes given as part of the objectives, although it may make more sense for the targets to be included with strategies and plans, because they are a means of accomplishing the goals and objectives.

Targets are typically described in prose in a media plan, but they should also include a numerical component. How many people (in thousands and as a percentage) are you aiming for, and how often will they be reached? Do these numbers make sense, and do they match up with the numerical targets?

Like every other section of the media plan, the targets should be fully explained and justified. They are important and deserve complete attention and treatment. Why these targets and not others? How were these decisions made and why?

In addition, the media planner must determine whether the targets are feasible. If the goal is to cover all 50 states, and the target is for only the top 10 or 15 markets in the country, that target may be too small a portion of the country to do an effective job. In addition, reaching only a small portion of the markets would make it difficult if not impossible to achieve sales-level goals.

Strategies

Strategies are plans—the plans that will be used to achieve the campaign objectives. As mentioned above, these strategies may include the targets. And the strategies will certainly include the media that are being recommended for inclusion in the campaign.

These media cannot possibly be selected before the objectives and the targets have been detailed. After all, a medium is by definition a go-between, so it must be clear what the goal is before any medium or go-between can be determined. Similarly, the target must be clearly defined before media can be selected, because it is not possible to know which media will reach those targets until the targets are clear.

The reasons for using each medium must be spelled out in detail. In addition, and just as important, is one fact that is too often overlooked: the reasons for not using other media. It should be clear that all possible media were considered and judged fairly in their applicability to the situation, to the campaign objectives, and to the targets to be reached.

It is not enough simply to give media types. For the media being recommended, what specific newspapers and magazines, which broadcast programs and stations, which cable networks are being suggested? And, as always, there must be compelling reasons to justify every decision, strategy, and tactic.

Budget

Now comes the money, an essential element in any campaign. Is there enough money to do an adequate job? Are the monies being spread too thinly across too many targets or too many media? Is there enough money to do an adequate job in each medium and against each target group?

It only makes sense to allocate money to each medium. In the case of local-market media, such as spot radio and local newspapers, the total sum for that medium must be reallocated to individual cities and markets. It makes no sense to allocate all the monies to individual markets if some of the media choices are national in scope, because then those individual-market allocations would have to be re-added together for the national buys.

Allocations to media and markets should be explained and justified. The budget should be given in a coordinated budgetary overview, and the allocation of funds to various types of media should be determined prior to the tactical phase of the plan.

Contingency Plan

Toward the end of the media plan, there should be a contingency plan, with details on what will be done if the proposed plan is not working as anticipated. Contingency plans are often too brief and oversimplified to be of any real use. In an emergency, there is no time to come up with alternative plans, so the contingency plan is vital.

Again, justification is needed.

Schedule

There also needs to be a schedule or calendar showing what advertising will be running during each phase of the campaign. This schedule is often given in the form of a flowchart because it can combine the media to be used, the weights for each medium, the time span, and the overlapping uses of various media. A presentation of the calendar in a flowchart or some other visually appealing graphic makes this information easier to communicate and easier to understand. (See Exhibits 29.1 through 29.5 for media checklists.)

Overall

General standards to consider include the following:

1. When information or data are provided, the sources of those facts should also be provided so the reader can judge the quality and reliability of the information. Keep in mind, too, that information gained from the Internet is often spurious or questionable.
2. When tables or figures or similar data are included, they should be related to the plans and objectives rather than simply dropped in with little apparent connection to the overall media plan.
3. When various terms are used, they should be clearly defined. Not everybody agrees on the meaning of every specialized term or expression.
4. The plan should not be too general or oversimplified. The more information and detail included, the better.
5. If a media plan starts strongly and then becomes much more general or just falls apart at the end, it is usually an indication that the planner started too late and ran out of time to complete the job.
6. Writing is important, too, so the written plan should use good grammar and correct spelling, with no typographical or punctuation errors. It might also be a good idea to avoid slang and abbreviations in formal business reports. Write from the advertiser's perspective, not your own; after all, this is the advertiser's plan and money.
7. Finally, as stressed earlier, justification is key to a successful media plan. An advertising budget may involve large sums of money, and the proposed expenditure of those funds needs to be sound.

Exhibit 29.1

Media Checklist

I.   Marketing goals
   A. Is the plan designed to:
      1. increase usage from existing user base?
      2. increase usage from lighter users?
      3. increase trial among nonusers?
      4. protect current user base from erosion?
II. Advertising goals
   A. Is the plan designed to:
      1. increase awareness among the target?
      2. change perception of the target(s)?
      3. generate an immediate response?
      4. generate an inquiry?
III. Timing
   A. Do you know the fiscal year?
   B. Is there a specific start date?
   C. What is the plan period?
IV. Target audience
   A. For consumer goods, have you defined the target(s)?
      1. usage (heavy, medium, light)
      2. demographics
      3. PRIZM clusters
      4. need-based segments
      5. drawn-out specific target segments with names
      6. looked at MRI, media audit
      7. looked at Spectra for packaged goods
      8. purchaser vs. user
      9. purchaser influencer
   B. For B2B clients, have you defined target(s)?
      1. standard industrialization classification code
      2. job description
      3. demographics
      4. need-based segments
      5. influencers in decision chain

(continued)

Exhibit 29.1 *(continued)*

V.   Seasonality
    A. Have you looked at the following:
       1. Sales by month or week?
       2. Category sales vs. brand sales?
       3. Competitive activity vs. sales?
VI. Geography
    A. Is the plan national, international, or local?
       1. Do you have sales by markets?
       2. Do you have category sales by market?
       3. Have you calculated BDI/CDI?
          a. Do you know distribution by market?
          b. ACV for packaged goods?
          c. Number of stores/units for retailers?
VII. Creative considerations
    A. Are creative units determined for media?
       1. If so, what are they?
       2. If not, what should they be?
       3. Are units in sync with goal and budget?
VIII. Budget
    A.   Do you know the total budget?
    B.   What is the media budget?
    C.   Is it net or gross?
    D.   How does it compare to last year?
    E.   How does it compare to competition?
    F.   Have you calculated share of market (SOM) to share of spending (SOS)?
    G.   What is the ad-to-sales ratio?
IX. Mandatories
    A. Are there any sacred cows?
    B. Has the client purchased anything on his or her own?
X.   Communications goals
    A. Have you set up specific communications goals?
       1. Reach/Frequency
          a. Is there an effective frequency level?
       2. Have you used the matrix?
       3. Is there a continuity goal?
       4. Is continuity more important than higher weight levels?

XI. Media strategies
    A. Do your media strategies include:
        1. Which media mix is best?
        2. How to best use each medium?
XII. Media tactics
    A. Do your tactics include:
        1. What is best vehicle and why?
        2. Cost analysis?
        3. Target audience analysis?
    B. Can you own a vehicle?
    C. Include a flowchart?
    D. Include a budget recap?
    E. Compare this year to last year?
    F. Have alternative plans?
XIII.Test options
    A. Is there the option of testing?
        1. Higher spend level?
        2. Alternative media mix?
        3. Different target?
        4. Different buying strategy?

Source: FKM.

Exhibit 29.2

Media Checklist: Retail

Retail advertising can be slightly more complicated than other advertising, and it is often different even when it is not more complicated. Here is a checklist for retail advertising media plans; use this checklist in addition to the checklist used for all advertising media plans.

1. Do you know what comp store sales goal is?
2. Do you have daily sales and know when key holidays are?
   • How have holidays changed vs. one year ago?
3. Do you know where the stores are located?
   • Have you defined a trading radius (e.g., 3 miles)?
4. Is the target audience different by trading area or market?
   • Are there pockets of consumer opportunity?
5. Do you know how print is planned?
   • What dates are they planned to run?
6. How was media planned year to year?
   • Many retailers comp on a weekly basis.
7. Competition is crucial for retail. Do you have a handle on when and where the competition spend?

Source: FKM.

Exhibit 29.3

Media Checklist: Packaged Goods

1. Do you know the source of volume for marketing mix?
   • Has a marketing-mix study been done?
2. Do you have volume and incremental volume goals?
3. Do you have target definitions from MRI and Spectra?
4. Do you have BDI/CDI for markets?
5. Are the markets listed IRI or Nielsen markets? (If so, do you have appropriate DMAs for these markets?)
6. Do you have ACV by market?
7. Do you know when consumer promotions are scheduled (particularly FSIs)?
8. Do you have category vs. brand seasonal sales and have you compared both to spending?
9. Have you done alternative plans on media mixes?
10. What is the role of advertising with the trade?
11. Is there a test component to the plan?
12. Do you know purchaser vs. user?
    • mom vs. kids

Source: FKM.

Exhibit 29.4

Media Checklist: B2B (Business-to-Business)

1. Do you have a clear understanding of the target?
   - The right standard industrial classification code?
   - The right job position?
   - The decision process?
2. Is there any weighting to be done by target or industry groups?
3. When are decisions made?
   - Are they ongoing or at a specific time of year?
4. Do they have a customer database of current and prospective customers?
   - Should there be a retention program?
5. Do you have the industry or job universes to better understand coverage of media?
6. Are there any key trade shows to support or consider?
7. Is direct marketing part of the program?
8. Have you considered the Internet as part of the mix?
9. Are there any vehicles you can own?
10. Are premium positions in magazines worth the cost?
11. Is driving website traffic an important part of the plan?
12. Is there anything that you can test?

Source: FKM.

Exhibit 29.5

Pay Attention to the Numbers

In any analysis of a proposed advertising media plan, it is crucial to pay attention to the numbers—to determine whether they make sense and to see if they all add up correctly. This checklist may be of help.

1. Is the budget adequate? Is there enough money to accomplish all the objectives?
2. Does the target audience size make sense? Will it account for a sizeable portion of the target groups?
3. Are there enough media types to cover a diverse audience?
4. Are enough markets used to cover most of the country or most of the region in question?
5. Is there enough media weight to achieve sales goals? Enough markets? Adequate portion of coverage?
6. Are larger markets getting more of the media allocations?
7. Over the course of the campaign (e.g., for the coming year), will advertising frequency be sufficient?
8. Are the advertising units affordable and sensible?
9. Are reach, frequency, and impact balanced? For example, expensive units (bigger print advertisements, longer broadcast commercials, using color in print) cost more, which leaves less for reach and frequency. The corollary is that less expensive units will provide more money for more reach and frequency.
10. Are reach and frequency sensibly balanced?
11. Are expensive media (e.g., television) slated to receive larger budgetary allocations than less expensive media (e.g., outdoor)?

Chapter 30

Impact of Media Ownership on Advertising Execution

Imagine working on an account at a large advertising agency. If you need research, you contact the research department, which knows about the major marketing research firms and the kinds of work they do. But if your advertising agency is owned or controlled by a large media holding company, perhaps you can simply pick up the telephone and contact a research firm that is owned by the same parent company.

In recent years, there have been many mergers and acquisitions of broadcast companies, advertising and public relations agencies, research firms, publishing houses, Internet marketing firms, and all other kinds of media-related businesses, with many of them sometimes controlled by the same media holding company or corporation, known as a media conglomerate. Table 30.1 shows some of the world's largest media conglomerates.

The benefits of media conglomeration are many, at least to the holding companies themselves. If a media firm has what are known as multiplatform operations they may have radio and television networks and stations, cable systems, magazine publishers, Internet operators, advertising agencies, newspaper publishers, outdoor companies, and even more—all under the same corporate umbrella. Perhaps the television network is producing a cartoon program, which can then be printed in comic books, offered on the Internet, shown as repeats on television stations or a cable network, and promoted on outdoor billboards, all working together smoothly, in an integrated fashion. That is why multiplatform media acquisitions have grown so important and fashionable in recent years.

As you can see in Table 30.2, there are many overlapping holdings and services, covering just about the entire media spectrum. And Time Warner is not even the largest of the media conglomerates.

Many of these parent firms operate in many countries. Look at the holdings of WPP in Table 30.3, a very large advertising holding company. The

Table 30.1

Some of the Largest Media Conglomerates (listed alphabetically)

Bertelsmann AG
CBS Corporation
E. W. Scripps Company
General Electric
Grupo Prisa
Hearst Corporation
Lagardère Group
Liberty Media
National Amusements
News Corporation
Organizações Globo
Sony
The Walt Disney Company
Time Warner
Viacom
Vivendi SA

Note: When this book was written, The Walt Disney Company was the world's largest media conglomerate, with News Corporation, Time Warner, and Viacom ranking second, third, and fourth, respectively, based on the *Fortune 500* list of largest corporations.

company is so large that it has operating headquarters in England, Ireland, the United States, Japan, China, India, and Latin America, and has more than 140,000 employees and operates in more than 100 countries.

An advertiser could buy just about all needed services from this one corporation: advertising, public relations, digital media services, research, production. Certainly there might be economies of scale, and the work of all these combined firms might operate more smoothly and with few snags, all of them sharing the same information. Yet if some research finding were in error, all the work would reflect that same mistake. And there might be pressure to save money and to cut corners, allowing the work to overlap from one firm to another instead of each doing its own work with its own preparations and its own due diligence.

Problems with Conglomeration

What if there is an advertising agency, a broadcast ratings research firm, a public relations firm, a publicity firm, and an Internet services firm all under the same corporate umbrella? Even though it may be illegal for a ratings firm to charge a corporate partner less than an outsider, it is possible that the ratings might be available a few days in advance to the partner agency, thus providing a real competitive advantage.

Table 30.2

Time Warner Media Holdings

Media holdings are often bought and sold, so any chart like this one cannot remain accurate and timely for very long. Still, this chart gives a good idea of the holdings of one of the world's largest media conglomerates, Time Warner.

Television

Network	CW Network (50% with CBS).
Cable	Home Box Office, Inc. (HBO, Cinemax, HBO Sports, HBO Pay-Per-View, HBO on Demand, Cinemax Multiplexes, Cinemax on Demand, HBO HD, Cinemax HD, as well as HBO channels around the world), TruTV, TBS, TBS HD, Boomerang, Cartoon Network, Turner Classic Movies, TCM Europe, TCM Asia Pacific, TNT, TNT HD, CNN Airport Network, CNN International, CNN Headline News, CNN en Español, CNN en Español Radio, CNN Pipeline.
Regional and local channels	NY1 News, NY1 Noticias, Sports Net, R News (Rochester, NY), Turner South, Capital News 9 Albany, MetroSports, News 8 Austin, News 10 Now-Syracuse, News 14 Carolina-Charlotte, News 14 Carolina-Raleigh.
International	CNN International, CNN Headline News in Asia Pacific, CNN Headline News in Latin America, CNN+, CETV (36%) (China), CNNj, CNN Turk, CNN-IBN, Cartoon Network Europe, Cartoon Network Latin America, Cartoon Network Asia Pacific, Cartoon Network Japan (70% share), Imagen, TCM Classic Hollywood in Latin America, TNT Latin America, TNT Serie, truTV, Nuts TV, Cartoonito, Pogo, 7 networks in Latin America.
Production and distribution	Warner Bros. Television Group, Warner Home Video, Warner Horizon Television, Warner Bros. Animation, Warner Bros. Digital Distribution, Telepictures Productions, HBO Video, HBO Independent Productions, New Line Television, Williams St. Studio, Cartoon Network Studios, CNN Newsource, Central Media Enterprises (31%).
Programming	CNN Newsroom, Live From The Situation Room, Lou Dobbs Tonight, Larry King Live, Anderson Cooper 360, NBA Games, MLB Playoffs, NASCAR, Entourage, Kids' WB, American Morning.

Internet

America Online — AOL, AOL.com, AOL Instant Messenger, AOL Wireless, AOL Music Now, AOL Local, McAfee VirusScan Online (bundled with AOL services), AOL by Phone, AOL Call Alert, AOL CityGuide, AOL PassCode, AOL Voicemail, AOL Europe (Germany and Luxembourg), America Online Latino (Brazil, Mexico, Argentina, Puerto Rico, Venezuela, Chile, AOL Global Web Services, AOL Latino).

Other online holdings — CNN.com, CNNMoney.com, CNNStudentNews.com, MapQuest, Moviefone, Movietickets.com, RED, Advertising.com, CompuServe, ICQ, KOL, SI.com, People.com, Pipeline, GameTap, CartoonNetwork.com, DCComics.com, Time.com, VeryFunnyAds.com, Cwtv.com, Golf.com, Truveo, Weblogs, TMZ.com, Momlogic.com, AIM, Bebo.com, NASCAR.com, NASCAR.com en Espanol, PGA.com, PGATour.com, Play On!, superdeluxe.com, MyRecipes.com, MyHomeIdeas.com, ThisOldHouse.com, buy.at, MedioTiempo.com, Goowy, Sphere Source, Mousebreaker.com.

Time Warner "operates" NBA.com until 2016.

Cinema

Production — Warner Bros. Pictures, New Line Cinema, Castle Rock, Warner Premiere, Picturehouse, Warner Bros. International Cinemas, Warner Independent Pictures, a joint venture with Village Roadshow Pictures, and a joint venture with Alcon Entertainment.

Distribution — Distribution to more than 125 international territories.

Print

Comics — DC Comics, E.C. Publications, Inc. (publisher of MAD magazine).

Publishing — Time Warner Book Group, with publishing companies The Mysterious Press, Time Warner Book Group UK, Warner Faith, Warner Vision, Warner Business Books, Aspect, and Little, Brown and Company (includes Little, Brown Adult Trade, Little, Brown Books for Young Readers, Back Bay, and Bulfinch Press); Oxmoor House, Inc.; Sunset Books; Book-of-the-Month Club, Inc.; Southern Progress Corporation; Grupo Editorial Expansion (publishes 15 magazines in Mexico).

(continued)

Table 30.2 *(continued)*

Magazines	*People, Time, Sports Illustrated, Fortune, This Old House, 25 Beautiful Homes, 25 Beautiful Kitchens, 4x4, Aeroplane, All You, Amateur Gardening, Amateur Photographer, Ambientes, Angler's Mail, Audi Magazine, Balance, Bird Keeper, Business 2.0, Cage & Aviary Birds, Caravan, Chat-Its Fate, Chilango, Classic Boat, Coastal Living, Cooking Light, Cottage Living, Country Homes & Interiors, Country Life, Cycle Sport, Cycling Weekly, Decanter, Entertainment Weekly, Essence (joint venture), Essentials, EXP, Expansion, European Boat Builder, Eventing, Family Circle (U.K.), Fortune Asia, Fortune Europe, FSB: Fortune Small Business, Golf Magazine, Golf Monthly, Guitar, Hair, Health, Hi-Fi News, Homes & Gardens, Horse, Horse & Hound, Ideal Home, In Style, In Style U.K., International Boat Industry, Land Rover World, Life, Manufactura, Marie Claire (joint venture), MBR-Mountain Bike Rider, MINI, MiniWorld, Model Collector, Money, Motor Boat & Yachting, Motor Boats Monthly, Motor Caravan, NME, Now, Nuts, Obras, Outdoor Life, Park Home & Holiday Caravan, People en Espanol, Pick Me Up, Practical Boat Owner, Practical Parenting, Prediction, Progressive Farmer, Quien, Quo (joint venture), Racecar Engineering, Real Simple, Rugby World, Ships Monthly, Shoot Monthly, Shooting Times, Soaplife, Southern Accents, Southern Living, Sporting Gun, Sports Illustrated for Kids, Stamp Magazine, Sunset, Superbike, Synapse, Targeted Media, Teen People, The Field, The Golf, The Golf+, The Railway Magazine, The Shooting Gazette, This Old House Ventures, Time Asia, Time Atlantic, Time Australia, Time Canada, Time for Kids, Time, Inc. Content Solutions, Time Pacific, TV & Satellite Week, TV Easy, TVTimes, Uncut, VolksWorld, Vuelo, Wallpaper, Webuser, Wedding, What Camera, What Digital Camera, What's on TV, Who, Woman, Woman & Home, Woman's Own, Woman's Weekly, World Soccer.*
Joint ventures	Groupe Marie Claire (U.K.).

Media Marketing and Other Media

Marketing businesses	Synapse Group Inc., Targeted Media, Inc., Media Networks, Inc., Third Screen Media, LLC, ADTECH AGTACODA LLC, Quigo Technologies.
Other	CNN Mobile, CNNRadio, Warner Bros. Interactive Entertainment Inc., Monolith Productions (game developer), GameTap, Warner Bros. Consumer Products Inc. (licensing), HBO Properties (licensing and merchandising), HBO distributed over AT&T Wireless, Warner Bros. Animation (including Hanna-Barbera and Looney Tunes), Time Warner Investments, Winamp.

Sources: Time Warner; Free Press; Fairness and Accuracy in Reporting; Los Angeles Independent Media Center, cjr.com.

Table 30.3

WPP: Advertising and Media Holdings

Like other media holdings, entities are often bought, sold, or merged, so this type of chart cannot remain accurate and timely for very long; but it does reflect the scope, size, and holdings of a large multinational advertising group, WPP.

Category	Company
Advertising	10AM Communications
	1861united
	ADK
	AdPeople
	Advertures
	APP (Agência Portuguesa de Produção)
	Bates 141
	Berlin Cameron United
	Blaze Advertising
	Blue Hive
	BPG Group
	BrandBuzz
	bsb comunicacion
	BTS United
	CHI&Partners
	Chime Communications Plc
	Cole & Weber United
	Contract Advertising
	Dawson
	DCSNET
	Dentsu, Y&R
	Diamond Ogilvy
	Diebitz, Stöppler, Braun & Kuhlmann (DSB&K)
	Digitaria
	Enfatico
	George Patterson Y&R
	Grey
	Grey Group
	HS Ad
	Jan Kelley Marketing
	JayGrey
	Johannes Leonardo
	JWT
	JWT Specialized Communications
	LDV United
	Les Ouvriers du Paradis United
	Master Comunicacao
	MetropolitanRepublic
	MONDAY
	Ogilvy & Mather Worldwide
	Ogilvy Noor
	Red Cell
	RedWorks

(continued)

Table 30.3 *(continued)*

	Santo
	SCPF
	Sharp Shooter Films
	Signposter.com
	Soho Square
	TAPSA
	TAXI
	Team Detroit
	Testardo Gram
	The Brand Shop
	the campaign palace
	The Jupiter Drawing Room
	The United Network
	True Worldwide
	Wildfire
	Y&R
	Young & Rubicam Brands
Branding and identity	Addison Corporate Marketing
	Always Marketing
	B to D Group
	BDG McColl
	BDGworkfutures
	Bisqit
	CAW Marketing
	CB'a
	Chime Communications Plc
	Coley Porter Bell
	Designworks
	Dovetail
	Fitch
	Lambie-Nairn
	Landor Associates
	Menacom
	Neo'@'ogilvy
	PeclersParis
	Penn Schoen Berland
	swat marketing
	Team Detroit
	The Partners
	The Brand Union
	VBAT
	Young & Rubicam Brands
Consumer insights	Added Value
	All Global
	All Global Viewing
	BMRB
	BPRI
	Center Partners
	Cheskin
	Cymfony

	Dynamic Logic
	Everystone Group
	Firefly
	Glass
	IdeaWorks
	IMRB International
	Japan Kantar Research
	JWTAction
	Kantar
	Kantar Health
	Kantar Media
	Kantar Operations
	Kantar Retail
	Kantar Video
	Kantar WorldPanel
	KMR Software
	Lightspeed Research
	Millward Brown
	ohal
	Red Dot Square Solutions
	SRDS
	The Focus Network
	The Futures Company
	TNS
	TNS Employee Insights
	TNS Gallup
	TNS Research International
	TNS-RMS
	TRU
Corporate/B2B	Chime Communications Plc
	Fitch
	Food Group
	MJM
	Ogilvy Primary Contact
	The PBN Company
	Penn Schoen Berland
	Young & Rubicam Brands Geneva
Demographic marketing	Bravo
	Etcom
	K&L Advertising
	UniWorld Group
	Wing
Digital	Blue State Digital
Digital, direct, viral, Ecommerce, and CRM	LaComunidad
Direct, digital, promotion, and relationship marketing	141 Premiere Sports & Entertainment
	20:20 Brand Action
	A.Eicoff
	Actionline
	Actis
	AGENDA

(continued)

Table 30.3 *(continued)*

all access ltd
Aqua Online
argonauten G2
BCG2
Big Idea Group
Blast Radius
Blue Hive
Brierley+Partners
Burrows
Catalyst Search Marketing
Comwerks
Designkitchen
Dialogue 141
Digit
ETECTURE GmbH
EWA Bespoke Communications
Forward
Futurecom interactive
G2
G2 Australia
G2 Knowledge Consulting
G2 Market Data
global3digital
Grass Roots
Grey Group
Headcount Field Marketing Limited
HeathWallace Ltd
HighCo
I-Behavior
i-Cherry
Kassius
KBM Group
Mando Brand Assurance
Maxx Marketing
MEC Access
MediaCom Interaction
Midia Digital
Neo@ogilvy
OgilvyAction
OgilvyOne Worldwide
Quisma
Reddion
RMG Connect
RTCRM
Smollan Group
Sonic Boom Creative Media
Spafax
Studiocom
TAPSA
tattoo
Teledirect

	These Days
	VML
	Wunderman
	Wunderman MENA
	XM Asia Pacific
	XM London
	Young & Rubicam Brands
	ZAAZ

Employer branding/ Recruitment	JWT Specialized Communications avh live communications
Event/Face-to-face marketing	Encompass facts+fiction Fitch Grass Roots IEG, LLC MJM Pro Deo
Foodservice marketing	Food Group
Healthcare communications	All Global All Global Viewing Chime Communications Plc Feinstein Kean Healthcare (FKH) GCI Health Grey Group Grey Healthcare LOb Conseils MJM Ogilvy CommonHealth Ogilvy CommonHealth Worldwide Ogilvy Healthworld Sudler & Hennessey WG Consulting Young & Rubicam Brands
Information, insight, and consultancy	IBOPE Media Information
Manufacturing Media and production services	Wire and Plastic Products Ltd Clockwork Capital Hogarth Worldwide Imagina Group Metro Plush Films Sprint Production The Farm
Media investment management	Blue Hive BrandAmp Chime Communications Plc Compas Data Intelligence GroupM

(continued)

Table 30.3 *(continued)*

	Happi Mindshare
	H-art
	Kinetic
	KR Media
	MAXUS
	MEC
	MEC Interaction
	MediaCom
	Menacom
	Meritus
	MindShare
	mInteraction
	Motivator
	oOh!media
	Outrider
	PQ Plakat Qualitaet
	TAPSA
	Team Detroit
	The Midas Exchange
Public relations and public affairs	Beyond Communications Hong Kong Limited
	Blanc & Otus
	Buchanan Communications
	Burson-Marsteller
	Carl Byoir & Associates
	Chime Communications Plc
	Clarion Communications
	Cohn & Wolfe
	Dewey Square Group, LLC
	Direct Impact
	Encoder Public Relations
	Essence Communications
	Finsbury
	GCI Canada
	Grey Group
	HERING SCHUPPENER
	Hill & Knowlton
	Intermarkets
	IPAN Hill and Knowlton
	Menacom
	Ogilvy Government Relations
	Ogilvy Public Relations Worldwide
	Penn Schoen Berland
	Polaris Public Relations
	PPR
	Prime Policy Group
	Proof Digital Media
	Proof Integrated Communications
	Public Strategies Inc
	Quinn Gillespie & Associates
	Robinson Lerer & Montgomery
	RPCA

Sonic Boom Creative Media
Triwaks Public Relations Consultants
Wexler & Walker Public Policy Associates
Young & Rubicam Brands

Real estate marketing	PACE
Social media and conversational marketing	SocialMedia8
Specialist communications	Communicator
Sports marketing	Alliance BIWIR, An Ogilvy PR Worldwide Company IEG, LLC PRISM
Technology marketing	Adgistics
	Banner
Viral and online video measurement	ViralTracker
WPP digital	24/7 Real Media Deliver Possible Worldwide Proclivity Syzygy The Media Innovation Group (MIG)
WPP digital partner companies	iconmobile JumpTap LiveWorld-WPP SAY Media Spot Runner Visible Technologies Visible World Wild Tangent Yield Software
WPP knowledge communities	The Channel The Store
Youth marketing	Geppetto Group

Source: WPP, "A full list of all WPP companies worldwide," http://www.wpp.com/wpp/companies/company-list.htm.

Think about a mid-sized American city where the local newspaper, two largest television stations, several radio stations, a homebuyers' guide, a weekly entertainment guide, and a retail discount coupon book all operate as part of the same company. Certainly they could save money by sending only one reporter to cover the local city council meetings, instead of a separate reporter for each media outlet. But then the news perspective is narrowed and the populace receives only one viewpoint on all local issues. This firm would have tremendous power in favoring certain political candidates. It would also have possible undue influence on advertising rates for both local and national advertisers who want to promote their services and product in that community. Advertising sales representatives could sell advertising for all the media at the same time, which might pressure local advertisers to buy more from these particular media vehicles.

Now imagine an advertising agency that is owned by the same corporation that also owns magazines. Could there be internal pressure to place more advertising in those company magazines than if there were no corporate ties? Could the magazine provide a better level of service to its agency partners than it does to outside vendors and purchasers? Might a single advertiser unduly influence both the agency and the magazine?

Future Impact

As you can see, small advertising agencies, independent publications, local broadcasters, and many other media operations could have trouble competing with these large conglomerates. Local firms might be neglected because they are too small to be of interest or to be profitable to large multinational corporations.

What if a large advertiser were to begin buying up media properties, and then running its advertising only in the media vehicles that it owns or controls? Independent media would suffer. Suppliers to the large advertiser might be pressured to purchase advertising in the media owned by the advertiser. The daytime television dramas, the so-called soap operas, were originally developed by the large soap and detergent manufacturers. Could it happen again?

What if the large advertiser also owned or controlled the advertising agencies that it uses? Could that ever happen? Today there are many "house" agencies owned by advertisers, sometimes working only on that advertiser's campaigns and in other cases also working on external work for other advertisers. But what if there are only a few large agencies remaining, all working under the same corporate umbrella with advertisers, media, research, and similar services? What is the future impact on the advertising media business if there is increasing partnering with large media companies and advertisers?

Chapter 31

Developing Test Plans

Every brand is looking for the optimum way to allocate its funds. Some brands spend a lot on advertising; others do not. Some use television; others use print. Because every brand is unique, it is important to develop a base of knowledge that, over time, guides the brand's support. That is why many brands develop test plans; it is a relatively safe and low-cost way to learn what works and what doesn't for your brand.

Test marketing is the use of controlled tests in one or more geographic areas to gather information about the brand, customers, and competitors. There are two basic reasons to test market. The first is to gain knowledge about a new product or line extension in a limited area before rolling it out nationally. The second is to test different marketing-mix strategies for an existing brand. These strategies can include a media-weight test, a media-mix test, a comparison of different copy strategies, or a test of a different blend of advertising-to-trade support.

Test marketing gives the brand management a lot of opportunities to learn as well as to fine-tune the brand strategy. It helps reduce the odds of failure for a future strategy, and it can lead the brand to a bolder strategy. Success depends on setting up an effective and representative test-market situation.

Establishing a worthwhile test-market scenario requires the proper research structure, appropriate test markets, and the ability to act on the information on a broad scale.

Guidelines for Test Marketing

It is terrible thing when you believe you have an appropriate test but actually something has muddied the water and you now can't read it or rely on it. It is important to set up the proper structure for having test markets that are reliable and projectable, that have the ability to broadcast to a broader area.

There are no hard-and-fast rules about what makes for a proper test, but there are some standards that over the years have served brand managers well. Table 31.1 lists the standards that are recommended for test marketing. There should be a minimum of two test markets in addition to a control market for most tests. If you are introducing a new brand, you would likely want three or four test markets in order to protect yourself from a regional bias.

Select markets that are geographically dispersed. If you concentrate your entire test in a certain region and the regional economy tanks, then you have an unreadable test.

Markets should be representative of the United States, unless there is a specific ethnic or demographic skew to your brand. Then you would want markets that mirror the category in which you compete. You also want the markets that you select to cover 3 percent or more of the country, so you'll have a sizable population base that has good projectability.

Most tests should run for at least six months. For most brands that have a four-week purchase cycle, a six-month test would allow for six complete purchase cycles and 26 individual data points that allow for statistical comparison to a baseline. If possible, it is desirable to schedule a test for 12 months to offer greater numbers of data points so that your test period can be statistically validated. If you have a product with a longer purchase cycle than four weeks, then you should consider testing for longer than a year in order to be able to read and trust the results.

If you are testing media-weight levels, you should look to increase or decrease the weight level by a minimum of 50 percent. If you adjust it less than this amount, you run the risk of not having data on which you can rely.

Selecting Test Markets

One of the most important elements in test marketing is selecting the right markets in which to test. For example, if you are testing a new baby formula and pick Fort Myers, Florida, where more than 50 percent of the population is over the age of 55, that might not pan out for you. The market must reflect the population of the United States or whatever the population base is in which your brand operates.

The second aspect to a test market is to select a market that is neither too small nor too big. Typically, a test market should be no less than 0.2 percent but no more than 2.0 percent of the United States. This usually translates to markets that range from 30 to 150 of the top 210 designated market areas. Table 31.2 shows some of the more popular test markets.

If you select a market that is too small, it might not have the appropriate number of media outlets to translate your test plan. If it is too

Table 31.1

Test Marketing Standards

2+ Test markets
1+ Control market
Geographically dispersed
Demographically representative of the United States
Test length at least 6 months
Weight levels tests at 50 percent ±

Table 31.2

Examples of Top Test Markets

Designated market area	Market rank	Percentage of United States
Oklahoma City	45	0.597
Louisville, KY	50	0.574
Tulsa	60	0.466
Toledo	68	0.406
Des Moines	72	0.376
Omaha	78	0.363
Syracuse	80	0.352
Rochester, NY	77	0.364
Spokane	79	0.357
Madison, WI	86	0.327
Colorado Springs	94	0.284

Source: Nielsen Media Research. U.S. TV Household Estimates.

big, it is not very cost efficient. Who wants to test a plan in New York, where media rates are sky high? As we discussed before, once you are in a few of the top 10 markets, you may have the media equivalent of a national brand.

Media Requirements

A test market must have a variety of media outlets available. It should be representative of the normal market. A market should have at least four television stations, which are basically the Big Four networks. Cable penetration should be no more than 10 percent above or below the national average; if it is outside this range, then you run the risk of a skewed viewing environment. The market should have a good range of radio stations covering a variety of formats. It should also have a dominant local newspaper that includes a daily and a Sunday edition. The Sunday newspaper should contain Sunday supplements and free-standing inserts. It is essential that the medium you want to test is contained in the test market.

Another aspect of test markets is their degree of media isolation. For example, San Angelo, Texas, receives more than 20 percent of its television viewing from Dallas/Fort Worth. You wouldn't want to purchase both San Angelo and Dallas stations for a test market. This is known as *spill-in,* when television signals from one market may be seen in another market.

Conversely, you don't want to air your commercials in one market and have them seen in another market where consumers can't get your product. You don't want to have consumers coming to your future retailing partner looking for a product that is not on the shelf. Television spill-in or spill-out should be restricted to less than 15 percent.

Marketing Criteria

If you are developing a test market for an existing product, you will want to find markets in which it makes sense to test. First, you want a market where you have solid distribution; it makes little sense to do a heavy spend test if you are not in 50 percent of the distribution outlets in the market. Once you have the proper distribution, then you should find markets that have average sales characteristics. If you have a 70 percent market share, the chance of pushing it up 20 percent, to 84 percent market share, is a lot less likely than if you picked a market where you start with only a 20 percent market share.

Use your brand and category development indexes (BDI and CDI) to help establish the criteria. For a test market, you should keep within a range of 115 to 85, or plus or minus 15 percentage points, from the average. The goal is to keep the markets as typical as possible, assuming that your test is designed to be rolled out nationally.

BehaviorScan Markets

For consumer packaged-goods (CPG) brands, one popular method of test marketing is to use Information Resources Inc.'s BehaviorScan test-marketing method. BehaviorScan uses a household panel in discrete designated marketing areas (DMAs) to measure the impact of advertising and actual product-sales movement of the test brand.

Respondents in the panel use a wand to scan their grocery and drug purchases. These same respondents also have their television viewing metered so you can understand their viewing behavior. In addition, respondents are profiled regarding their other media habits as well as their purchase behavior.

BehaviorScan has markets that cut across the country. You can choose from markets such as Cedar Rapids, Iowa; Midland, Texas; and Pittsfield, Massachusetts. When you choose to use a BehaviorScan test, obviously the test-market criteria are already taken care of. If you elect to do your own study, then stick to the criteria in the previous section.

Test-Market Translations

When you are developing a test plan, you should start with how your plan will ultimately be executed. For example, testing a plan that might translate to a $50 million national plan is a waste of time if you know you can't afford such a plan. If your goal is to be a national brand, start with the objective of how you would execute the tested plan on a national basis; if your goal is to be a regional brand, focus on executing the plan on a system-wide basis.

Assuming that your goal is to be a national brand, or to implement your test nationally, let's review the techniques for doing just that. There are two commonly used techniques for translating national media plans into local test plans. The two techniques are called "Little USA" and "As It Falls."

"Little USA," sometimes called "Little America," assigns each test market the average national rating-point level. This technique assumes that the local market will behave similarly to the whole United States. So if a national media plan calls for 100 network television rating points and 100 magazine rating points, then each test market would be assigned those weight levels. The plan at the local level is a replication of the plan at the national level.

The "As It Falls" method is a bit different from the "Little USA" approach. In the "As It Falls" method, each test market's media delivery is based on what that delivery would be if the plan were to be implemented nationally. So if the national plan calls for 100 network television rating points and your test market normally delivers 10 percent above the average in terms of network delivery, then the test market would receive 110 rating points. The purpose of the "As It Falls" method is to replicate as precisely as possible the actual national plan that would be implemented.

There are reasons to select one method over the other. "Little USA" is best used when the advertiser is testing a new brand and has no benchmark category sales data available on a local market level. In this case, you want to understand the performance of the product and not necessarily the media variation. On the other hand, if a brand has a good amount of historical sales data, then the "As It Falls" method is preferable because it is closer to what will actually happen once the plan is implemented nationally. You may want to compromise if you find that the "As It Falls" test markets produce abnormally low or high rating-point delivery compared to the national plan. Then you either go to a "Little USA" method or reexamine your test markets.

Translating National Media to the Local Level

You've figured out what you want to test. The media group has developed the perfect national plan. You've selected your test markets. Now you have to take that hypothetical national media plan and execute it in the test markets. In doing so, you need to make some media decisions. Unfortunately, the process is not as simple as taking one plan and executing it. National media and local media are different. Each medium has its own nuances. Getting the stars to align takes some work. Let's examine the four major national media, starting with network television.

In scheduling commercials, the biggest difference between network television and spot or local television is that network purchases are usually made within an actual program whereas spot purchases are made between the programs. For example, if you use CBS's *Two and a Half Men,* your commercial will run within the actual program, either at the 10-minute or 20-minute commercial break after the show begins. Spot television, on the other hand, offers commercials at the program break, so your commercial would air between *Two and a Half Men* and the following program. Why is this important? Research shows that retention of commercials at the between-program break drops 20 to 30 percent compared to commercials within a program. Therefore, you may want to boost your test plan to compensate for this inequity.

Unlike network television, 15-second commercials are immediately preemptable in spot television. This means that unless a local station has another advertiser running a 15-second unit during the same program that you are, your commercial will not air. There are few natural breaks for 15-second commercials on a local basis, so the chances of your commercial not running can be great. As a result, you may want to schedule 30-second commercials on a spot basis to guard against being bumped off the air.

Cable television is difficult to translate to a local market. Many local cable operators sell advertising only on selected channels, which may not be the ones you would purchase. Even on those channels that they do sell, they may offer only broad rotation schedules so you cannot pick the time you want. In some areas, local cable operators may not sell advertising. Local cable is problematic at best. If national cable is a part of an overall plan, you should consider purchasing that test weight on over-the-air television. Local early fringe, late fringe, and/or weekend times can be good substitutes for cable weight.

Network radio translates well to the local level. In radio, it is important to ensure that whatever station format you plan on using nationally, you end up purchasing locally. The only other nuance to radio is the cost implications of 60-second commercials versus 30-second commercials. Usually, :30s are half the price of :60s nationally, yet many local stations charge the same for :60s and :30s locally.

Magazine placement has its own set of issues as well. Depending upon the publication, it may not have a large enough circulation to offer a test-market edition. Most large circulation publications such as *Good Housekeeping, Time,* and *TV Guide* offer very detailed local editions. But if your strategy is to be in more "niche" publications such as *Chili Pepper,* then you are going to run into problems. All you can do is to find publications that are similar in nature to what you plan on scheduling.

The other major issue with magazines is the type of unit that can be scheduled in a test-market edition of a national publication. Because publications must actually make a mechanical plate change in the printing process to accommodate your advertisement, they usually allow only full-page advertisements to be in a test-market edition. So if your test plan calls for checkerboard advertisements or a fractional unit, you may want to rethink your test. A checkerboard is scheduling quarter-page ads in each of the four corners of a two-page spread; fractional units are anything less than a full page, such as a two-thirds-page or half-page unit. Regardless of your creative wishes, you must use some practical sense when testing in magazines.

Developing test plans does take some serious thought. You need to have your objectives honed with the understanding that what you test can actually be rolled out. Then, select the proper test markets and develop your test translation. Finally, work the local plan so that it fits the national plan as closely as possible.

Tactical Testing

This chapter has focused on developing classical test-market plans typically used with CPG brands. The basic tenets of this type of planning can apply to any brand situation regardless of category. However, you don't have to develop classic test-market scenarios to have a valid test.

As a brand manager, you should always be looking at ways to improve your advertising and media program. Learning what works or doesn't work provides a golden opportunity to further your brand's cause in the marketplace. There are plenty of areas to do small tactical tests that can reap big rewards: all you have to do is isolate the variable to be tested and have test and control markets.

For example, suppose that you are a retail brand that relies on weekly inserts to drive traffic to your store. You could test if you want your ad to be inserted in the weekday or Sunday newspaper. Or you could see if paid newspapers outperformed free distribution papers. A home accessories retail chain recently ran a test where they changed their insert drop from Sunday to Thursday. They found that their sales had no change by moving the date but they saved nearly 30 percent on their media costs since the Sunday paper had a higher cost per thousand than the daily, plus it distributed more copies. By doing this small tactical test, this retailer saved millions of dollars for the company.

The same is true for business-to-business marketing. You can isolate a market or a particular job title to do a test. One business-to-business marketer had a publication sort his database with their circulation. For the customers that they had in common, he sent one message; to the prospects, he sent another. This led to an increase in both new customer acquisition as well as retention of existing customers.

If you have an online component to your marketing plan, you are in a constant state of testing. Most online campaigns are built similar to direct marketing campaigns with message, creative, offer, and media testing all available. It is like being in a test kitchen for a restaurant chain. Just about anything that can be thought of can be tested in the online arena. Online media can be an effective laboratory to test ideas before rolling them out to offline media.

Whether you are developing classic test-market scenarios or you want to understand how one media vehicle performs, test marketing should be a part of any media plan. As a brand manager, you want to continually add to the brand's knowledge base. Test marketing is one consistent method of doing just that.

Chapter 32

Agency Compensation Structures

What does a media planner have to do with agency compensation? The answer is plenty. Media is a direct and indirect generator of agency income and ultimately profitability. Historically, advertising agencies were compensated on media commission. The business began as an agent for the print media and grew from there. Even if media isn't the direct measure of compensation, it usually forms the basis for other forms of compensation. The advertising budget is a barometer of the agency's compensation. And the media budget is typically the lion's share of the advertising budget.

Media can also impact the agency's profitability indirectly. Media becomes cash flow that an agency can earn interest on. In the halcyon years of moderate or high inflation, media budgets in the multimillion-dollar range at 5 percent interest could generate a significant amount of profit for the agency. In a traditional advertising agency, media billing is typically the largest portion of the dollars flowing through the agency.

With the ever-expanding array of media and the rise of media-only agencies, media planning and buying have become big businesses. The top media planning and buying agencies are larger than the top-billing public relations agencies. They command a large place in the advertising world.

You don't have to be a financial genius to be a media planner. But you do need to understand the fundamentals of how the agency is compensated. The compensation philosophy of the agency will have a large impact on your media plan and how you manage the execution of that plan.

Compensation Structures and Philosophy

Compensation is the cornerstone of any business. The approach to compensation is as much philosophical as it is methodological. There is an underlying method to doing business that involves how you charge for your services and what you give the client. There is a philosophical approach to each method that ensures that each side is fairly rewarded.

Although methods and philosophies can vary from agency to agency, there are three fundamental methods for developing agency compensation.

- Commission based
- Fee based
- Value based

Each of these methods has media planning implications. Let's review each method and how it impacts the media planner's job.

Commission Based

The advertising industry is based on media commission as the revenue engine. Fifteen percent commission was the standard. That means for every $100 placed in media, the agency would get $15. This was a simple form of compensation because it was a rebate from the media rather than a direct payment from the client.

During the 1960s through the 1980s, this form of compensation also had a simple philosophy. The philosophy was based on the success of the advertising. The greater the success, the more the client would spend and the more the agency would make. In an era when there were limited media choices, a more homogeneous population, and broad-based products, it was a formula for success.

The implication of the commission system for the media planner is that all media would be billed at gross. This means that it contains the 15 percent commission. Other variations on the commission system include a sliding scale based on the level of advertising. For example, the agency may get 15 percent commission on the first $10 million of advertising, 10 percent commission on the next $10 million, and 5 percent on the next $10 million. This sliding scale assumed that there was a point where the agency gained economies of scale with the placement of advertising.

With the compensation of the agency tied to the media spending, it was in the best interest of the agency to protect and/or grow the media budget. So, there was pressure on the media team to find new ways to increase the budget. This might be through test markets or other areas where gaining a greater budget was possible. Of course, the budget growth was based on growing the client's business but the agency was driven to constantly increase budgets.

These led clients to sometimes question agency motives. The solution to corporate growth is not always to advertise more. Yet, with agency compensation based on advertising, it was in the agency's best interest to maintain and grow advertising budgets. This potential conflict of interest led to our second form of compensation, the agency fee.

Fee Based

Fee-based agency compensation models are usually based on manpower. This means that the advertising agency estimates how many people and how much time those people will spend working on the client's account. The philosophy is that the agency charges the client based on the time it takes to do the task. So, the client only pays for the time spent working on his or her behalf.

There are a variety of fee models. Some are capped at a certain number of hours so that there is a ceiling to the amount the client will be charged. Other models are project based, where each task is estimated in advance so that the client knows what he is paying for.

The media implication to the fee-based model is twofold. One implication is that most fee-based models require that media be placed at net, or without commission. This means that a media budget may go further because the agency is rebating the 15 percent commission to the client. The second implication is that the agency is usually rewarded for efficiency. Many times a flat fee is negotiated so that if the agency is more time efficient, it will make more money.

The fee-based system is the most common form of agency compensation. The benefit is that the client and agency both know what they are receiving. It takes the pressure off the agency to be more objective in its viewpoint regarding recommending advertising as a solution. It puts the agency more in a management consultant role.

There is also a hybrid system where an agency may establish a fee for the day-to-day people working on the client's business along with either a commission or a discounted commission for media placed. The idea of the hybrid is to cover daily costs but to have a variable cost for media placement. Typically this scenario focuses on a discounted commission to fund the hours of the media placement.

The downside of the fee-based system is that there is no reward for the agency for doing a great job. If the advertising program works well, the agency receives the same compensation it would get if the program were only moderately successful. It also puts the emphasis on efficiency rather than on taking whatever time is needed to generate a big idea. This lack of an upside has led to another form of compensation.

Value Based

Value-based compensation is based on the value delivered. For example, you may negotiate that for every new dollar of revenue you generate, you get 10 cents. So, if the client generates $100 million of revenue, you would receive $10 million. The more you can generate new revenue, the more you make. It is similar to a sales commission.

Another value-based method is to put a number on the program or idea. The agency pegs a value to the idea. It may be $1 million or it may be $5 million. There may be a formula based on agreed-upon metrics for the final value of the idea. But the philosophy is the same. Pay us for what we generate and not the activity that we do.

The media implication for this method is similar to the fee-based system. Media would be placed at net or no commission. The bigger implication for the media team is that they are under the gun to make the program a success or their work will be for naught.

Ideally, value-based compensation does put the agency and the client on common ground. The goal is to succeed. Each party should be driven to succeed because the more the client succeeds, the more the agency succeeds. On the other hand, whereas value-based compensation sounds ideal, few clients embrace it because it is sometimes daunting to have to determine the actual impact of advertising on the business.

More agencies and clients are experimenting with a hybrid of value-based compensation and fee-based compensation as the model for the future. With more tools that track accountability, this is the area toward which the industry is migrating.

With more and more emphasis on accountability from clients and profitability from the agency, the media planner must understand not only how the client's business works but also how the agency works. Of course the media planner must do what is right for the client, but selection of media does have agency financial implications.

Impact of Media Selection

The kinds of media selected for a campaign have different degrees of execution efficiency. For example, it takes just one network buyer a small amount of time to place a $3 million commercial on the Super Bowl. It takes a wide variety of people a much longer time to place a $3 million mix of local television, newspaper, and online display.

If the agency is compensated the same for each of these activities, it should make a lot more money when placing the one network television commercial versus a mix of media. So, what does this mean for media planning? Do you have to constantly consult with your CFO before doing a media plan? Should you take into account the manpower necessary to complete a media plan?

While it is incumbent upon the media strategist to develop the right plan for the client, it is equally as important to understand the economic impact of that plan on the agency. The media strategist isn't consulting with the CFO on the best plan, but may be alerting the CFO to any significant change in media strategy that could impact future agency workload. If the agency doesn't make money, then the media strategist will not have a job.

There are some fundamental aspects to media execution that warrant discussion.

National versus Local Media

As a rule of thumb national media are more time efficient to purchase than local media. This goes for broadcast as well as print and online. The more complex the media purchase, the longer it takes. The implication for you as media planner is that your agency management may request a higher fee or commission rate based on a local versus national media plan.

Online Media Tracking

Online display and search engine marketing (pay-per-click) are both highly measurable. You can measure the impact of the media weekly, daily, even hourly. Most digital media plans do analytical reports after a few weeks to determine what is working and what isn't. Based on these data, the media purchase is adjusted. Each time a media planner does an analysis and adjusts a plan, he or she is spending time doing it. So, the more extensively you track the plan, the more it may cost the client. The media implication for digital media is that you need to have an agreement with the client on the parameters of the analytics prior to a purchase. The time spent tracking and analyzing will weigh on agency compensation.

Promotional Media

Sometimes you purchase media that contain promotional elements. For example, you may buy a schedule on a radio station that contains both airtime and a caller give-away. To coordinate this give-away may take obtaining prizes, getting sponsorship rules approved, governing the contest, and then providing the prizes to the winners. All of this takes time and money. The media implication of promotional media is that there may need to be a co-ordination fee built into the program.

The media strategist must keep one eye on what is right and one eye on what is profitable. It would be naïve to think otherwise. The client and the agency must make money to survive. The media team can have a significant impact on the agency's profitability, so it is a key aspect of the media strategist's role to understand the fundamentals of how the agency makes money.

How the Agency Makes Money

The advertising agency business is a pretty simple one. There are three components. The first is revenue from the client. That is the income side of the equation. The two variables that the agency controls to make a profit are personnel salaries and overhead to keep the business going.

In Table 32.1, there is a very basic review of how an agency makes money. Let's take a look at each item.

Revenue

Every business must have revenue to survive. As we have said before, agency revenue can come in many forms. Sometimes it comes from agency commissions through media or production. Sometimes it comes through fees. Sometimes it comes through bonuses. All of these are direct forms of agency compensation.

There are also indirect forms of compensation. One area is interest income. There may be a month's lag between getting paid for media by the client and paying the media vendors. This large amount of money accrues interest before being paid out just like money in your own money market fund. When interest rates are high, this can be a great income source for an advertising agency. Whereas the media team has no direct impact on this income, it highlights the importance of media billing.

Regardless of where income comes from, the agency builds a financial budget based on what it forecasts as its annual income. This becomes the basis for allocating costs. Many agencies have short-term projects or potential new-business opportunities, and so they routinely update these forecasts and balance costs against them.

Salaries and Benefits

In an advertising agency, the majority of costs are those folks who go up and down in the elevator. It is all about people and their salaries. Managing payroll is a key aspect of agency management. Too much payroll and you don't make any profit. Too few people and payroll, and you will likely burn your employees out.

Table 32.1

How an Agency Makes Money

Revenue from client	100%
Salaries and benefits of employees	50%
Overhead of agency (rent, stat services, supplies, management)	30%
Gross profit	20%
Net profit after tax	10%

This means that if your salary-to-revenue percentage is above 60 percent you will not make much, if any, money. If your salary-to-revenue percentage is below 45 percent it is likely you are not staffed properly. Most agencies target 50 percent salary-to-revenue percentage as their goal. This typically translates to a 20 percent pretax profit. This percent of pretax profit is the level in the top 25 percent of advertising agencies as reported by the American Association of Advertising Agencies.

When we discuss salary and benefits, we refer to how much a person earns in wages as well as their corresponding benefits. Benefits are made up of a variety of elements depending upon the company. The standard benefits include medical and life insurance, profit sharing, and possibly a 401K program.

The media implications for salaries and benefits relate to the media staff and task to complete. If a media plan shifts to tactics that require more manpower, that has an impact on overall company salaries. Conversely, if the plan shifts to a less-manpower-intensive plan, that can also have financial implications for the company.

The management of the media department works with the CFO to determine the optimum number of people and salary load depending upon the workload and the revenue available. Salary is the key aspect of any service organization. As you move into a management role in the organization, you will deal with salary matters.

Agency Overhead

The other expenses of an advertising agency or media company are just like any other service business. There is rent, supplies, utilities, and equipment necessary to operate the business. Agency management is also factored in to overhead costs.

The media team has a significant impact on overhead costs. To run a sophisticated media operation requires having access to the latest research tools and data. These tools and data cost quite a bit of money. For many advertising agencies that have full-service media departments, the cost to subscribe to rating information from Nielsen and Arbitron—along with additional subscriptions to MRI, SMRB, and others—can run in the hundreds of thousands of dollars.

The media team is asked to negotiate contract terms with research vendors and to work with the agency CFO on how to optimize those costs. Sometimes clients are billed directly or indirectly for the costs of these research tools. Understanding these costs plus the costs of the necessary computer hardware to operate these research tools is an important aspect of media management.

Overhead also plays into how an agency charges a client for personnel fees. Let's assume that the agency and client agree on a fee compensation plan that is based on an hourly rate for agency personnel who work on the client's business. That hourly rate, then, is made up of the salary and benefits of the personnel along with an overhead factor. This factor is the portion of all the costs necessary to conduct business that are added to the salary and benefits of the agency personnel. Clients are sensitive to what is included in overhead because ultimately they will be paying for it.

The two cost elements the agency must contend with are salary/benefits and overhead. Those are the two areas that the agency manages. Media is a key aspect of both of these costs. Media people will be asked to play a role in optimizing the cost side of the agency balance sheet.

Profit

The agency, like any business, needs to make a profit to survive. There are two profit numbers that every business evaluates. The first is gross profit. This is the money made after subtracting the costs from the revenue. So, if the agency had a revenue of $1 million and it cost $800,000 to manage the business, the gross profit would be $200,000 ($1,000,000 − $800,000 = $200,000).

Gross profit is also called pretax profit. Gross profit is the money made prior to filing the company's income tax. Net profit, on the other hand, is the profit reported after taxes. This is the money retained by the company for the cash portion of the balance sheet. This net profit or cash then builds up into retained earnings. Basically, retained earnings are like your personal savings account. The company uses retained earnings as a cushion for an emergency. It also uses retained earnings to borrow money and to ease any type of cash crunch.

The media team impacts the gross profit of the company. This is the key measure of success. Net profit is much more driven by financial decisions made by the company. Some companies elect to retain their profits and others disburse them to their shareholders. These decisions are out of the day-to-day control of the typical media person.

But, every employee should have a basic grasp of how profitable the agency is and how they contribute to that profitability. Generating a profit is the cornerstone of the agency business. Continually making a profit is the key to long-term growth. Without it, there would be no future media plans.

Summary

The media team has a big impact on the agency's financial success. Every aspect of the financial performance of the agency is impacted. The top-line revenue is many times a direct result of a media plan or purchase. How the senior media leadership manages the department payroll and media resources impacts the profitability of the agency. Media is a financial cornerstone of many successful advertising agencies. Media companies are devoted solely to the media planning and purchasing skills to make a living. Although you don't need to be a financial genius to be a media strategist, you should have a basic understanding of financial practices.

Appendix
How the Advertising Business Is Organized

Every business, including every advertising agency, has its own unique organization. It is simply not possible to discuss or demonstrate all the various organizational plans and schemes and designs that are used in advertising.

Still, understanding how the media operations in advertising fit in with the overall advertising operations will help you comprehend how the business functions and how the media operations mesh with the rest of the advertising work.

In advertising agencies, there are two major themes used in agency organization. In the *departmental organization,* the various advertising functions are grouped together in departments. The advertising work flows go from one department to the next: from research to media and copywriting and art, all controlled through account services by the account executive or account supervisor. (See Exhibits A.1 and A.2. Exhibit A.2 shows a common type of departmental arrangement.) Nevertheless, as stated before, each agency is different, so no two organizational charts will be exactly alike.

Each department is composed of specialists in given activities who work on a variety of accounts. The work is spread out to keep the pace more even. Thus, the media department can handle the media planning, estimating, buying, and checking for all of the advertiser clients, moving from one account to another as necessary.

In an *account team organization,* the agency is organized into small teams, almost like small agencies within the bigger agency. Each account team has a mix of specialists who work on their own parts of the advertising campaign, and the entire team handles one or a few advertiser accounts. The entire list of accounts is split up among the various account teams, each team working on only a few of the accounts. In Exhibit A.3, a sample of the account teams' organization is diagrammed, but the actual composition of an account team might be larger or smaller; the diagram shows only one possible type of team specialty combination.

The advantage of the account team setup is that the teams become accustomed to working together and know their own accounts quite well. The disadvantages include getting stale from working on the same account all the time, as well as enduring some periods of time with high workloads and others with low workloads. The advertising media personnel may handle the entire load without much contact with other media staffers.

A small advertising agency may be organized in a manner similar to that shown in Exhibit A.3, but with a few differences. An organizational chart from an actual advertising agency, using the account team plan, is shown in Exhibit A.4.

A larger advertising agency will, of course, be more complex. Exhibit A.5 shows a medium-sized advertising agency with a departmental arrangement. Note that this is not the entire organizational chart for the agency, only the media department's organization.

Very large advertising agencies will be even more complex. A large advertising agency will have many more specializations and, consequently, many more specialists. Only the media department of a large advertising agency is shown in Exhibit A.6.

Advertisers—the clients of advertising agencies—are organized quite differently. They do not need media estimators, media planners, or media buyers because that work is normally handled at the agency, not at the advertiser (client) company.

A small national company's advertising department is portrayed in Exhibit A.7. Note that even though the titles deal with advertising, the emphasis appears to be on marketing in general. The media portion of the client company's advertising effort is handled primarily by the media director, who oversees the agency's work and serves as the direct liaison between the advertiser and the agency.

A large firm will have a more complex advertising department. In Exhibit A.8, the advertising operations of a large industrial company are displayed as an entire division of the corporation. This division works on a variety of media efforts unique to the corporation and its industry, which requires multiple departments and staff. Even though an advertising agency handles media estimating, planning, and buying, there is still a lot of detailed media work done by this advertiser's media department.

Although each of the organizational charts displayed here is unique to an individual firm, together they should provide you with a solid overview of the types of organizations used to manage and control advertising media operations in a variety of firms and settings.

Exhibit A.1

Organizational Charts

Large organizations draw charts to show how they are organized. These organizational charts indicate levels of authority, lines of communication and control, and names and job titles or descriptions.

The higher a position is on an organizational chart, the more important it is. People in top spots have more authority over personnel and decision making for their firm. (See the organizational chart.) Thus, the board chairperson or president is typically at the top of the organizational chart, and the middle and lower management positions are further down.

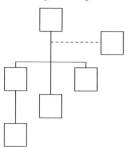

On the organizational chart, positions are joined by lines that are either solid or dotted. Solid lines indicate both communication and control, and they are thus called line positions. Dotted lines indicate staff positions, meaning that communication exists but control does not. Line positions, then, have a say in how things are done, as well as the ability to communicate with those connected by organizational lines, whereas staff positions are usually advisory in nature, and although they still have communication with those connected by dotted lines, staff positions do not have a say in how things are done.

Generally, formal communication between two distant persons on the chart just goes through the intermediaries—that is, through the positions intercepted by the lines joining the two original individuals. In practice, of course, people can send e-mail messages and make telephone calls to most of the others in the organization, but formal requests and approvals go through the other positions that come between them along the lines that connect them.

Individual boxes usually indicate certain positions, including both the job title and the name of the person currently filling that position.

Exhibit A.2

Departmental Organization

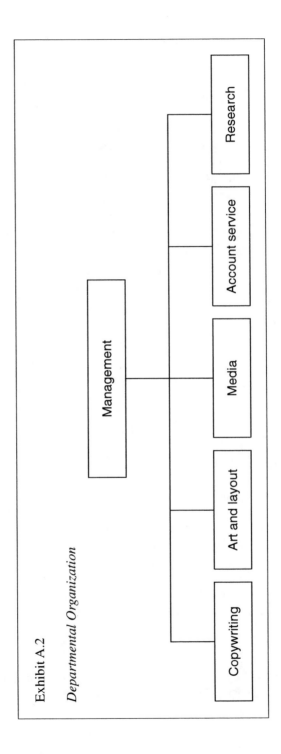

Exhibit A.3

Account Team Organization

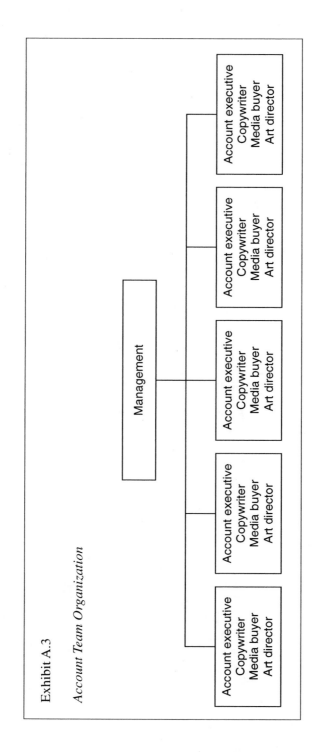

Exhibit A.4

Small Advertising Agency

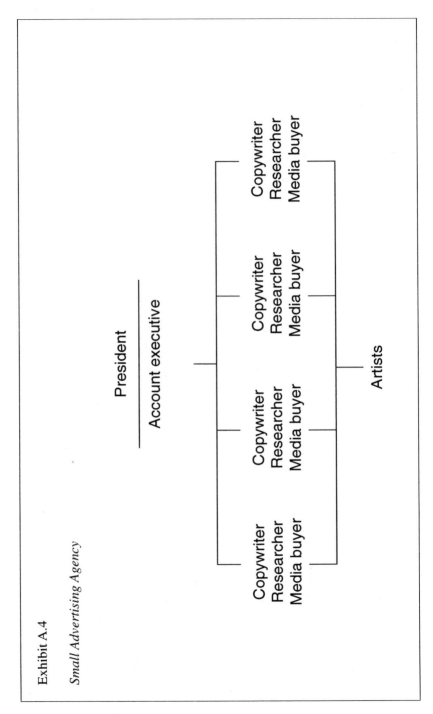

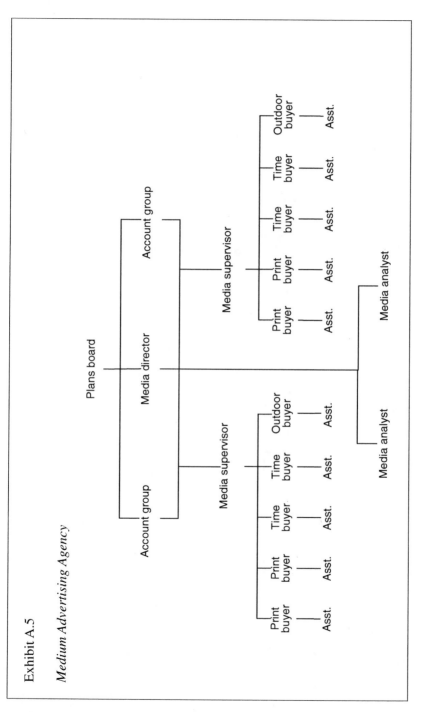

Exhibit A.5

Medium Advertising Agency

274

Exhibit A.6

Large Advertising Agency

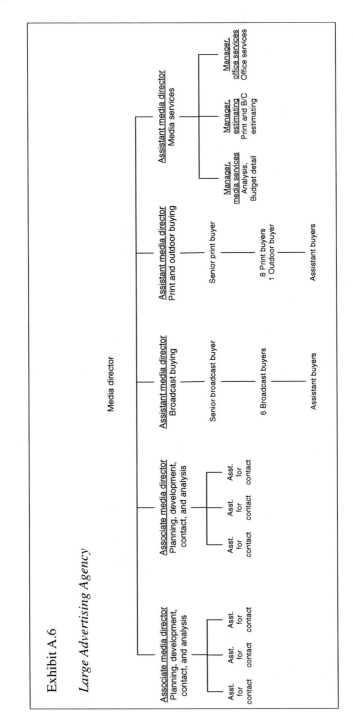

Exhibit A.7

Advertising Department, Smaller Company

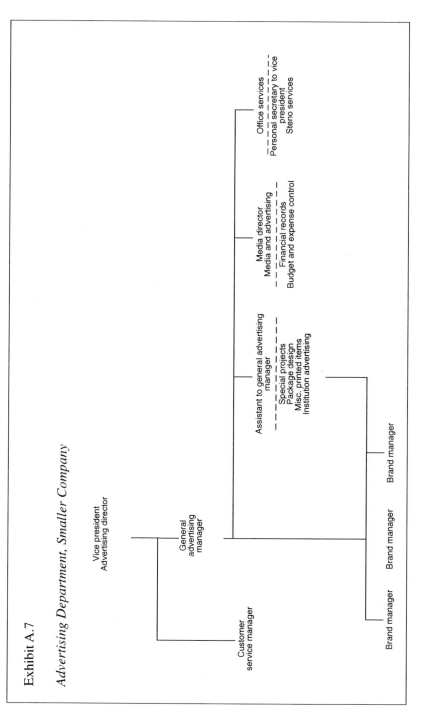

Exhibit A.8

Advertising Division, Larger Company

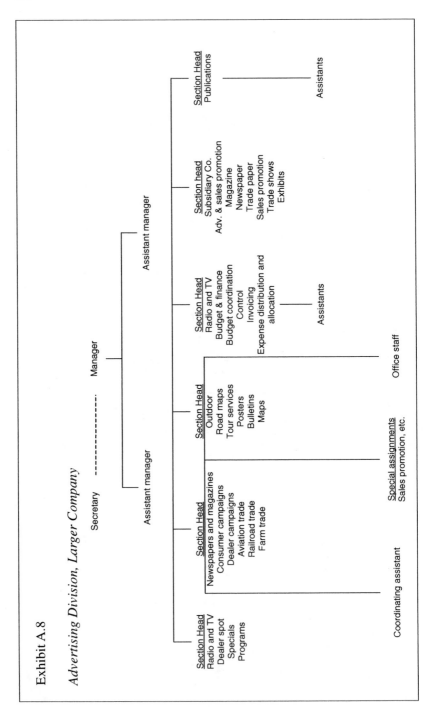

Index

About the Authors

Larry D. Kelley is professor of advertising at the Valenti School of Communication at the University of Houston. His teaching specialties are advertising media planning, advertising account planning, and advertising campaigns. He is the advisor for the University of Houston AAF National Student Advertising Competition team.

Mr. Kelley is a partner at FKM advertising agency where he is the chief planning officer responsible for research and planning.

Mr. Kelley has held senior management positions in media and research at Publicis, Bozell & Jacobs, and BBD&O prior to joining FKM in 1990. He has worked on a wide variety of accounts that span consumer and business-to-business categories on an international basis. A sample of his account activity has been: ConAgra Foods, Coca-Cola Foods, Conoco/Phillips, Dell, Exxon, Southwest Airlines, and Waste Management.

Mr. Kelley is widely quoted in trade publications such as *Adweek* and *Advertising Age*. He has co-authored six advertising textbooks in advertising media planning, advertising account planning, advertising and public relations research, and advertising management. All have been published by M.E. Sharpe.

Mr. Kelley is on numerous boards including Retail Marketing Institute, the Advisory Council for Radio Measurement, and the American Association of Advertising Agencies Media Council.

He holds a Bachelor of Science in strategic communication from the University of Kansas and a Master's Degree in advertising from the University of Texas at Austin.

Dr. Donald W. Jugenheimer is an author, researcher, consultant, and educator. His specialties are both interpersonal and mass communications, with an emphasis on personal communication, advertising and media management, media economics, and advertising media.

As a consultant, Dr. Jugenheimer has worked with such firms including American Airlines, IBM, Century 21 real estate, Aetna insurance, Pacific Telesis, and the U.S. Army Recruiting Command, and currently consults on a variety of research and advisory projects in advertising and marketing, including advertising media plans for class-action lawsuits. He has also conducted research for a variety of enterprises including the U.S. Department of Health, Education and Welfare, the International Association of Business Communicators, and National Liberty Life Insurance.

Dr. Jugenheimer is author or co-author of twenty-five books and many articles and papers. He has spoken before a variety of academic and professional organizations, including the World Advertising Congress in Tokyo. He also served as president and as executive director of the American Academy of Advertising and as advertising division head of the Association for Education in Journalism and Mass Communication. He also was business manager for the founding of the *Journal of Advertising*. He has testified about advertising before the U.S. House of Representatives Armed Forces Committee, as well as in federal and state court proceedings.

Since earning his PhD in communications from the University of Illinois with a specialization in advertising and a minor in marketing, Dr. Jugenheimer has been a tenured member of the faculties at the University of Kansas, Louisiana State University (where he was the first person to hold the Manship Distinguished Professorship in Journalism), Fairleigh Dickinson University, Southern Illinois University, and Texas Tech University. At most of those universities he also served as an administrator. His bachelor's degree was in advertising with a minor in economics and his master's degree was also in advertising with a minor in marketing, and all three degrees are from the University of Illinois at Urbana-Champaign. He worked at several advertising agencies in Chicago and downstate Illinois. He also served in the U.S. Air Force, first in aero-medical evacuation and later as a medical administrative officer.

Dr. Jugenheimer has lectured and conducted workshops in several countries and served on the guest faculty of the Executive Media MBA program for the Turku School of Economics and Business Administration in Finland. In addition, he has held a Kellogg National Fellowship, is listed in *Who's Who in America, Who's Who in Advertising, Who's Who in Education,* and in several other biographical references.

Dr. Jugenheimer is currently a partner and principal in the research, writing, and consulting firm In-Telligence, Inc., which concentrates on communications, marketing, and advertising.

Dr. Kim Bartel Sheehan is professor of advertising at the University of Oregon, and directs the Master's program in strategic communication. Her teaching specialties are advertising management, research, and media planning.

Before earning her PhD in communications from the University of Tennessee, Dr. Sheehan worked for more than a dozen years at advertising agencies including Darcy, McManus and Masius in St. Louis; Foote, Cone and Belding in Chicago; and LRBP in Boston, where she was vice president, associate media director working on accounts including McDonald's and Wendy's. She also planned and bought media for the retail chain Laura Ashley. She holds a Bachelor of Science in speech from Northwestern University, and an MBA from Boston University.

She has published extensively in academic journals such as the *Journal of Advertising,* the *Journal of Advertising Research,* and *Journal of Public Policy and Marketing.* She is the author or co-author of several books, and most recently has published two books focusing on word-of-mouth communications and social media for small businesses. She lectures frequently at industry conferences, and contributes to the website www.grabbinggreen. com, a small business information site.

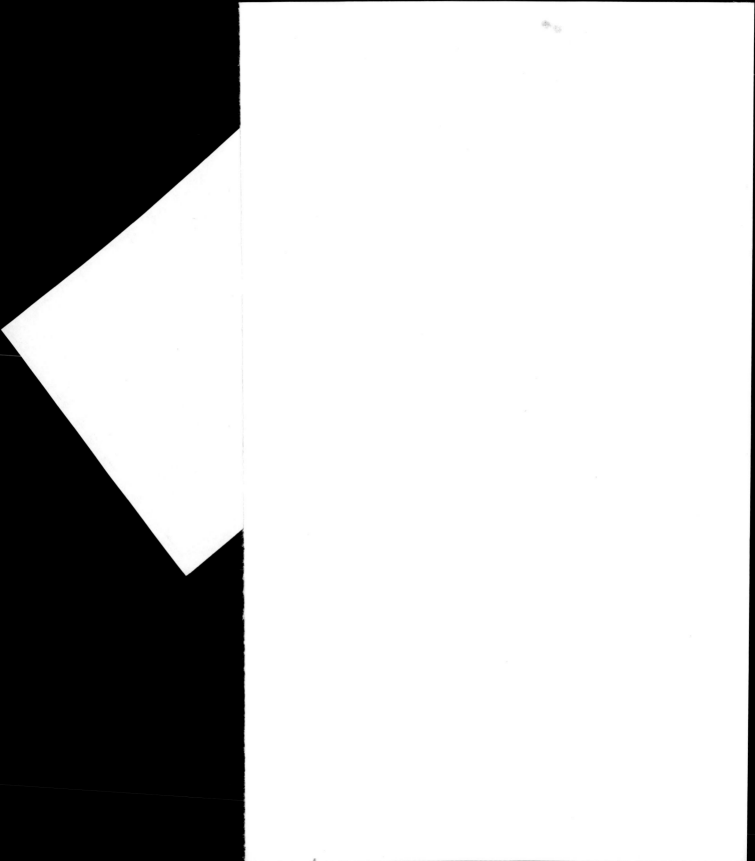

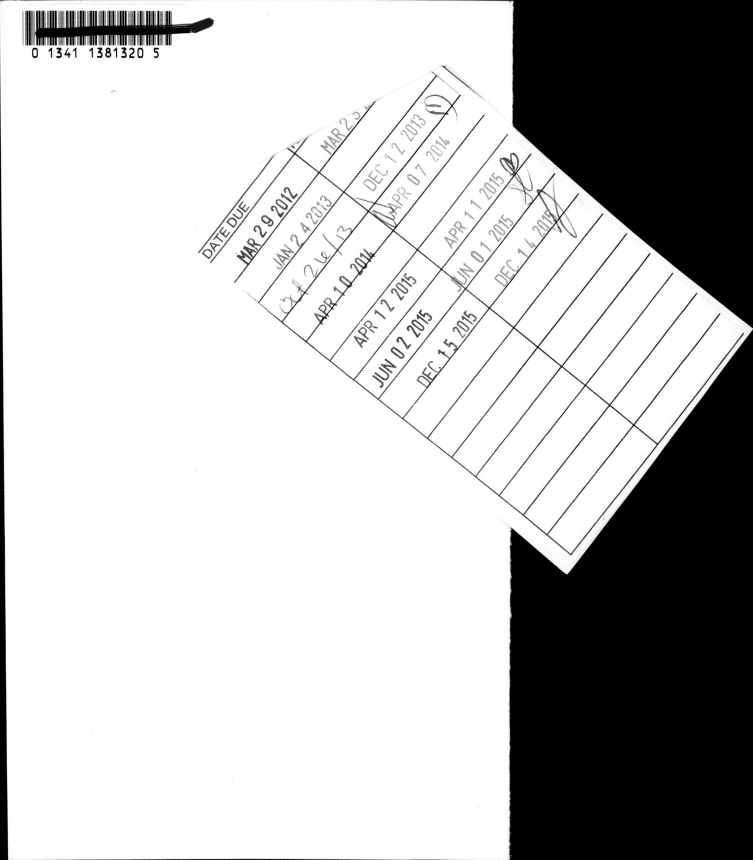

DATE DUE

DATE DUE				
MAR 29 2012	MAR 2 3	DEC 1 2 2013		
JAN 2 4 2013		APR 0 7 2014	APR 1 1 2015	
Oct 26/13			JUN 0 1 2015	
APR 1 0 2014	APR 1 2 2015		DEC 1 4 2015	
	JUN 0 2 2015	DEC 1 5 2015		